John Milton, Thomas Newton

Paradise Regain'd

a poem in four books; to which is added Samson Agonistes and poems upon several

occasions

John Milton, Thomas Newton

Paradise Regain'd
a poem in four books; to which is added Samson Agonistes and poems upon several occasions

ISBN/EAN: 9783337951085

Printed in Europe, USA, Canada, Australia, Japan

Cover: Foto ©Thomas Meinert / pixelio.de

More available books at **www.hansebooks.com**

IOANNES MILTON

Ætatis   Suæ. 21

PARADISE REGAIN'D.

A

P O E M,

IN

F O U R B O O K S.

To which is added

S A M S O N A G O N I S T E S:

AND

POEMS upon SEVERAL OCCASIONS:

The AUTHOR

J O H N M I L T O N.

The THIRD EDITION,
With NOTES of various AUTHORS,
By *THOMAS NEWTON*, D.D.

VOLUME *the* FIRST.

PREFACE.

IT hath been recommended to me by fome great perfons, as well as by feveral friends, to complete the edition of Milton's poetical works : for tho' the Paradife Loft be the flower of epic poefy, and the nobleft effort of genius ; yet here are other poems which are no lefs excellent in their kind, and if they have not that fublimity and majefty, are at leaft equally beautiful and pleafing to the imagination. And the fame method that was taken in the publication of the Paradife Loft, is purfued in this edition of the Paradife Regain'd and other poems, firft to exhibit the true and genuin text according to Milton's own editions, and then to illuftrate it with notes critical and explanatory of various authors. Of the Paradife Regain'd and Samfon Agoniftes there was only one edition in Milton's life-time, in the year 1671 ; and this we have made our ftandard, correcting only what the author himfelf would have corrected. Dr. Bentley pronounces it to be without faults, but there is a large table of Errata at the end, which inftead of being emended have rather been augmented in the following editions, and were never corrected in any edition that I have feen before the prefent. Of the other poems there were two editions in Milton's life-time, the firft in 1645 before he was blind, and the other with fome additions in 1673. Of the Mafk there was likewife an edition publifh'd by Mr. Henry Lawes in 1637 : and of the Mafk and feveral other poems there are extant copies in Milton's own hand writing, preferved in the library of Trinity College in Cambridge : and all thefe copies and editions have

been

been carefully collated and compared together, the differences and variations are noted, and even the poet's corrections and alterations in his Manuscript are specified for the satisfaction of the curious critical reader. The Manuscript indeed hath been of singular service in rectifying several passages, and especially in the Sonnets, some of which were not printed till many years after Milton's death, and were then printed imperfect and deficient both in sense and meter, but are now by the help of the Manuscript restored to their just harmony and original perfection. From the Manuscript too we have given the plan of Paradise Lost, as Milton first designed it, in the form of a tragedy, and likewise the subjects which he had sketched out for other tragedies, whether with an intention ever to finish them or not we cannot be certain. They were printed before in the Historical and Critical Life of Milton prefixed to his prose works by the learned and ingenious Mr. Birch, who is continually adding something new to the stock of learning: but it was judged proper to reprint them from the Manuscript in this edition, as they bear a nearer relation to the author's poetical works.

The notes, as upon the Paradise Lost, so likewise upon the Paradise Regain'd and other poems, are of various authors and of various kinds: but these, excepting only a few, were never printed before, and have therefore novelty to recommend them, as well as some names of the first rank and greatest eminence in the republic of letters. The truth of my assertion will be fully justify'd by mentioning only the names of Mr. Warburton and Mr. Jortin, who while they

are

are employ'd in writing the moſt learned and elabo-
rate defenſes of religion, yet find leiſure to cultivate
the politer arts, and to promote and improve both in
themſelves and others a claſſical taſte of the fineſt
authors: and whatever may be the ſucceſs, I can never
repent of having engaged in this undertaking, which
hath given me ſo many convincing proofs of their
friendſhip and kindneſs, and at the ſame time hath
happily conjoined (what perhaps might never elſe
have been joined together) my ſtudies and my name
with theirs. I am equally obliged too to Mr. Thyer
for the continuation of his friendly aſſiſtance; and
the reader will find the ſame good ſenſe, and learn-
ing, and ingenuity in theſe, as in his former remarks
upon the Paradiſe Loſt. And now he hath gone thro'
Milton's poetical works, I hope he will do the ſame
juſtice to another of our greateſt Engliſh poets, and
gratify the public with a complete edition of Spen-
ſer's works, or at leaſt with his equally learned equally
elegant obſervations upon them. I would not be un-
derſtood by this to diſparage in the leaſt Mr. Upton's
intended edition, or Mr. Sympſon's, who is my friend,
and hath kindly aſſiſted me in this edition, as well as
in that of the Paradiſe Loſt. Mr. Upton is certainly
a man of great learning, and ſo likewiſe is Mr. Symp-
ſon, and particularly well read in our old Engliſh au-
thors, as appears from his ſhare in the late excellent
edition of Beaumont's and Fletcher's works: but I
know no man, who hath a juſter and more delicate
taſte of the beauties of an author than Mr. Thyer,
or is a greater maſter of the Italian language and Ita-
lian poetry, which in Spenſer's time was the ſtudy

and

and delight of all the men of letters, and Spenſer him-
ſelf hath borrowed more from that ſource than from
almoſt any other, and ſometimes hath tranſlated two
or three ſtanza's together. Mr. Richardſon likewiſe
hath continued his good offices, and communicated
his comment upon Lycidas and his marginal notes
and obſervations upon the other poems, together with
a very fine head of Milton done by his father after a
drawing of Cooper: and both the Richardſons father
and ſon deſerve the thanks of all lovers of the ſiſter
arts, for their inſtructive eſſays on painting, as well as
for ſeveral ingenious remarks on Milton. I had the
honor of all theſe for my aſſociates and aſſiſtants be-
fore, but I have been farther ſtrengthen'd by ſome
new recruits, which were the more unexpected, as
they were ſent me from gentlemen, with whom I
never had the pleaſure of a perſonal acquaintance. The
reverend Mr. Meadowcourt, Canon of Worceſter,
in 1732 publiſhed a Critical Diſſertation with notes
upon the Paradiſe Regain'd, a ſecond edition of which
was printed in 1748; and he likewiſe tranſmitted to
me a ſheet of his manuſcript remarks, wherein he
hath happily explained a moſt difficult paſſage in Ly-
cidas better than any man had done before him. The
reverend Mr. Calton of Marton in Lincolnſhire hath
contributed much more to my aſſiſtance: he favor'd
me with a long correſpondence; and I am at a loſs
which to commend moſt, his candor as a friend, or
his penetration and learning as a critic and divine.
Beſides all theſe helps I have pickt out ſome grain
from among the chaff of Mr. Peck's remarks, and
have gleaned up every thing which I thought might
any

any ways be ufeful towards illuftrating our author; and in the conclufion have added an index of the lefs common words occafionally explained in the notes.

The Latin poems I cannot fay are equal to feveral of his Englifh compofitions : but yet they are not without their merit; they are not a Cento like moft of the modern Latin poetry; there is fpirit, invention, and other marks and tokens of a rifing genius; for it fhould be confidered, that the greater part of them were written while the author was under twenty. They are printed correctly according to his own editions in 1645 and 1673; and as they can be read only by the learned, there is the lefs occafion for any notes and obfervations upon them. Some few are added, which were thought no more than neceffary. ——But it is time to have done with thefe things, and to apply to other works, more important and more ufeful, if the execution prove anfwerable to the intention.

December 31, 1751.

THE

TABLE of CONTENTS.

THE

THE

FIRST BOOK

OF

PARADISE REGAIN'D.

Vol. I.   B

F. Hayman inv.   *C. Grignion sculp.*

PARADISE REGAIN'D.

B O O K I.

I Who ere while the happy garden fung,
By one man's difobedience loft, now fing
Recover'd Paradife to all mankind,

By

Milton's Paradife Regain'd has not met with the approbation that it deferves. It has not the harmony of numbers, the fublimity of thought, and the beauties of diction, which are in Paradife Loft. It is compofed in a lower and lefs ftriking ftile, a ftile fuited to the fubject. Artful fophiftry, falfe reafoning, fet off in the moft fpecious manner, and refuted by the Son of God with ftrong unaffected eloquence, is the peculiar excellence of this poem. Satan there defends a bad caufe with great fkill and fubtlety, as one thoroughly verfed in that craft;

Qui facere affuerat
    Candida de nigris, et de candentibus atra.

His character is well drawn. *Jortin.*

1. *I who ere while &c.*] Milton begins his Paradife Regain'd in the fame manner as the Paradife Loft; firft propofes his fubject, and then invokes the affiftance of the Holy Spirit. The beginning *I who ere*

while &c is plainly an allufion to the *Ille ego qui quondam* &c attributed to Virgil: but it doth not therefore follow, that Milton had no better tafte than to conceive thefe lines to be genuin. Their being fo well known to all the learned was reafon fufficient for his imitation of them, as it was for Spenfer's before him:

Lo, I the man, whofe Mufe
    whileom did mafk,
As time her taught, in lowly
    fhepherd's weeds,
Am now enforc'd a far unfitter
    tafk,
For trumpets ftern to change
    mine oaten reeds &c.

2. *By one man's difobedience*] The oppofition of *one man's difobedience* in this verfe to *one man's obedience* in ver. 4. is fomewhat in the ftile and manner of St. Paul. Rom. V. 19. *For as by* one man's difobedience *many were made finners; fo by* the obedience of one *fhall many be made righteous.*

3. *Recover'd Paradife*] It may

B 2   feem

By one man's firm obedience fully try'd

Through all temptation, and the tempter foil'd   5

In all his wiles, defeated and repuls'd,

And Eden rais'd in the waſte wilderneſs.

Thou Spi'rit who ledſt this glorious eremite

Into the deſert, his victorious field,

Againſt the ſpiritual foe, and brought'ſt him thence

By

seem a little odd at firſt, that Milton ſhould impute the recovery of Paradiſe to this ſhort ſcene of our Saviour's life upon earth, and not rather extend it to his agony, crucifixion &c; but the reaſon no doubt was, that *Paraaiſe regain'd* by our Saviour's reſiſting the temptations of Satan might be a better contraſt to *Paradiſe loſt* by our firſt parents tco eaſily yielding to the ſame ſeducing Spirit. Beſides he might very probably, and indeed very reaſonably, be apprehenſive, that a ſubject ſo extenſive as well as ſublime might be too great a burden for his declining conſtitution, and a taſk too long for the ſhort term of years he could then hope for. Even in his Paradiſe Loſt he expreſſes his fears, leſt he had begun too late, and left *an age too late, or cold climate, or years ſhould have damp'd his intended wing*; and ſurely he had much greater cauſe to dread the ſame now, and be very cautious of lanching out too far.   *Thyer.* It is hard to ſay whether Milton's wrong notions in divinjty led him

to this defective plan; or his fondneſs for the plan influenced thoſe notions.   That is whether he indeed ſuppoſed the redemption of mankind (as he here repreſents it) was procured by Chriſt's triumph over the Devil in the wilderneſs; or whether he thought that the ſcene of the deſert oppoſed to that of Paradiſe, and the action of a temptation withſtood to a temptation fallen under, made *Paradiſe Regain'd* a more regular ſequel to *Paradiſe Loſt.*   Or if neither this nor that, whether it was his being tired out with the labor of compoſing Paradiſe Loſt made him averſe to another work of length (and then he would never be at a loſs for fanciful reaſons to determin him in the choice of his plan) is very uncertain. All that we can be ſure of is, that the plan is a very unhappy one, and defective even in that narrow view of a ſequel, for it affords the poet no opportunity of driving the Devil back again to Hell from his new conqueſts in the air. In the mean time nothing

By proof th' undoubted Son of God, infpire, 11
As thou art wont, my prompted fong elfe mute,
And bear through highth or depth of nature's bounds
With profp'rous wing full fumm'd, to tell of deeds
Above heroic, though in fecret done, 15
And unrecorded left through many an age,
Worthy t' have not remain'd fo long unfung.

Now

nothing was eafier than to have in-
vented a good one, which fhould
end with the refurrection, and com-
prife thefe four books, fomewhat
contracted, in an epifode, for which
only the fubject of them is fit.
Warburton.
7. *And Eden rais'd in the wafte
wildernefs.*] There is, I think,
a particular beauty in this line,
when one confiders the fine allu-
fion in it to the curfe brought upon
the Paradifiacal earth by the fall of
Adam, —— *Curfed is the ground for
thy fake* —— *Thorns alfo and thiftles
fhall it bring forth.* Thyer.
8. *Thou Spi'rit who ledft this glo-
rious eremite*] The invocation
is properly addref'd to the Holy
Spirit, not only as the infpirer of
every good work, but as the leader
of our Saviour upon this occafion
into the wildernefs. For it is faid
Mat. IV. 1. *Then was Jefus led up
of the Spirit into the wildernefs, to be
tempted of the Devil.* And from the
Greek original εϱημος the defert,
and εϱημιτης an inhabitant of the
defert, is rightly formed the word

eremite, which was ufed before by
Milton in his Paradife Loft III.
474.
Embrio's and idiots, *eremites* and
friers:
and by Fairfax in his tranflation of
Taffo, Cant. 11. St. 4.
Next morn the bifhops twain,
the *eremite:*
and in Italian as well as in Latin
there is *eremita,* which the French,
and we after them, contract into
hermite, hermit.
13. —— *of nature's bounds*] To
which he confines himfelf in this
poem, not as in Paradife Loft,
where he foars above and without
the bounds of nature. VII. 21.
Richardfon.
14. *With profp'rous wing full
fumm'd,*] We had the like ex-
preffion in Paradife Loft VII. 421.
They *fumm'd* their pens ——
and it was noted there that it is a
term in falconry. A hawk is faid
to be *full fumm'd,* when all his fea-

B 3 thers

Now had the great Proclamer, with a voice
More awful than the found of trumpet, cry'd
Repentance, and Heav'n's kingdom nigh at hand 20
To all baptiz'd: to his great baptifm flock'd
With awe the regions round, and with them came
From Nazareth the fon of Jofeph deem'd
To the flood Jordan, came as then obfcure,
Unmark'd, unknown; but him the Baptift foon 25
Defcry'd, divinely warn'd, and witnefs bore

As

thers are grown, when he wants nothing of the *fum* of his feathers, cui nihil de *fumma* pennarum deeft, as Skinner fays. There was therefore no occafion for reading as fome body propofed,

With profp'rous wing full *plum'd*.

14. —— *to tell of deeds
Above heroic*,] Alluding perhaps in the turn of expreffion to the firft verfe of Lucan,

Bella per Emathios *plufquam ci-vilia* campos,
Jufque datum fceleri canimus,
Thyer.

19. —— *cry'd
Repentance, and Heav'n's kingdom
nigh at hand
To all baptiz'd*:] John preached repentance and the approach of Chrift's kingdom. Ask—to whom? and the anfwer is—*to all baptiz'd.* Doth not this feem to imply, that the great prophet baptized *before* he

preached? and that none could be admitted to hear him without this previous immerfion? Whereas in the nature of things as well as the Gofpel hiftory, his preaching muft be, and was preparatory to his baptifm.   One might read

—— nigh at hand,
Baptizing all ——

But this may be thought too diftant from the common lection; and a lefs change will effect the cure, Read therefore

And all baptiz'd:

The prophet preached repentance and the approach of Chrift's kingdom, *and* baptized *all*, that is multitudes of people, who were difpofed by his preaching to prepare their hearts for that great event.

Calton.

There is fomething plaufible and ingenious in this emendation: but I conceive the conftruction to be
not

As to his worthier, and would have refign'd
To him his heav'nly office, nor was long
His witnefs unconfirm'd : on him baptiz'd
Heav'n open'd, and in likenefs of a dove   30
The Spi'rit defcended, while the Father's voice
From Heav'n pronounc'd him his beloved Son.
That heard the Adverfary, who roving ftill
About the world, at that affembly fam'd
Would not be laft, and with the voice divine   35
                                            Nigh

not that he *cry'd to all baptiz'd re-*
pentance &c. but *Heav'n's kingdom*
nigh at hand to all baptiz'd. Hea-
ven's kingdom was nigh at hand to
all fuch as were baptized with
John's baptifm; they were thereby
difpofed and prepared for the re-
ception of the Gofpel.

24. *To the flood Jordan, came as*
then obfcure,] In Mr. Fenton's and
moft other editions it is pointed
thus,

> To the flood Jordan came, as
> then obfcure,

but we have followed the punctua-
tion of Milton's own edition ; for
there is very little force in the re-
petition, *and with them came, to the*
flood Jordan came; but to fay that
he *came with them to the flood Jor-*
dan, and *came as then obfcure,* is
very good fenfe, and worthy of the
repetition.

25. ——*but him the Baptift foon*
Defcry'd, divinely warn'd,] John

the Baptift had notice given him
before, that he might certainly
know the Meffiah by the Holy
Ghoft defcending and abiding upon
him. *And I knew him not, but he*
that fent me to baptize with water,
the fame faid unto me, Upon whom
thou fhalt fee the Spirit defcending
and remaining on him, the fame is he
which baptizeth with the Holy Ghoft.
John I. 33. But it appears from
St. Matthew, that the Baptift knew
him and acknowledged him, before
he was baptized and before the
Holy Ghoft defcended upon him.
Mat. III. 14. *I have need to be bap-*
tized of thee, and comeft thou to me?
To account for which we muft ad-
mit with Milton, that another di-
vine revelation was made to him
at this very time, fignifying that
this was the perfon, of whom he
had had fuch notice before.

26. —— *divinely warn'd*] To
comprehend the propriety of this
word *divinely* the reader muft have
                                          his

Nigh thunder-ſtruck, th' exalted man, to whom

Such high atteſt was giv'n, a while ſurvey'd

With wonder, then with envy fraught and rage

Flies to his place, nor reſts, but in mid air

To council ſummons all his mighty peers,　　　40

Within thick clouds and dark ten-fold involv'd,

A gloomy conſiſtory; and them amidſt

With looks aghaſt and ſad he thus beſpake.

　O ancient Powers of air and this wide world,

For much more willingly I mention air,　　　45

This our old conqueſt, than remember Hell,

Our hated habitation; well ye know

How

his eye upon the Latin *divinitus*, *from Heaven*, ſince the word *divinely* in our language ſcarce ever comes up to this meaning. Milton uſes it in much the ſame ſenſe in Paradiſe Loſt. VIII. 500.

　She heard me thus, and though *divinely* brought.　*Thyer.*

　41. *Within thick clouds &c*] Milton in making Satan's reſidence to be *in mid air, within thick clouds and dark*, ſeems to have St. Auſtin in his eye, who ſpeaking of the region of clouds, ſtorms, thunder &c ſays —— ad iſta caliginoſa, id eſt, ad hunc aerem, tanquam ad carcerem, damnatus eſt diabolus &c. Enarr. in Pſ. 148. S. 9. Tom. 5. p. 1677. Edit. Bened.　*Thyer.*

　42. *A gloomy conſiſtory;*] This in imitation of Virgil Æn. III. 677.

　Cernimus aſtantes nequicquam lumine torvo
　Ætneos fratres, cœlo capita alta ferentes,
　Concilium horrendum:

By the word *conſiſtory* I ſuppoſe Milton intends to glance at the meeting of the Pope and Cardinals ſo nam'd, or perhaps at the epiſcopal tribunal, to all which ſort of courts or aſſemblies he was an avow'd enemy. The phraſe *concilium horrendum* Vida makes uſe of upon a like occaſion of aſſembling the infernal powers. Chriſt. Lib. 1.

Protinus

How many ages, as the years of men,
This univerſe we have poſſeſs'd, and rul'd
In manner at our will th' affairs of earth,   50
Since Adam and his facil conſort Eve
Loſt Paradiſe deceiv'd by me, though ſince
With dread attending when that fatal wound
Shall be inflicted by the ſeed of Eve
Upon my head: long the decrees of Heav'n   55
Delay, for longeſt time to him is ſhort;
And now too ſoon for us the circling hours
This dreaded time have compaſs'd, wherein we
Muſt bide the ſtroke of that long threaten'd wound,

At

Protinus acciri diros ad regia
   fratres
Limina, *concilium horrendum.*

And Taſſo alſo in the very ſame
manner. Cant. 4. St. 2.

   Che ſia comanda il popol ſuo
      raccolto
   (*Concilio horrendo*) entro la regia
   foglia.   *Thyer.*

   44. *O ancient Pow'rs of air and
      this wide world,*] So the
Devil is call'd in Scripture, *the
prince of the power of the air*, Eph.
II. 2. and evil Spirits *the rulers of
the darkneſs of this world*, Eph. VI.
12. Satan here ſummons a coun-
cil, and opens it as he did in the
Paradiſe Loſt: but here is not that

copiouſneſs and variety which is in
the other; here are not different
ſpeeches and ſentiments adapted
to the different characters; it is a
council without a debate; Satan is
the only ſpeaker. And the author,
as if conſcious of this defect, has
artfully endevored to obviate the ob-
jection by ſaying, that their danger

—— admits no long debate,
But muſt with ſomething ſudden
   be oppos'd,

and afterwards

—— no time was then
For long indulgence to their
   fears or grief.

The true reaſon is, he found it
impoſſible to exceed or equal the
                        ſpeeches

At leaſt if ſo we can, and by the head   60
Broken be not intended all our power
To be infring'd, our freedom and our being,
In this fair empire won of earth and air;
For this ill news I bring, the woman's ſeed
Deſtin'd to this, is late of woman born: 65
His birth to our juſt fear gave no ſmall cauſe,
But his growth now to youth's full flow'r, diſplaying
All virtue, grace, and wiſdom to achieve
Things higheſt, greateſt, multiplies my fear.
Before him a great prophet, to proclame   70
His coming, is ſent harbinger, who all
Invites, and in the conſecrated ſtream
Pretends to waſh off ſin, and fit them ſo
Purified to receive him pure, or rather
To do him honour as their king; all come,   75

                                                        And

ſpeeches in his former council, and
therefore has aſſign'd the beſt rea-
ſon he could for not making any
in this.

74. *Purified to receive him pure,*]
Alluding to the Scripture expreſſion
1 John III. 3. *And every man that
hath this hope in him, purifieth him-
ſelf even as he is pure.*

83. *A perfect dove deſcend,*] He
had expreſſed it before ver. 30. *in
likeneſs of a dove,* agreeably to

St. Matthew, *the Spirit of God de-
ſcending like a dove,* III. 16. and to
St. Mark, *the Spirit like a dove de-
ſcending upon him,* I. 10. But as
Luke ſays, that *the Holy Ghoſt de-
ſcended in a bodily ſhape,* III. 22.
the poet ſuppoſes with Tertullian,
Auſtin, and others of the fathers,
that it was a real dove, as the
painters always repreſent it.

91. *Who this is we muſt learn.*]
Our author favors the opinion of
                                              thoſe

And he himfelf among them was baptiz'd,
Not thence to be more pure, but to receive
The teftimony' of Heav'n, that who he is
Thenceforth the nations may not doubt; I faw
The prophet do him reverence, on him rifing   80
Out of the water, Heav'n above the clouds
Unfold her cryftal doors, thence on his head
A perfect dove defcend, whate'er it meant,
And out of Heav'n the fovran voice I heard,
This is my Son belov'd, in him am pleas'd.   85
His mother then is mortal, but his fire
He who obtains the monarchy of Heaven,
And what will he not do to' advance his Son?
His firft be-got we know, and fore have felt,
When his fierce thunder drove us to the deep;   90
Who this is we muft learn, for man he feems

In

thofe writers, Ignatius and others among the Ancients, and Beza and others among the Moderns, who believed that the Devil, tho' he might know Jefus to be fome extraordinary perfon, yet knew him not to be the Meffiah, the Son of God: and the words of the Devil *If thou be the Son of God* feem to exprefs his uncertainty concerning that matter. The Devils indeed afterwards knew him and proclamed him to be the Son of God, but they might not know him to be fo at this time, before this temptation, or before he had enter'd upon his public miniftry, and manifefted himfelf by his miracles. And our author, who makes the Devil to hear the voice from Heaven *This is my beloved Son.* ftill makes him doubt in what fenfe Jefus was fo called. See IV. 514.

In all his lineaments, though in his face
The glimpfes of his father's glory fhine.
Ye fee our danger on the utmoft edge
Of hazard, which admits no long debate,   95
But muft with fomething fudden be oppos'd,
Not force, but well couch'd fraud, well woven fnares,
Ere in the head of nations he appear
Their king, their leader, and fupreme on earth.
I, when no other durft, fole undertook   100
The difmal expedition to find out
And ruin Adam, and th' exploit perform'd
Succefsfully; a calmer voyage now
Will waft me; and the way found profp'rous once
Induces beft to hope of like fuccefs.   105
                                        He

Thenceforth I thought thee worth my nearer view,
And narrower fcrutiny, that I might learn
In what degree or meaning thou art call'd
The Son of God, which bears no fingle fenfe; &c.

94. *Ye fee our danger on the utmoft edge Of hazard*,] An expreffion borrowed from Shakefpear. All's well, that ends well. Act III. Sc. 5.

———— Sir, it is
A charge too heavy for my ftrength; but yet

We'll ftrive to bear it for your worthy fake,
To *th' extreme edge of hazard.*

113. *To him their great dictator,*] Milton applies this title very properly to Satan in his prefent fituation, as the authority he is now vefted with is quite dictatorial, and the expedition on which he is going of the utmoft confequence to the fall'n Angels.   *Thyer.*

119. *So to the coaft of Jordan he directs His eafy fteps, girded with fnaky wiles*,] For as Lightfoot obferves Vol. II. p. 299. the wildernefs,

He ended, and his words impreffion left
Of much amazement to th' infernal crew,
Diſtracted and ſurpris'd with deep diſmay
At theſe ſad tidings; but no time was then
For long indulgence to their fears or grief: 110
Unanimous they all commit the care
And management of this main enterprize
To him their great dictator, whoſe attempt
At firſt againſt mankind ſo well had thriv'd
In Adam's overthrow, and led their march   115
From Hell's deep-vaulted den to dwell in light,
Regents and potentates, and kings, yea Gods
Of many a pleaſant realm and province wide.
So to the coaſt of Jordan he directs

His

neſs, where our Saviour underwent his forty days temptation, was on the ſame bank of Jordan where the baptiſm of John was, St. Luke witneſſing it, that Jeſus being now baptized ὑπιςρεψιι απο τɤ Ιορδανɤ, *returned from Jordan*, namely from the ſame tract, whereby he came thither. *His eaſy ſteps*, for here was not that danger and difficulty as in his firſt expedition to ruin mankind. It is ſaid in reference to what he had ſpoken before,

I, when no other durſt, ſole un-
dertook
The diſmal expedition to find out

And ruin Adam ———
——— a calmer voyage now
Will waft me &c.

Girded with ſnaky wiles, alluding to the habit of ſorcerers and ne-cromancers, who are repreſented in ſome prints as girded about the middle with the ſkins of ſnakes and ſerpents; a cincture totally op-poſit to that recommended by the Apoſtle Eph. VI. 14. *having your loins girt about with truth*; and worn by our Saviour Iſa. XI. 5. *And righteouſneſs ſhall be the girdle of his loins, and faithfulneſs the girdle of his reins.*

120 ——— *girded*

His eafy fteps, girded with fnaky wiles,   120
Where he might likelieft find this new-declar'd,
This man of men, attefted Son of God,
Temptation and all guile on him to try;
So to fubvert whom he fufpected rais'd
To end his reign on earth fo long enjoy'd: 125
But contrary unweeting he fulfill'd
The purpos'd counfel pre-ordain'd and fix'd
Of the moft High, who in full frequence bright
Of Angels, thus to Gabriel fmiling fpake.

    Gabriel, this day by proof thou fhalt behold, 130
Thou and all Angels converfant on earth
With man or mens affairs, how I begin

                            To

120 — *girded with fnaky wiles,*] 'The imagery very fine, and the circumftance extremely proper. Satan is here figured engaging on a great expedition, fuccinct, and his habit girt about him with a girdle of fnakes; which puts us in mind of the inftrument of the fall.
           Warburton.

  122. *This man of men, attefted Son of God,*] The phrafe is low and idiotic; and I wifh the poet had rather written

    This man, *of Heav'n* attefted Son of God.

In the holy Scriptures *God of Gods,* and *Heaven of Heavens* are truly grand expreffions: but then there is an idea of greatnefs in the words themfelves to fupport the dignity of the phrafe: which is wanting in Milton's *man of men.*   Calton.

  129. — *Thus to Gabriel fmiling fpake.*] This fpeech is properly addrefs'd to *Gabriel* particularly among the Angels, as he feems to have been the Angel particularly employed in the embaffies and tranfactions relating to the Gofpel. Gabriel was fent to inform Daniel of the famous prophecy of the feventy weeks; Gabriel notified the conception of John the Baptift to
                   his

To verify that folemn meſſage late,
On which I fent thee to the Virgin pure
In Galilee, that ſhe ſhould bear a fon   135
Great in renown, and call'd the Son of God;
Then toldſt her doubting how theſe things could be
To her a virgin, that on her ſhould come
The Holy Ghoſt, and the pow'r of the Higheſt
O'er-ſhadow her : this man born and now up-grown,
To ſhow him worthy of his birth divine   141
And high prediction, henceforth I expoſe
To Satan ; let him tempt and now aſſay
His utmoſt ſubtlety, becauſe he boaſts
And vaunts of his great cunning to the throng 145

                                                     Of

his father Zacharias, and of our
bleſſed Saviour to his virgin mo-
ther. And the Jewiſh Rabbi's fay,
that Michael was the miniſter of
feverity, but Gabriel of mercy:
and accordingly our poet makes
Gabriel the guardian Angel of Pa-
radiſe, and employs Michael to
expel our firſt parents out of Para-
diſe: and for the fame reaſon this
fpeech is directed to Gabriel in
particular. And God's being re-
prefented as *ſmiling* may be juſtified
not only by the Heathen poets, as
Virg. Æn. I. 254.

    Olli *ſubridens* hominum fator
    atque deorum ;

but by the authority of Scripture
itſelf. See Paradife Loſt, V. 718.

   131. *Thou and all Angels conver-*
      ſant on earth
With man or mens affairs,] This
feems to be taken from the verſes
attributed to Orpheus.

Αγγελοι, ὑ-τι μεμηλε βροτοις ὡς
   παιҭα τελειται.

   144.   — *becauſe he boaſts*
   and vaunts &c.] This alludes
to what Satan had juſt before faid
to his companions, ver. 100.

   I, when no other durſt, fole un-
dertook &c.   *Thyer.*

                            163. *That*

Of his apoſtaſy; he might have learnt
Leſs overweening, ſince he fail'd in Job,
Whoſe conſtant perſeverance overcame
Whate'er his cruel malice could invent.
He now ſhall know I can produce a man   150
Of female ſeed, far abler to reſiſt
All his ſolicitations, and at length
All his vaſt force, and drive him back to Hell,
Winning by conqueſt what the firſt man loſt
By fallacy ſurpris'd.   But firſt I mean   155
To exerciſe him in the wilderneſs,

There

163. *That all the Angels and ethe-
real Powers*, &c] Not a word
is ſaid here of the Son of God, but
what a Socinian would allow. His
divine nature is artfully concealed
under a partial and ambiguous re-
preſentation; and the Angels are
firſt to learn the myſtery of the in-
carnation from that important con-
flict, which is the ſubject of this
poem. They are ſeemingly invited
to behold the triumphs of the *man*
Chriſt Jeſus over the enemy of man-
kind; and theſe ſurpriſe them with
the glorious diſcovery of the *God*

— inſhrin'd
In fleſhly tabernacle, and human
form.

That Chriſt was *perfect man* is a
partial truth, and ſerves to keep the
higher perfection of his divine na-
ture, for the preſent, out of ſight,
without denying or excluding it.
It is likewiſe very truly ſaid of this
perfect man, that he is by *merit* call'd
the *Son of God*. Juſtin Martyr ob-
ſerves in his ſecond Apology [p. 67.
Ed. Col.] that Chriſt, conſidered
only as man, deſerved for his ſu-
perior wiſdom to be called the Son
of God. Ὑιὸς δε Θεᾳ ὁ Ιησᾳς λε-
γομενᾳ, ει και κοινως μονον ανθρω-
πᾳ, δια σοφιαν αξιᾳ ὑιᾳ Θεᾳ λε-
γεσθαι. In either capacity of *God*
or *Man* he had a clame of *merit*
to the title. The Father, ſpeaking
to his eternal Word in Paradiſe
Loſt, III. 308. on his generous un-
dertakings for mankind, ſaith

—— and haſt been found
By merit more than birthright
Son of God.

Again,

There he fhall firft lay down the rudiments
Of his great warfare, ere I fend him forth
To conquer Sin and Death, the two grand foes,
By humiliation and ftrong fufferance :   160
His weaknefs fhall o'ercome Satanic ftrength,
And all the world, and mafs of finful flefh ;
That all the Angels and ethereal Powers,
They now, and men hereafter may difcern,
From what confummate virtue I have chofe   165
This perfect man, by merit call'd my Son,
To earn falvation for the fons of men.

So

Again, the words *confummate vir-tue* are ambiguous, and may be re-ferred to the *divine* nature of Chrift as well as the *human*. Their pre-fent connexion applies them direct-ly to the *human* nature : but they had a fecret reference, I conceive, in the poet's meaning to the ma-jefty of that heavenly part of him, which denominates Chrift in the holy Scriptures the wifdom of God and the power (or *virtue*) of God, Θεȣ δυναμιν, Dei *virtutem*, Lat. Vulg. 1 Cor. I. 24. Hunc tamen folum primogenitum divini nomi-nis appellatione dignatus eft, patria fcilicet *virtute*, ac majeftate pollen-tem. Effe autem fummi Dei filium, qui fit poteftate maxima præditus, non tantùm voces prophetarum, fed etiam Sibyllarum vaticinia de-monftrant. Lactantius. Div. Inft. Lib. IV. 6. Cum igitur a prophetis idem manus Dei, & *virtus*, & fer-mo dicatur. ibid. 29. Paradife Loft. VI. 713.

— Into thee fuch *virtue* and grace
Immenfe I have transfus'd.

Chrift fhow'd his heavenly wif-dom upon every trial: but his *divine virtue* broke out, to the amazement of the tempter, in the laft. Note that the præpofition *from*,

From what confummate virtue..
is ufed here as ἰπο and præ, to fignify *for* or *becaufe of.*
Calton.

So fpake th' eternal Father, and all Heaven
Admiring ftood a fpace, then into hymns
Burft forth, and in celeftial meafures mov'd,   170
Circling the throne and finging, while the hand
Sung with the voice, and this the argument.
   Victory' and triumph to the Son of God
Now entring his great duel, not of arms,

                                   But

168. *So fpake th' eternal father, and all Heaven Admiring ftood a fpace,*] We cannot but take notice of the great art of the poet in fetting forth the dignity and importance of his fubject. He reprefents all beings as interefted one way or other in the event. A council of Devils is fummon'd; an affembly of Angels is held upon the occafion. Satan is the fpeaker in the one, the Almighty in the other. Satan expreffes his diffidence, but ftill refolves to make trial of this Son of God; the Father declares his purpofe of proving and illuftrating his Son. The infernal crew are diftracted and furpriz'd with deep difmay; all Heaven ftands a while in admiration. The fiends are filent thro' fear and grief; the Angels burft forth into finging with joy and the affured hopes of fuccefs. And their attention is thus engaged, the better to engage the attention of the reader.

171.   *—— while the hand*

Sung with the voice,] We have pretty near the fame phrafe in Tibullus. III. IV. 41.

Sed poftquam fuerant *digiti cum voce locuti,*
   Edidit hæc dulci triftia verba modo.

And the word *hand* is ufed by Milton once again in this poem, and alfo in the Arcades, to diftinguifh inftrumental harmony from vocal. IV. 254.

There thou fhalt hear and learn the fecret power
Of harmony in tones and numbers hit
By voice or hand.

Arcades, 77.

If my inferior *hand or voice* could hit
Inimitable founds.

I have fometimes indulg'd a fufpicion, that the poet dictated,
            —while

But to vanquifh by wifdom hellifh wiles.   175
The Father knows the Son ; therefore fecure
Ventures his filial virtue, though untry'd,
Againft whate'er may tempt, whate'er feduce,
Allure, or terrify, or undermine.
Be fruftrate all ye ftratagems of Hell,   180
And devilifh machinations come to nought.

So

——— while the *harp*
Sung with the voice ; ———

but the few authorities alledged put
the prefent reading out of queftion.
Calton.

174. *Now entring his great duel,*]
There is, I think, a meannefs in
the cuftomary fenfe of this term
that makes it unworthy of thefe
fpeakers and this occafion; and yet
it is obfervable, that Milton in his
Paradife Loft makes Michael ufe
the very fame word where he is
fpeaking to Adam of the fame
thing. XII. 386.

To whom thus Michael. Dream
not of their fight,
As of a *duel*, &c.

The Italian *duello*, if I am not
miftaken, bears a ftronger fenfe,
and this, I fuppofe, Milton had in
view.   *Thyer.*
If it be not a contradiction, it is
inaccurate at leaft in Milton, to
make an Angel fay in one place,
Dream not of their fight as of a duel;
and afterwards to make the Angels

exprefs it by the metaphor of a
duel, *Now entring his great duel.*

175. *But to vanquifh by wifdom*]
He lays the accent on the laft fyl-
lable in *vanquifh*, as elfewhere in
triumph; and in many places, in
my opinion, he imitates the Latin
and Greek profody, and makes a
vowel long before two confonants.
Jortin.

176. *The Father knows the Son;*
therefore fecure
Ventures his filial virtue, though
untry'd,] Could this have been
faid by the Angels, if they alfo had
known this Son to be the eternal
Word, who created all things; and
who had before driven this Temp-
ter, and all his Powers out of Hea-
ven? The incarnation was gene-
rally believed by the Fathers to
have been a fecret to Angels, till
they learned it from the Church.
See Huetii Origeniana. Lib. 2.
Cap. 2. Quæft. 5. 18. As to the
time and means of their informa-
tion, Milton feems to be particular.
Calton.

C 2   182. *S,*

So they in Heav'n their odes and vigils tun'd:
Mean while the Son of God, who yet some days
Lodg'd in Bethabara where John baptiz'd,
Musing and much revolving in his breast,   185
How best the mighty work he might begin
Of Saviour to mankind, and which way first
Publish his God-like office now mature,
One day forth walk'd alone, the Spirit leading,
And his deep thoughts, the better to converse   190
With solitude, till far from track of men,

> Thought

182. *So they in Heav'n their odes and vigils tun'd:*
Mean while the Son of God——] How nearly does the poet here ad-here to the same way of speaking he had used in Paradise Lost on the same occasion. III. 416.

Thus they in Heav'n above the starry sphere
Their happy hours in joy and hymning spent.
Mean while &c.   *Thyer.*

182.—*their odes and vigils tun'd:*] This is a very uncommon expres-fion, and not easy to be understood, unless we suppose that by *vigils* the poet meant those songs which they sung while they kept their watches. Singing of hymns is their manner of keeping their *wakes* in Heaven. And I see no reason why their evening service may not be called *vigils*, as the morning service is

called *mattins*. Mr. Sympson pro-poses a flight alteration,

——their odes *in* vigils tun'd,

that is, each watch when reliev'd sung so and so: but as we have explain'd the word, there seems to be no occasion for any alteration.

183. ——*who yet some days*
Lodg'd in Bethabara where John baptiz'd,] The poet, I presume, said this upon the authority of the first chapter of St. John's Gospel, where several particulars, which happened several days together, are related concerning the Son of God, and it is said ver. 28. *These things were done in Bethabara beyond Jor-dan, where John was baptizing.*

189. *One day forth walk'd alone,*
the Spirit leading,
And his deep thoughts.] This is wrong pointed in all the editions thus,

> One

Thought following thought, and ſtep by ſtep led on,
He enter'd now the bord'ring deſert wild,
And with dark ſhades and rocks environ'd round,
His holy meditations thus purſu'd.   195
    O what a multitude of thoughts at once
Awaken'd in me ſwarm, while I conſider
What from within I feel myſelf, and hear
What from without comes often to my ears,
Ill ſorting with my preſent ſtate compar'd!   200
When I was yet a child, no childiſh play

                                            To

One day forth walk'd alone, the
    Spirit leading;
And his deep thoughts, &c.

But at moſt there ſhould be only a
comma after *leading*, for the con-
ſtruction is, *his deep thoughts lead-
ing* as well as the Spirit. And as
Mr. Thyer obſerves, what a fine
light does Milton here place that
text of Scripture in, where it is ſaid,
that *Jeſus was led up of the Spirit
into the wilderneſs*, and how excel-
lently adapted to embelliſh his
poem! He adheres ſtrictly to the
inſpir'd hiſtorian, and yet without
any ſort of profanation gives it a
turn which is vaſtly poetical.

    191.—*till far from track of men,
Thought following thought*, &c] I
hope it won't be thought too light
to obſerve, that our author might
probably in theſe lines have in view

his favorite romances, where the
muſing knights are often deſcrib'd
loſing themſelves in foreſts in this
manner. *Thyer.*

    195.——*meditations*] This is the
reading in Milton's own edition;
in all the reſt that I have ſeen it is
meditation.

    201. *When I was yet a child, no
childiſh play
To me was pleaſing*;] How finely
and conſiſtently does Milton here
imagin the youthful meditations of
our Saviour? how different from
and ſuperior to that ſuperſtitious
trumpery which one meets with in
the *Evangelium Infantiæ*, and other
ſuch apocryphal traſh? Vid. Fa-
bricii Cod. Apoc. N. Teſt. *Thyer*.
He ſeems to allude to Callimachus,
who ſays elegantly of young Jupi-
ter, Hymn. in Jov. 56.
    C 3   Οξυ

To me was pleafing; all my mind was fet
Serious to learn and know, and thence to do
What might be public good; myfelf I thought
Born to that end, born to promote all truth,   205
All righteous things: therefore above my years,
The law of God I read, and found it fweet,
Made it my whole delight, and in it grew
To fuch perfection, that ere yet my age
Had meafur'd twice fix years, at our great feaft 210
I went into the temple, there to hear
The teachers of our law, and to propofe

What

Οξυ δ'αναβησας, ταχινοι δε τοι
ηλθον ιυλοι.
Αλλ' ετι παιδι☉ εων εφρασσαο
παιλα τελεια.

Swift was thy growth, and early
    was thy bloom,
But earlier wifdom crown'd thy
    infant days.   *Jortin.*

Henry Stephens's tranflation of
the latter verfe is very much to our
purpofe,

    Verum ætate, puer, digna es
        meditatus adulta:

or rather his more paraphraftical
tranflation,

    Verum ætate puer, puerili haud
        more folebas
    Ludere; fed jam tum tibi feria
        cuncta placebant,

Digna ætate animus jam tum
    volvebat adulta.

And Pindar in like manner praifes
Demophilus. Pyth. Od. IV. 501.
κεινῳ☉ γαρ εν παισι νεῳ☉, εν δε βελαις
πρεσβυς. Our author might allude
to thefe paffages, but he certainly
alluded to the words of the Apoftle
1 Cor. XIII. 11. only inverting
the thought. *When I was a child,
I fpake as a child* &c.

204.   ―― *myfelf I thought
Born to that end, born to promote
    all truth,*] Alluding to our
Saviour's words John XVIII. 37.
*To this end was I born, and for this
caufe came I into the world, that I
fhould bear witnefs unto the truth.*

210.―― *at our great feaft*] The
feaft of the paffover, Luke II. 41.
    214. *And*

What might improve my knowledge or their own;
And was admir'd by all: yet this not all
To which my fpi'rit afpir'd; victorious deeds   215
Flam'd in my heart, heroic acts, one while
To refcue Ifrael from the Roman yoke,
Then to fubdue and quell o'er all the earth
Brute violence and proud tyrannic power,
Till truth were freed, and equity reftor'd: 220
Yet held it more humane, more heav'nly firft
By winning words to conquer willing hearts,
And make perfuafion do the work of fear;

At

214. *And was admir'd by all:*]
For *all that heard him were aftonifh-
ed at his underftanding and anfwers.*
Luke II. 47.

219. *Brute violence*] So again in
the Mafk

And noble grace that dafh'd *brute
violence.*   Thyer.

221. *Yet held it more humane,
more heav'nly firft* &c.] Here
breathes the true fpirit of tolera-
tion in thefe lines, and the fenti-
ment is very fitly put into the
mouth of him, who *came not to
deftroy mens lives but to fave them.*
The allitteration of w's in this
line, and the affonance of *winning*
and *willing* have a very beautiful
effect;
By winning words to conquer
willing hearts.

—— victorque volentes
Per populos dat jura, viamque
affectat Olympo.

Our author was always a declar'd
enemy to perfecution, and a friend
to liberty of confcience. He rifes
above himfelf, whenever he fpeaks
of the fubject; and he muft have
felt it very ftrongly, to have ex-
prefs'd it fo happily. For as Mr.
Thyer juftly remarks upon this
paffage, there is a peculiar foftnefs
and harmony in thefe lines, exact-
ly fuited to that gentle fpirit of
love that breathes in them; and
that man muft have an inquifito-
rial fpirit indeed who does not feel
the force of them.

222.—*to conquer willing hearts,*]
Virgil Georg. IV. 561.
—— victorque

At leaft to try, and teach the erring foul

Not wilfully mif-doing, but unware   225

Mifled; the ftubborn only to fubdue.

Thefe growing thoughts my mother foon perceiving

By words at times caft forth inly rejoic'd,

And faid to me apart, High are thy thoughts

O Son, but nourifh them and let them foar   230

To what highth facred virtue and true worth

Can raife them, though above example high;

By matchlefs deeds exprefs thy matchlefs Sire.

For know, thou art no fon of mortal man;

Though men efteem thee low of parentage,   235

Thy father is th'eternal King who rules

All Heav'n and Earth, Angels and Sons of men;

A meffenger from God foretold thy birth

Conceiv'd in me a virgin, he foretold

Thou

——victorque volentes
Per populos dat jura——
which expreffion of Virgil's, by
the way, feems to be taken from
Xenophon, Oeconomic. XXI. 12.
Ου γαρ παιν μοι δοκει ολον τετι το
αγαθον αιθρωπινον ειναι, αλλα θειον,
το εθελονλωι αρχειν. I could add
other paffages of Xenophon, which
Virgil has manifeftly copied.
                    Jortin.
226.—*the ftubborn only to fubdue.*]
We cannot fufficiently condemn the

negligence of the former editors
and printers, who have not fo
much as correcled the Errata point-
ed out to them by Milton himfelf,
but have carefully followed all the
blunders of the firft edition, and
increafed the number with new
ones of their own. This paffage
affords an inftance. In all the
editions we read.

— the ftubborn only to *deftroy*;
and this being good fenfe, the
                        miftake

Thou fhould'ft be great, and fit on David's throne,

And of thy kingdom there fhould be no end. 241

At thy nativity a glorious quire

Of Angels in the fields of Bethlehem fung

To fhepherds watching at their folds by night,

And told them the Meffiah now was born 245

Where they might fee him, and to thee they came,

Directed to the manger where thou lay'ft,

For in the inn was left no better room:

A ftar, not feen before, in Heav'n appearing

Guided the wife men thither from the eaft, 250

To honor thee with incenfe, myrrh, and gold,

By whofe bright courfe led on they found the place,

Affirming it thy ftar new grav'n in Heaven,

By which they knew the king of Ifrael born.

Juft Simeon and prophetic Anna, warn'd 255

By

miftake is not fo eafily detected: but in the firft edition the reader is defired in the table of Errata for *deftroy* to read *fubdue*; and if we confider it, this is the more proper word, more fuitable to the humane and heavenly character of the fpeaker; and befides it anfwers to the *fubdue and quell* in ver. 218. *The fon of man came not to deftroy mens lives* &c. Luke IX. 56.

227. —*my mother foon perceiving*
—— *inly rejoic'd,*]

Virgil. Æn. I. 502.

Latonæ tacitum pertentant gaudia pectus. *Jortin.*

241. ——*there fhould be no end.*] We have reftored the reading of Milton's own edition, *fhould* not *fhall*, as before

Thou *fhouldft* be great ——

255. *Juft Simeon and prophetic Anna,*] It may not be impro- per to remark how ftrictly our au- thor

By vifion, found thee in the temple', and fpake
Before the altar and the vefted prieft,
Like things of thee to all that prefent ftood.

This having heard, ftrait I again revolv'd
The law and prophets, fearching what was writ 260
Concerning the Meffiah, to our fcribes
Known partly, and foon found of whom they fpake
I am; this chiefly, that my way muft lie
Through many a hard affay ev'n to the death,
Ere 1 the promis'd kingdom can attain, 265
Or work redemption for mankind, whofe fins
Full weight muft be transferr'd upon my head.

Yet

thor adheres to the Scripture hif-
tory, not only in the particulars
which he relates, but alfo in the
very epithets which he affixes to
the perfons; as here *Juft Simeon*,
becaufe it is faid Luke II. 25. *and
the fame man was juft:* and *pro-
phetic Anna*, becaufe it is faid Luke
II. 36. *and there was one Anna a
prophetefs*. The like accuracy may
be obferved in all the reft.

262.——*and foon found of whom
they fpake
I am*;] The Jews thought that
the Meffiah, when he came, would
be without all power and diftinc-
tion, and *unknown even to himfelf*,
till Elias had anointed and declared

him. Χριϛ⊙· δε ει και γεγενηται,
και εϛι πȣ, αγιωϛ⊙· εϛι, και ȣδε
αυτⷦ· πω ἑαυτον επιϛαται, ȣδε εχει
δυναμιν τινα, μεχρις αν ελθων Ηλιας
χριση αυτον, και Φανερον πασι ποιηση.
Juft. Mart. Dial. cum Tryph. p.
226. Ed. Col. *Calton*.

266. ——*whofe fins
Full weight muft be transferr'd
upon my head.*] Ifaiah LIII. 6.
*The Lord hath laid on him the ini-
quity of us all.*

271. *Not knew by fight*] Tho'
Jefus and John the Baptift were
related, yet they were brought up
in different countries, and had no
manner

Yet neither thus diſhearten'd or diſmay'd,

The time prefix'd I waited, when behold

The Baptiſt (of whoſe birth I oft had heard, 270

Not knew by ſight) now come, who was to come

Before Meſſiah and his way prepare.

I as all others to his baptiſm came,

Which I believ'd was from above; but he

Strait knew me, and with loudeſt voice proclam'd

Me him (for it was ſhown him ſo from Heaven) 276

Me him whoſe harbinger he was; and firſt

Refus'd on me his baptiſm to confer,

As much his greater, and was hardly won:

But as I roſe out of the laving ſtream, 280
                                        Heav'n

manner of intimacy or acquain-
tance with each other. John the
Baptiſt ſays expreſsly John I. 31,
33. *And I knew him not*; and he
did not ſo much as know him by
ſight, till our Saviour came to his
baptiſm; and afterwards it doth not
appear that they ever converſed
together. And it was wiſely or-
dered ſo by Providence, that the
teſtimony of John might have the
greater weight, and be freer from
all ſuſpicion of any compact or
colluſion between them.

278. *Refus'd on me his baptiſm to
confer,*

As much his greater,] Here Mil-
ton uſes the word *greater* in the
ſame manner as he had done be-
fore, Parad. Loſt, V. 172.

Thou Sun, of this great world
    both eye and ſoul,
Acknowledge him *thy greater*.

And this, I think, is a proof that
the preſent reading there is right,
and that both Dr. Bentley's emen-
dation and mine ought abſolutely
to be rejected.   *Thyer.*

280. —*out of the laving ſtream,*]
Alluding, I fancy, to the phraſe
laver of regeneration ſo frequently
applied to baptiſm. It may be ob-
ſerved in general of this ſoliloquy
of our Saviour, that it is not only
excellently well adapted to the pre-
                                        ſent

Heav'n open'd her eternal doors, from whence
The Spi'rt defcended on me like a dove,
And laft the fum of all, my Father's voice,
Audibly heard from Heav'n, pronounc'd me his,
Me his beloved Son, in whom alone   285
He was well pleas'd; by which I knew the time
Now full, that I no more fhould live obfcure,
But cpenly begin, as beft becomes

Th'authority

fent condition of the divine fpeaker, but alfo very artfully introduc'd by the poet to give us a hiftory of his hero from his birth to the very fcene with which the poem is open'd.   *Thyer.*

281. ——— *eternal doors*] So in Pfal. XXIV. 7, 9. *everlafting doors.*

286.   ——— *the time Now full,*] Alluding to the Scripture phrafe, *the fulnefs of time. When the fulnefs of time was come* &c Gal. IV. 4.

293. *For what concerns my knowledge God reveals.*] Jefus was led by an inward impulfe to retire into the defert: and he obey'd the motion, without knowing the purpofe of it, for that was not reveal'd to him by God. The whole foliloquy is form'd upon an opinion, which hath authorities enough to give it credit, viz. *that Chrift was not, by virtue of the perfonal union of the two natures, and from the firft moment of that union, pof-*

fefs'd of all the knowledge of the ΛΟΓΟΣ, *as far as the capacity of a human mind would admit.* [See Le Blanc's Elucidatio Status Controverfiarum &c. Cap. 3.] In his early years he —— *increas'd in wifdom,* and in ftature. St. Luke II. 52. And Beza obferves upon this place, that —— ipfa Θιότητθ plenitudo fefe, prout & quatenus ipfi libuit, humanitati affumtæ infinuavit: quicquid garriant matæologi, & novi Ubiquitarii Eutychiani. Gerhard, a Lutheran profeffor of divinity, has the fame meaning, or none at all, in what I am going to tranfcribe. —— Anima Chrifti, juxta naturalem, & habitualem fcientiam vere profecit, λόγω omnifcio ἐνέργειαν fuam, quæ eft actu omnia fcire & cognofcere, per affumtam humanitatem non femper exerente. [Joh. Gerhardi Loci Theol. Tom. 1. Loc. 4. Cap. 12.] Grotius employs the fame principle, to explain St. Mark XIII. 32. —— Videtur mihi, ni meliora docear, hic locus non
impie

Th' authority which I deriv'd from Heaven.

And now by fome ftrong motion I am led   290

Into this wildernefs, to what intent

I learn not yet, perhaps I need not know;

For what concerns my knowledge God reveals.

    So fpake our Morning Star then in his rife,

And looking round on every fide beheld   295

A pathlefs defert, dufk with horrid fhades;

                                        The

impie poffe exponi hunc in mo-
dum, ut dicamus *divinam Sapien-*
tiam, menti humanæ Chrifti effec-
tus fuos impreffiffe *pro temporum ra-*
tione. Nam quid aliud eft, fi verba
non torquemus, προεκοπίι σοφια,
Luc. II. 52? And our Tillotfon
approv'd the opinion. —— " It is
" not unreafonable to fuppofe, that
" the *Divine Wifdom,* which dwelt
" in our Saviour, did communi-
" cate itfelf to his *human foul* ac-
" cording to his pleafure, and fo
" his *human Nature* might at fome
" times not know fome things.
" And if this be not admitted,
" how can we underftand that
" paffage concerning our Saviour,
" Luke II. 52. that *Jefus grew in*
" *wifdom and ftature?* [Sermons
Vol. IX. P. 273.] Grotius could
find fcarce any thing in antiquity
to fupport his explication: but
there is fomething in Theodoret
very much to his purpofe, which
I owe to Whitby's Stricturæ Pa-
trum, P. 190. —— τη; [δελε μοφ-

Φης, ut videtur,] τοιαυτα κατ' εκεινο
τε καιρε γινωσκεση:, οσα η εποικεσα
Θεοτης απεκαλυψε. —— Non eft Dei
Verbi ignorantia, fed Formæ fer-
vi, quæ tanta per illud tempus
fciebat, quanta Deitas inhabitans
revelabat. Repreh. Anath. quarti
Cyrilli, Tom 4 P. 713. If fome
things might be fuppos'd unknown
to Chrift, without prejudice to the
union, being not reveal'd to him
by the *united Word,* it will follow
that, till fome certain time, even
the *union* itfelf *might* be unknown
to him.   This time feems to have
been, in Milton's fcheme, after
the foliloquy; but before the forty
days of fafting were ended, and
the Demon enter'd upon the fcene
of action: and then was a fit occa-
fion to give him a feeling of his
own ftrength, when he was juft
upon the point of being attack'd
by fuch an adverfary. *Calton.*
    294. *So fpake our Morning Star*]
So our Saviour is called in the Re-
velation XXII. 16. *the bright and*
                        morning

The way he came not having mark'd, return
Was difficult, by human steps untrod;
And he still on was led, but with such thoughts
Accompanied of things past and to come   300
Lodg'd in his breast, as well might recommend
Such solitude before choicest society.
Full forty days he pass'd, whether on hill
Sometimes, anon in shady vale, each night
Under the covert of some ancient oak,   305
Or cedar, to defend him from the dew,
Or harbour'd in one cave, is not reveal'd;
Nor tasted human food, nor hunger felt
Till those days ended, hunger'd then at last

Among

morning star: and it is properly applied to him here at his first rising.

302. *Such solitude before choicest society.*] This verse is of the same measure as one in the Paradise Lost, IX. 249. and is to be scann'd in the same manner.

  For soli|tude some|times is | best so|ciety.
  Such soli|tude be|fore choi'|cest so|ciety.

Or we must allow that an Alexandrine verse (as it is called) may be admitted into blank verse as well as into rime.

307. — *one cave*] Read — *some* cave. *Jortin.*

310. —— *they at his sight grew mild,*] All this is very common in description, but here very judiciously employ'd as a mark of the returning Paradisiacal state.
                 Warburton.

312. —— *and noxious worm*] This beautiful description is formed upon that short hint in St. Mark's Gospel I. 13. *and was with the wild beasts.* A circumstance not mention'd by the other Evangelists, but excellently improv'd by Milton to show how the ancient prophecies began to be fulfill'd, Isa. XI. 6—9. LXV. 25. Ezek. XXXIV. 25; and how *Eden* was *rais'd in the waste*

Among wild beafts: they at his fight grew mild, 310
Nor fleeping him nor waking harm'd, his walk
The fiery ferpent fled, and noxious worm,
The lion and fierce tiger glar'd aloof.
But now an aged man in rural weeds,   314
Following, as feem'd, the queft of fome ftray ewe,
Or wither'd fticks to gather, which might ferve
Againft a winter's day when winds blow keen,
To warn him wet return'd from field at eve,
He faw approach, who firft with curious eye
Perus'd him, then with words thus utter'd fpake. 320
    Sir, what ill chance hath brought thee to this place
So far from path or road of men, who pafs

In

wafte wildernefs. But the word *worm*, tho' joined with the epithet *noxious*, may give too low an idea to fome readers: but as we obferved upon the Paradife Loft, IX. 1068, where Satan is called *falfe worm*, it is a general name for the reptil kind, and a ferpent is called *the mortal worm* by Shakefpear. 2 Henry VI. Act III. and fo likewife by Cowley in his Davideis. Book I.

——— With that fhe takes
One of her worft, her beft beloved fnakes,
Softly dear *worm*, foft and unfeen
(faid fhe).

314. *But now an aged man* &c] As the Scripture is entirely filent about what perfonage the Tempter affum'd, the poet was at liberty to indulge his own fancy; and nothing, I think, could be better conceived for his prefent purpofe, or more likely to prevent fufpicion of fraud. The poet might perhaps take the hint from a defign of David Vinkboon's, where the Devil is reprefented addreffing himfelf to our Saviour under the appearance of an old man. It is to be met with among Vifcher's cuts to the Bible, and is ingrav'd by Landerfelt. *Thyer.*

323. *In*

In troop or caravan? for single none
Durst ever, who return'd, and dropt not here
His carcafs, pin'd with hunger and with drouth. 325
I afk the rather, and the more admire,
For that to me thou feem'ft the man, whom late
Our new baptizing Prophet at the ford
Of Jordan honor'd fo, and call'd thee Son
Of God; I faw and heard, for we fometimes   330
Who dwell this wild, conftrain'd by want, come forth
To town or village nigh (nigheft is far)
Where ought we hear, and curious are to hear,
What happens new; fame alfo finds us out.   —

    To whom the Son of God. Who brought me hither,
Will bring me hence; no other guide I feek.   336
                          By

323. *In troop or caravan?*] A caravan, as Tavernier fays, is a great convoy of merchants, which meet at certain times and places, to put themfelves into a condition of defenfe from thieves, who ride in troops in feveral defert places upon the road   A caravan is like an army, confifting ordinarily of five or fix hundred camels, and near as many horfes, and fometimes more. This makes it the fafeft way of traveling in Turky and Perfia with the caravan, though it goes indeed flower, than in lefs company, or with a guide alone, as fome will do.   See Travels into Perfia in Harris Vol. II. B. 2. ch. 2.

339. —*tough roots and ftubs*] This muft certainly be a miftake of the printer, and inftead of *ftubs* it ought to be read *fhrubs*. It is no uncommon thing to read of hermits and afcetics living in deferts upon roots and fhrubs, but I never heard of *ftubs* being ufed for food, nor indeed is it recorcileable to common fenfe. Some have thought that the ακριδες, which the Scripture fays were the meat of the Baptift, were the tops of plants or fhrubs.   *Thyer.* I find the word *ftubs* ufed in Spenfer. Faery Queen B. 1. Cant. 9. St. 34.

                             And

By miracle he may, reply'd the fwain,
What other way I fee not, for we here
Live on tough roots and ftubs, to thirft inur'd
More than the Camel, and to drink go far,   340
Men to much mifery and hardfhip born;
But if thou be the Son of God, command
That out of thefe hard ftones be made thee bread,
So fhalt thou fave thyfelf and us relieve
With food, whereof we wretched feldom tafte. 345
 He ended, and the Son of God reply'd.
Think'ft thou fuch force in bread ? is it not written
(For I difcern thee other than thou feem'ft)
Man lives not by bread only, but each word
Proceeding from the mouth of God, who fed 350
                                                             Our

And all about old ftocks and *ftubs* of trees :

but this only proves the ufe of the word, and not of the thing as food, which feems impoffible, and therefore I embrace the former ingenious conjecture.

340. *More than the camel,*] It is commonly faid that camels will go without water three or four days. Sitim & quatriduo tolerant. Plin. Nat. Hift. Lib. 8. Sect. 26. But Tavernier fays, that they will ordinarily live without drink eight or nine days. See Harris ibid. And therefore, as Dr. Shaw juftly ob-

ferves in his phyfical obfervations on Arabia Petræa p. 389 we cannot fufficiently admire the great care and wifdom of God in providing the camel for the traffic and commerce of thefe and fuch like defolate countries. For if this serviceable creature was not able to fubfift feveral days without water, or if it required a quantity of nourifhment in proportion to its bulk, the travelling in thefe parts would be either cumberfome and expenfive, or altogether impracticable.

350 *Proceeding from the mouth of God, who fed*
Our fathers here with Manna?]

Our fathers here with Manna ? in the mount
Mofes was forty days, nor eat nor drank ;
And forty days Elijah without food
Wander'd this barren wafte ; the fame I now :
Why doft thou then fuggeft to me diftruft,   355
Knowing who I am, as I know who thou art ?
    Whom thus anfwer'd th'Arch-Fiénd now undif-
'Tis true, I am that Spirit unfortunate,   [guis'd.
Who leagu'd with millions more in rafh revolt
Kept not my happy ftation, but was driven   360
                                With

The feventh and perhaps fome other editions have pointed it thus,

> Proceeding from the mouth of
> God ? who fed
> Our fathers here with Manna ;

In the firft and fecond editions there is a femicolon in both places, which is ftill worfe. A comma would be fufficient after *God*, and the mark of interrogation fhould clofe the period after *Manna*.
                 Calton.

356. *Knowing who I am.*] This is not to be underftood of Chrift's *divine* nature. The Tempter knew him to be the perfon *declar'd the Son of God* by a voice from Heaven, ver. 385. and that was all that he knew of him.   *Calton.*

358. *'Tis true, I am that Spirit unfortunate, &c.*] Satan's franknefs in confeffing who he was, when he found himfelf difcovered, is remarkable. Hitherto he has been called *an aged man*, and *the fwain* ; and we have no intimation from the poet, that Satan was concealed under this appearance, which adds to our pleafure by an agreeable furprife upon the difcovery. In the firft book of the Æneid, Æneas being driven by a ftorm upon an unknown coaft, and going in company with Achates to take a furvey of the country, is met in a thick wood by a lady, in the habit of a huntrefs. She inquires of them if they had feen two fifters of hers in a like drefs, employed in the chace. Æneas addreffes her as Diana, or one of her nymphs, and begs fhe would tell him the name and ftate of the country the tempeft had thrown him upon. She declines his compliment, informs him fhe was no Goddefs, but only a
                 Tyrian

With them from blifs to the bottomlefs deep,

Yet to that hideous place not fo confin'd

By rigor unconniving, but that oft

Leaving my dolorous prifon I enjoy

Large liberty to round this globe of earth,   365

Or range in th'air, nor far from the Heav'n of Heav'ns

Hath he excluded my refort fometimes.

I came among the fons of God, when he

Gave up into my hands Uzzean Job

To prove him, and illuftrate his high worth ;   370

And

Tyrian maid, gives an account of the place, and a full relation of Dido's hiftory and fettlement there. In return, Æneas acquaints her with his ftory, and particularly the lofs of great part of his fleet in the late ftorm. Upon which fhe affures him, from an omen which appeared to them, that his fhips were fafe, bids him expect a kind reception from the queen ; and then turning to go away, Æneas difcovers her to be his mother, the Goddefs of love. If Virgil had not informed us of her being Venus, till this time, and in this manner, it would have had an agreeable effect in furprifing the reader, as much as fhe did Æneas : but his conduct has been quite the reverfe, for in the beginning of the ftory, he lets the reader into the fecret, and takes care every now and then to remind him.

Cui mater media fefe tulit obvia fylva, &c.

See *An Effay upon Milton's imitations of the Ancients*, p. 60.

360. *Kept not my happy ftation,*] A manner of fpeaking borrowed from the Scripture. Jude 6. *And the Angels which kept not their firft eftate.*

365. —*to round this globe of earth,*] Milton ufes the fame phrafe in his *Paradife Loft* X. 684. fpeaking of the fun :

Had *rounded* ftill th'horizon—
Thyer.

368. *I came among the fons of God, &c*] Job I. 6. *Now there was a day when the fons of God came to prefent themfelves before the Lord, and Satan came alfo among them.* See too II. 1.

D 2   372. To

And when to all his Angels he propos'd
To draw the proud king Ahab into fraud
That he might fall in Ramoth, they demurring,
I undertook that office, and the tongues
Of all his flattering prophets glibb'd with lies   375
To his destruction, as I had in charge,
For what he bids I do : though I have lost
Much lustre of my native brightnes, lost
To be beloved of God, I have not lost
To love, at least contemplate and admire   380
What I see excellent in good, or fair,
Or virtuous, I should so have lost all sense.

                   What

372. *To draw the proud king Ahab into fraud*] That is, into mischief, as *fraus* sometimes means in Latin. *Jortin.* The reader may see an instance of *fraud* and *fraus* used in this sense in the Paradise Lost, IX. 643, and the note there. And this story of Ahab is related 1 Kings XXII. 19 &c. *I saw the Lord sitting on his throne, and all the host of Heaven standing by him, on his right hand and on his left. And the Lord said, Who shall perfuade Ahab, that he may go up and fall at Ramoth-gilead? And one said on this manner, and another on that manner. And there came forth a Spirit and stood before the Lord, and said, I will perfuade him. And* the Lord said unto him, Wherewith? *And he said, I will go forth, and I will be a lying spirit in the mouth of all his prophets. And he said, Thou shalt perfuade him, and prevail also : go forth, and do so.* And this symbolical vision of Micaiah, in which heavenly things are spoken of after the manner of men in condescension to the weaknes of their capacities, our author was too good a critic to understand litterally, tho' as a poet he represents it so.

385. —— *To hear attent Thy wisdom,*] Milton seems to have borrowed this word and this emphatical manner of applying it from Spenser, Faery Queen B. 6. Cant. 9. St. 26.

                Whilst

What can be then lefs in me than defire

To fee thee and approach thee, whom I know

Declar'd the Son of God, to hear attent   385

Thy wifdom, and behold thy Godlike deeds?

Men generally think me much a foe

To all mankind: why fhould I? they to me

Never did wrong or violence; by them

I loft not what I loft, rather by them   390

I gain'd what I have gain'd, and with them dwell

Copartner in thefe regions of the world,

If not difpofer; lend them oft my aid,

Oft my advice by prefages and figns,

And

Whilft thus he talk'd, the knight with greedy ear Hung ftill upon his melting mouth *attent*.   Thyer.

394. *Oft my advice by prefages and figns,*

And anfwers, oracles, portents and dreams,] 1. *Portents* are but odly thrown in here betwixt *oracles* and *dreams*; befides that the meaning of the word had been fully exprefs'd before by *prefages* and *figns*. Thefe comprehend all the imagin'd notes of futurity in *auguries* in *facrifices*, in *lightnings*, and in all the varieties of *portents, oftents, prodigies*. That *portent* at Aulis, which fhowed the Greeks the fuccefs and

duration of the war they were going upon, is called by Homer μεγα σημα a great fign, Iliad. II. 308. What were the Lacedæmonians profited before, (faith Cicero De Div. II. 25.) or our own countrymen lately by the *oftents* and their interpreters? which, if we muft believe them to be *figns* fent by the Gods, why were they fo obfcure? Quid igitur aut *oftenta*, aut corum interpretes, vel Lacedæmonios olim, vel nuper noftros adjuverunt? quæ fi *figna* Deorum putanda funt, cur tam obfcura fuerunt? This paffage of Cicero will lead us to the fenfe of the next word, which very naturally follows *prefages* and *figns*, and is con-

nected

And anfwers, oracles, portents and dreams,   395
Whereby they may direct their future life,
Envy they fay excites me thus to gain
Companions of my mifery and woe.
At firft it may be; but long fince with woe

Nearer

nected with them. In Cicero we
have *figns* and their *interpreters*,
and here *figns* and their *interpreta-
tions* ; for this I take to be the
meaning of *anfwers*. The *haruf-
picum refponfa* amongft the Romans
are obvious authorities. 2. There
are three fpecies of divination, dif-
tinguifhed from the former by *figns*,
in Cicero's firft book on that fub-
ject, viz. *dreams, vaticinations* or
prophecies, and *oracles*. Carent au-
tem arte ii, qui non ratione, aut
conjectura, obfervatis ac notatis
fignis, fed concitatione quadam ani-
mi, aut foluto liberoque motu fu-
tura praefentiunt ; quod & *fomnian-
tibus* faepe contingit, & nonnun-
quam *vaticinantibus* per furorem
&c. Cujus generis oracula etiam
habenda funt. De Div. l. 18. Thefe
three frequently occur together ; as
again in this firft book. 51. Item
igitur *fomniis, vaticinationibus, ora-
culis*, &c. And again in de Nat.
Deor. II. 65. Multa cernunt ha-
rufpices : multa augures provident:
multa *oraculis* declarantur, multa
vaticinationibus. multa *fomniis*, (and
I will fairly add, tho' it may be
thought to make againft me) mul-
ta *portenti*. Here *portents* are join'd
with *oracula, vaticinationes*, and

fomnia ; and why might not Milton
join them with *oracles* and *dreams* ?
In anfwer to this I obferve, that
the word *portents* in our poet is not
only irregularly inferted, but ex-
cludes another fpecies of divina-
tion out of a place, where the au-
thority of Cicero himfelf. and in
this very paffage too, would make
one expect to find it ; which can-
not be faid of *portentis*. And now
perhaps a conjecture may appear
not void of probability, that the
poet dictated,

And anfwers, oracles, *prophets,*
and dreams. *Calton.*

I have given this learned note at
length, though I can by no means
agree to the propos'd alteration.
My greateft objection to it is, that
I conceive Milton would not have
inferted *prophets* between *oracles* and
dreams, any more than Cicero would
have inferted *vates* between *oracula*
and *fomnia*. Cicero has faid *oracula,
vaticinationes. fomnia* ; and Milton
in like manner would have faid
by *prefages and figns*, and *anfwers,
oracles, prophecies*, not prophets, *and
dreams*. But I fuppofe the poet was
not willing to afcribe *prophecy* to the
Devil ; he might think, and very
juftly

Nearer acquainted, now I feel by proof,   400
That fellowſhip in pain divides not ſmart,
Nor lightens ought each man's peculiar load.
Small conſolation then, were man adjoin'd :
| This wounds me moſt (what can it leſs ?) that man,

Man

juſtly think, that it lay not within his ſphere and capacity : and by *portents,* he plainly underſtands ſomething more than *preſages* and *ſigns,* as *portenta* are rank'd with *monſtra* and *prodigia* in the beſt Latin authors.   The gentleman ſeems apprehenſive that his laſt quotation from Cicero may be turned againſt him : and indeed that paſſage and this reflect ſo much light on each other, as would incline one to believe that Milton had it in mind as he was compoſing. Multa cernunt haruſpices : multa augures provident: theſe are the *preſages and ſigns and anſwers* : multa oraculis declarantur, multa vaticinationibus, multa ſomniis, multa portentis : here *portents* are annumerated with *oracles and dreams* : quibus cognitis, multæ ſæpe res *hominum ſententia atque utilitate partæ* (or as Lambin reads, *ex animi ſententia atque utilitate partæ*) multa etiam pericula depulſa ſunt : the ſenſe of which is very well expreſſed by the following line in *Milton,*

Whereby they may direct their future life.

400. —— *now I feel by proof,*

That fellowſhip in pain divides not ſmart,] Our author here had in his eye this line of the poet,

Solamen miſeris ſocios habuiſſe doloris.   *Thyer.*

402. *Nor lightens ought each man's pecul ar load.*] I think it will not be caviling to ſay, that *each* man's *peculiar load* ſhould not be put in the mouth of Satan, who was no man, who had confeſſed to Chriſt that he was the unfortunate Arch-Fiend, and who ſpeaks of himſelf. If Milton had been aware of it, he would have corrected it thus,

Nor lightens ought each *one's* peculiar load,

or in ſome other manner. Beſides the word *man* is repeated here too often.

Nor lightens ought each *man's* peculiar load.
Small conſolation then, were *man* adjoin'd :
This wounds me moſt (what can it leſs ?) that *man,*
Man fall'n ſhall be reſtor'd, I never more.   *Jortin.*

404. *This wounds me moſt &c*]
D 4   Very

Man fall'n ſhall be reſtor'd, I never more.   405
　To whom our Saviour ſternly thus reply'd.
Deſervedly thou griev'ſt, compos'd of lies
From the beginning, and in lies wilt end ；
Who boaſt'ſt releaſe from Hell, and leave to come
Into the Heav'n of Heav'ns : thou com'ſt indeed, 410
As a poor miſerable captive thrall
Comes to the place where he before had ſat
Among the prime in ſplendor, now depos'd,
Ejected, emptied, gaz'd, unpity'd, ſhunn'd,
A ſpectacle of ruin or of ſcorn   415
To all the hoſt of Heav'n : the happy place
Imparts to thee no happineſs, no joy,
Rather inflames thy torment, repreſenting
Loſt bliſs to thee no more communicable,

　　　　　　　　　　　　　　　So

Very artful. As he could not ac-
quit himſelf of envy and miſchief
he endevors to ſoften his crimes
by aſſigning this cauſe of them.
　　　　　　　　　　Warburton.
　This wounds me moſt (what can it
　　leſs ?) that man,
　Man fall'n ſhall be reſtor'd, I ne-
　　ver more.
The poet very judiciouſly makes
the Tempter conclude with theſe
lines concerning the reſtoration of
fall'n man, in order to lead our Sa-
viour to ſay ſomething about the
manner of it, to know which was

one great part of his deſign, that
he might be able, if poſſible, to
counterplot and prevent it.　With
no leſs judgment is our Saviour re-
preſented in the following anſwer
taking no other notice of it than by
replying _Deſervedly thou griev'ſt_ &c
　　　　　　　　　　　Thyer.
　416.—_the happy place_ &c] The
ſame noble ſentiment we find alſo
in Paradiſe loſt. IX. 467.
　But the hot Hell that always in
　　him burns,
　Though in mid Heav'n, &c.
　　　　　　　　　　Thyer.
　417. _Im-_

So never more in Hell than when in Heav'n.   420
But thou art ferviceable to Heav'n's King.
Wilt thou impute t'obedience what thy fear
Extorts, or pleafure to do ill excites ?
What but thy malice mov'd thee to mifdeem
Of righteous Job, then cruelly to' afflict him   425
With all inflictions ? but his patience won.
The other fervice was thy chofen tafk,
To be a liar in four hundred mouths ;
For lying is thy fuftenance, thy food.
Yet thou pretend'ft to truth ; all oracles   430
By thee are giv'n, and what confefs'd more true
Among the nations ? that hath been thy craft,
By mixing fomewhat true to vent more lies.
But what have been thy anfwers, what but dark,

Ambiguous

417. *Imparts to thee*] In all the
editions it is printed *Imports to thee*,
but in the Errata of the firft edition
we are defired to read *Imparts to
thee.* It is no wonder that the er-
rors of the firft edition are conti-
nued in the fubfequent ones, when
thofe errors do not much difturb the
fenfe : but even where they make
downright nonfenfe of the paffage,
they are ftill continued ; and we had
a moft remarkable inftance a little
before in ver. 400. *Never acquaint-
ed* for *Neurer acquainted.*

426. *With all inflictions ? but his
patience won.*] So Mr. Fenton
points this paffage in his edition,
and fo it fhould be pointed.   And
the verb *won* I think is not often
ufed as a verb neuter, but I find
it fo in Spenfer's Faery Queen.
B. 1. Cant. 6. St. 39.

And he the ftouteft knight that
ever *won.*

434. *But what have been thy an-
fwers, what but dark,*] The
oracles were often fo obfcure and
dubious,

Ambiguous and with double fenfe deluding, 435
Which they who afk'd have feldom underftood,
And not well underftood as good not known?
Who ever by confulting at thy fhrine
Return'd the wifer, or the more inftruct
To fly or follow what concern'd him moft, 440
And ruin not fooner to his fatal fnare?

For

dubious, that there was need of
other oracles to explain them. Sed
jam ad te venio,

Sanɛte Apollo qui umbilicum cer-
tum terrarum obfides,
Unde fuperftiticfa primum fæva
evafit vox fera,

tuis enim oraculis Chryfippus to-
tum volumen implevit, partim fal-
fis, ut ego opinor, partim cafu ve-
ris, ut fit in omni oratione fæpiffi-
me ; partim *flexiloquis, & obfcuris,*
ut interpres egeot interprete, & fo's
ipfa ad fortes referenda fit ; partim
ambiguis, & quæ ad dialecticum de-
ferenda fint. Cicero De Div. II. 56.
Caiton.

Milton in thefe lines about the
Heathen oracles feems to have had
in view what Eufebius fays more
copioufly upon this fubject in the
fifth book of his Præparatio Evan-
gelica. That learned father rea-
fons in the very fame way about
them, and gives many inftances
from hiftory of their delufive and
double meanings. It may not per-
haps be impertinent to mention

one by way of illuftration. Crœ-
fus fending to confult the Delphic
oracle about the fuccefs of his in-
tended expedition againft the Per-
fian received this anfwer,

Κρεσῶ Αλυν διαβας μεγαλην αρχην
καταλυσει.
Crœfus Halym penetrans magnam
pervertet opum vim,

which by the ambiguity of one
word might either fignify the con-
queft of the Perfian empire, or the
ruin of his own : but he, as it was
natural enough for an ambitious
prince to do, conftruing it accord-
ing to his own flattering hopes, was
overcome and loft his kingdom.
Thyer.

447. *But from him or his Angels*
prefident]Utitur etiam eis Deus
(Dæmonibus, ad veritatis manife-
ftationem per ipfos fiendam, dum
divina myfteria eis per Angelos re-
velantur. The words are quoted
from Aquinas (2da 2dæ Queft. 172.
Art. 6) but the opinion is as old at
leaft as St. Auftin, whofe authority
he

For God hath juftly giv'n the nations up
To thy delufions ; juftly, fince they fell
Idolatrous : but when his purpofe is
Among them to declare his providence   445
To thee not known, whence haft thou then thy truth,
But from him or his Angels prefident
In every province ? who themfelves difdaining

T'approach

he and Peter Lombard alledge for
it.   *Calton.*
This notion Milton very probably
had from Tertullian and St. Auftin.
Tertullian fpeaking of the Gods of
the Heathens and their oracles fays
— Difpofitiones etiam Dei & tunc
prophetis concionantibus exceperunt, & nunc lectionibus refonantibus carpunt, ita & hinc fumentes
quafdam temporum fortes æmulantur divinitatem, dum furantur divinationem. In oraculis autem, quo
ingenio ambiguitates temperent in
eventus, fciunt Crœfi, fciunt Pyrrhi.
Apol. C. 22. St. Auftin more appofitely to our prefent purpofe, anfwering the Heathen boafts of their
oracles fays —— tamen nec ifta ipfa, quæ ab eis vix raro & clanculo
proferuntur, movere nos debent, fi
cuiquam Dæmonum extortum eft
id prodere cuitoribus fuis, quod didicerat ex eloquiis prophetarum,
vel oraculis Angelorum. Aug. De
Div. Dæmonum. Sect. 12. Tom. 6.
Ed. Bened. And again Cum enim
vult Deus etiam per infimos infernofque fpiritus aliquem vera cog-

nofcere, temporalia dumtaxat atque
ad iftam mortalitatem pertinentia,
facile eft, et non incongruum, ut
omnipotens et juftus ad eorum pœnam, quibus ifta prædicuntur, ut
malum quod eis impendet ante
quam veniat prænofcendo patiantur, occulto apparatu minifteriorum fuorum etiam fpiritibus talibus
aliquid divinationis impertiat, ut
quod audiunt ab Angelis, prænuntient hominibus. De Div. Queft.
ad Simpl. L. 2. S. 3. Tom. 6. The
following paffage from the fame
place of St. Auftin may ferve to
illuftrate what Milton fays above at
ver. 432.

—— that hath been thy craft,
By mixing fomewhat true to vent
        more lies.

Mifcent tamen ifti (Dæmones) fallacias, & verum quod noffe potuerint, non docendi magis quam decipiendi fine prænunciant. *Thyer.*

447. — *or his Angels prefident
In every province ?*] Milton has
here follow'd the Septuagint reading

T' approach thy temples, give thee in command
What to the smalleſt tittle thou ſhalt ſay   450
To thy adorers ; thou with trembling fear,
Or like a fawning paraſite obey'ſt ;
Then to thyſelf aſcrib'ſt the truth foretold.
But this thy glory ſhall be ſoon retrench'd ;

No

ing in Deuteronomy. Ὅτι ὁ ἐμε-
ρίζεν ὁ ὑψιςῶ ἔθνη —ἐςησεν ὅρια ἐθνων
κατα αριθμον αζγελων Θεȣ.
                Warburton.

453. *Then to thyſelf aſcrib'ſt the
    truth foretold.*] The Demons
(Lactantius ſays) could certainly
foreſee, and truly foretel many
future events, from the knowledge
they had of the diſpoſitions of
Providence before their fall. And
then they aſſumed all the honor to
themſelves, pretending to be the
authors. and docrs of what they
predicted. Nam cum diſpoſitiones
Dei præſentiant, quippe qui mi-
niſtri ejus fuerunt, interponunt ſe
in his rebus ; ut quæcunque à Deo
vel facta ſunt, vel fiunt, ipſi potiſ-
ſimum facere, aut feciſſe videantur.
Div. Inſt. II. 16.   *Calton.*

456. —— *henceforth oracles are
    ceas'd.*] I would not cenſure
Milton for mentioning the ſilence
of oracles, at our Saviour's appear-
ing in the world, both here and in
his elegant hymn on Chriſt's nati-
vity, becauſe it adorns the poems,
tho' it be a vulgar error. *Jortin.*
As Milton had before adopted the

ancient opinion of oracles being
the operations of the fall'n Angels,
ſo here alſo again he follows the
ſame authority in making them
ceaſe at the coming of our Sa-
viour. See this matter fully diſ-
cuſs'd in Fontenelle's hiſtory of
oracles, and father Baltus's anſwer
to him.   *Thyer.*

458. —— *at Delphos*] In the fa-
mous controverſy about ancient and
modern learning Mr. Wotton re-
proves Sir William Temple, for
putting *Delphos* for *Delphi*, every
where in his Eſſays. Mr. Boyle
juſtifies it, and ſays that it is uſed
by all the fineſt writers of our
tongue, and beſt judges of it, par-
ticularly Waller, Dryden, Creech,
&c. If theſe authorities may ju-
ſtify Sir William Temple, they
may alſo juſtify Milton ; but cer-
tainly the true way of writing is
not *Delphos* in the accuſative caſe,
but *Delphi* in the nominative. And
though one would not condemn
thoſe excellent writers, who have
unawares fallen into the common
error, yet to defend *Delphos* upon
this only pretence, that it has been
the cuſtom of our Engliſh writers
                  to

No more fhalt thou by oracling abufe   455
The Gentiles; henceforth oracles are ceas'd,
And thou no more with pomp and facrifice
Shalt be inquir'd at Delphos or elfewhere,
At leaft in vain, for they fhall find thee mute.
God hath now fent his living oracle   460

Into

to call it fo ; is, as Dr. Bentley re-
plies, like the Popifh Prieft, who
for 30 years together had read
Mumpfimus in his breviary inftead
of *Sumpfimus* ; and when a learned
man told him of his blunder, I'll
not change, fays he, my old *Mumpfi-
mus* for your new *Sumpfimus*.

  460. *God hath now fent his living
  oracle*
Into the world] This heavenly
oracle delivers himfelf here, in
terms clear enough to alarm the
Tempter : but it was not time yet
to put an end to the temptation by
giving him full conviction. Tan-
tum vero ei innotuit (Chriftus)
quantum voluit : tantum autem vo-
luit, quantum oportuit. [Aug. De
Civ. Dei IX. 21. I have put *ei*
for eis to fuit it to my prefent pur-
pofe] The Son of God was fent,
a man amongft men to teach them
viva voce, conveying his inftruc-
tions to the underftanding by the
ear. In this view he was *a living
oracle*, and diftinguifh'd from the
other oracle, the Holy Spirit, who
communicates himfelf by filent im-
preffions upon the mind within.

But Chrift had a nobler meaning.
In the Greek Fathers he is ftil'd
αυτεζων, ζωσα βυλη, λογ☉ ζων,
effential life, the living counfel,
and the living word of God. And
St. John fays that *in him was life,
and the life was the* light *of men.*
1. 4. This meaning was not unob-
ferved by the Tempter. He eafily
perceived that the eternal Word
might be the living oracle intend-
ed : and his words a little below
ver. 475. feem to be a feign'd ac-
knowledgment of what he would
not yet believe, tho' he feared it
might be true.

But thou art plac'd above me, thou
  art *Lord* ;
From thee I can and muft fubmifs
  indure
Check or reproof, *and glad to
  'fcape fo quit.*

Thou art the firft begotten of God,
and *Lord* of all things ; and thou
canft remand me to that dreadful
deep, whither thy thunder drove
me out of Heaven.   *Calton.*

  460. —— *his living oracle*] We
                                have

Into the world to teach his final will,
And fends his Spi'rit of truth henceforth to dwell
In pious hearts, an inward oracle
To all truth requifite for men to know.

    So fpake our Saviour ; but the fubtle Fiend,   465
Though inly ftung with anger and difdain,
Diffembled, and this anfwer fmooth return'd.

    Sharply thou haft infifted on rebuke,
And urg'd me hard with doings, which not will
But mifery hath wrefted from me : where   470
Eafily canft thou find one miferable,
And not enforc'd oft-times to part from truth ;
If it may ftand him more in ftead to lie,
Say and unfay, feign, flatter, or abjure ?
But thou art plac'd above me, thou art Lord ;   475
From thee I can and muft fubmifs indure
Check or reproof, and glad to 'fcape fo quit.
Hard are the ways of truth, and rough to walk,

                     Smooth

have here corrected an error, which has prevailed in moft of the editions, *loving* oracle inftead of *living* oracle ; and another a little afterward, *and* inward oracle inftead of *an* inward oracle.

474. *Say and unfay, feign, flatter, or abjure ?*] Might not Milton poffibly intend here, and particularly by the word *abjure*, to lafh fome of his complying friends, who renounc'd their republican

Smooth on the tongue difcours'd, pleafing to th'ear,

And tuneable as fylvan pipe or fong;   480

What wonder then if I delight to hear

Her dictates from thy mouth ? moft men admire

Virtue, who follow not her lore : permit me

To hear thee when I come (fince no man comes)

And talk at leaft, though I defpair to'attain.   485

Thy Father, who is holy, wife and pure,

Suffers the hypocrite or atheous prieft

To tread his facred courts, and minifter

About his altar, handling holy things,

Praying or vowing, and vouchfaf'd his voice   490

To Balaam reprobate, a prophet yet

Infpir'd; difdain not fuch accefs to me.

    To whom our Saviour with unalter'd brow.

Thy coming hither, though I know thy fcope,

I bid not or forbid; do as thou find'ft   495

Permiffion from above; thou can'ft not more.

                                        He

---

publican principles at the reftora-
tion ?   *Thyer.*

482.   —— *moft men admire*
Virtue, who follow not her lore :]
Imitated from the well known

faying of Medea. Ov. Met. VII.
20.

    —Video meliora, proboque;
Deteriora fequor.

                        497.—*and*

He added not ; and Satan bowing low
His gray diffimulation, difappear'd
Into thin air diffus'd : for now began
Night with her fullen wings to double-fhade   500
The defert ; fowls in their clay nefts were couch'd ;
And now wild beafts came forth the woods to roam.

497.—*and Satan bowing low*
His gray diffimulation,] An ex-
preffion this, which your little
word-catching critics will very pro-
bably cenfure, but readers of true
tafte admire. It is a true inftance
of the *feliciter audet*. There is
another of the fame kind in this
book, where the poet fays, fpeak-
ing of the angelic quire, ver. 170.

   —— and in celeftial meafures
     mov'd,
Circling the throne and finging,
   while the hand
Sung with the voice. Thyer.

498.   —— *difappear'd*
Into thin air diffus'd :] So Virgil
of Mercury. Æn. IV. 278.

Et procul in tenuem ex oculis
   evanuit auram.

500.   —— *to double fhade*
The defert ;] He has expreffed
the fame thought elfewhere

In double night of darknefs, and
   of fhades.

And tho reader will naturally ob-
ferve how properly the images
are taken from the place, where
the fcene is laid. It is not a de-
fcription of night at large, but of
a night in the defert ; and as
Mr. Thyer fays, is very fhort, tho'
poetical. The reafon no doubt
was, becaufe the poet had before
labor'd this fcene to the utmoft per-
fection in his Paradife Loft.

The end of the Firft Book.

THE

SECOND BOOK

OF

PARADISE REGAIN'D.

VOL. I.   E

PARADISE REGAIN'D.

B O O K II.

MEAN while the new-baptiz'd, 'who yet re-
main'd
At Jordan with the Baptift, and had feen
Him whom they heard fo late exprefly call'd
Jefus Mefiiah Son of God declar'd,

And

1. *Mean while the new-baptiz'd*
&c.] The greateft and indeed jufteft
objeftion to this poem is the nar-
rownefs of its plan, which being
confin'd to that fingle fcene of our
Saviour's life on earth, his tempta-
tion in the defert, has too much
famenefs in it, too much of the
reafoning, and too little of the de-
fcriptive part, a defeft moft cer-
tainly in an epic poem, which
ought to confift of a proper and
happy mixture of the inftruftive
and the delightful. Milton was
himfelf, no doubt, fenfible of this
imperfeftion, and has therefore
very judicioufly contriv'd and in-
troduc'd all the little digreffions
that could with any fort of pro-
priety conneft with his fubjeft, in
order to relieve and refrefh the
reader's attention. The following
converfation betwixt Andrew and
Simon upon the miffing our Saviour
fo long, with the Virgin's reflec-
tions on the fame occafion, and the

council of the Devils how beft to
attack their enemy, are inftances
of this fort, and both very happily
executed in their refpeftive ways.
The language of the former is not
glaring and impaffion'd, but cool
and unaffefted, correfponding moft
exaftly to the humble pious cha-
rafter of the fpeakers. That of
the latter is full of energy and ma-
jefty, and not a whit inferior to
their moft fpirited fpeeches in the
Paradife Loft. This may be given
as one proof out of many others,
that, if the Paradife Regain'd is
inferior, as indeed I think it muft
be allow'd to be, to the Paradife
Loft, it cannot juftly be imputed,
as fome would have it, to any de-
cay of Milton's genius, but to his
being cramp'd down by a more
barren and contrafted fubjeft.
Thyer.
4. *Jefus Mefiah Son of God de-
clar'd,*] This is a great miftake
in the poet. All that the people

could

And on that high authority had believ'd,   5
And with him talk'd, and with him lodg'd, I mean
Andrew and Simon, famous after known,
With others tho' in holy writ not nam'd,
Now miffing him their joy fo lately found,
So lately found, and fo abruptly gone,   10
Began to doubt, and doubted many days,

And

could collect from the declarations of John the Baptift and the voice from Heaven was that he was a great prophet, and this was all they did in fact collect; they were uncertain whether he was their promis'd Meffiah.   *Warburton.*

6.   —— *I mean Andrew and Simon.*] This founds very profaic; but I find a like inftance or two in Harrington's tranflation of the Orlando Furioio. Cant. 31. St. 46.

And calling ftill upon that noble name,
That often had the Pagans overcome,
(*I mean* Renaldo's houfe of Montalbane.)

And again St. 55.

Further fhe did to Brandimart recount,
How fhe had feen the bridge the Pagan made,
(*I mean* the cruel Pagan Rodomount.)

The particulars here related are founed upon the firft chapter of St John. Two of John's difciples, upon his teftimony, *followed Jefus:* and *they came and faw where he dwelt, and abode with him that day.* One *of the two was Andrew, Simon Peter's brother. He firft findeth his own brother Simon, and faith unto him, We have found the Meffias; and he brought him to Jefus.* Thefe incidents our author improves to great advantage; and as his fubject was fcanty and barren, he fhoweth his fkill and judgment in embellifhing it with as many particulars, and interefting as many perfons in it, as he poffibly could.

13. *Sometimes they thought he might be only fhewn,*] Virg. Æn. VI. 870.

Oftendent terris hunc tantùm fata nec ultra
Effe finent.

16. *And the great Thifbite*] Or *Tifhbite* as he is called in Scripture, 1 Kings XVII. 1. Elijah, a native of

And as the days increas'd, increas'd their doubt :
Sometimes they thought he might be only shown,
And for a time caught up to God, as once
Mofes was in the mount, and miffing long ;   15
And the great Thifbite, who on fiery wheels
Rode up to Heav'n, yet once again to come.
Therefore as thofe young prophets then with care

Sought

of Thifbe or Tifhbe, a city of the
country of Gilead beyond Jor-
dan. *Yet once again to come.* For
it hath been the opinion of the
church, that there would be an
Elias before Chrift's fecond com-
ing as well as before his firft :
and this opinion the learned Mr.
Mede fupports from the prophecy
of Malachi IV. 5. *Behold I will
fend you Elijah the prophet, before
the coming of the great and dreadful
day of the Lord* &c : and from what
our Saviour fays Mat. XVII. 11.
*Elias truly fhall firft come, and re-
ftore all things.* Thefe words our
Saviour fpake when John Baptift
was beheaded, and yet fpeaks as
of a thing future, αποκαταςτςτι
παντα, *and fhall reftore all things.*
But as it was not Elias in perfon,
but only in fpirit, who appeared
before our Saviour's firft coming,
fo will it alfo be before his fecond.
The reader may fee the argu-
ments at large in Mr. Mede's Dif-
courfe XXV. which no doubt Mil-
ton had read, not only on account
of the fame and excellence of the

writer, but as he was alfo his fel-
low-collegian.
18. *Therefore as thofe young pro-
phets then with care
Sought loft Elijah,* &c] 2 Kings
II. 17. *They fent fifty men, and they
fought three days, but found him not.*
So in each place thefe nigh to Betha-
bara : fuch ellipfes, as Mr. Symp-
fon obferves, are frequent, and
efpecially in our author. *In Jeri-
cho the city of palms,* fo it is called
Deut. XXXIV. 3. and Jofephus,
Strabo, Pliny, and all writers de-
fcribe it as abounding with thofe
trees. *Ænon,* mention'd John III.
23 as is likewife *Salim* or *Salem.*
And *John alfo was baptizing in
Enon near to* Salim. But there ap-
pears to be no particular reafon for
our author's calling it *Salem old,*
unlefs he takes it to be the fame
with the *Shalem* mention'd Gen.
XXXIII. 18. or confounds it with
the *Salem* where Melchizedeck was
king. *Machærus,* a caftle in the moun-
tainous part of *Peræa* or the coun-
try beyond Jordan, which river is
well known to run thro' the lake of

Gene-

Sought loft Elijah, fo in each place thefe
Nigh to Bethabara; in Jericho   20
The city' of palms, Ænon, and Salem old,
Machærus, and each town or city wall'd
On this fide the broad lake Genezaret,
Or in Peræa ; but return'd in vain.

Then on the bank of Jordan, by a creek,   25
Where winds with reeds and ofiers whifp'ring play,
Plain fifhermen, no greater men them call,
Clofe in a cottage low together got,
Their unexpected lofs and plaints out breath'd.

   Alas, from what high hope to what relapfe   30
Unlook'd for are we fall'n ! our eyes beheld
Meffiah certainly now come, fo long
Expected of our fathers ; we have heard
His words, his wifdom full of grace and truth ;
Now, now, for fure, deliverance is at hand,   35
                         The

Genezareth, or the fea of Tiberias, or the fea of Galilee, as it is otherwife called. So that they fearched in each place *on this fide* Jordan, or in *Peræa*, πιραν Ιορδανε, *beyond it.*

  27. *Plain fifhermen, no greater men them call.*] Imitated from the beginning of Spenfer's Shepherd's Calendar.

A fhepherd's boy, no better do him call.

  30. *Alas, from what high hope &c*] So we read in the firft edition ; in moft of the others it is abfurdly printed

Alas, from *that* high hope to what relapfe.

                    Va-

The kingdom fhall to Ifrael be reftor'd :
Thus we rejoic'd, but foon our joy is turn'd
Into perplexity and new amaze :
For whither is he gone, what accident
Hath rapt him from us ? will he now retire   40
After appearance, and again prolong
Our expectation ? God of Ifraël,
Send thy Meffiah forth, the time is come ;
Behold the kings of th' earth how they opprefs
Thy chofen, to what highth their pow'r unjuft   45
They have exalted, and behind them caft
All fear of thee ; arife and vindicate
Thy glory, free thy people from their yoke.
But let us wait ; thus far he hath perform'd,
Sent his Anointed, and to us reveal'd him,   50
By his great Prophet, pointed at and fhown
In public, and with him we have convers'd ;

Let

Væ mifero mihi, quanta de fpe decidi! Terence Heaut. II. III. 9.

34. —— *full of grace and truth* ;] Quoted from John I. 14. *The Word was made fiefh, and dwelt among us, —full of grace and truth.*

36. *The kingdom fhall to Ifrael be reflor'd* :] They are properly made to talk in the language, and according to the expectations of the Jews. *Lord, wilt thou at this time reflore again the kingdom to Ifrael* ? Acts I. 6.

42. *God of Ifraël*, &c.] This fudden turn, and breaking forth into prayer to God is beautiful as it is furprifing : and the prayer itfelf is conceived very much in the fpirit of the Pfalms, and almoft in the words of fome of them.

L 4   56. *Mock*

Let us be glad of this, and all our fears
Lay on his providence ; he will not fail,
Nor will withdraw him now, nor will recall,   55
Mock us with his bleſt ſight, then ſnatch him hence ;
Soon we ſhall ſee our hope, our joy return.

Thus they out of their plaints new hope reſume
To find whom at the firſt they found unſought :
But to his mother Mary, when ſhe ſaw   60
Others return'd from baptiſm, not her ſon,
Nor left at Jordan, tidings of him none,
Within her breaſt though calm, her breaſt though pure,
Motherly cares and fears got head, and rais'd
Some troubled thoughts, which ſhe in ſighs thus clad.

O

56. *Mock us with his bleſt ſight,*
then ſnatch him hence ;] Virgil
Æn. I. 407.

——— ſalſis
Ludis imaginibus.

Æn. VI. 870.

Oſtendent terris hunc tantùm fa-
ta. neque ultra
Eſſe ſinent.   *Jortin.*

60. *But to his mother Mary*] The
meaning of the common reading
(if it have any, and be not a blun-
der of the preſs) muſt be ——— ad
matrem quod attinct ——— *as for* or
as to his mother Mary ——— for her
part. Or the meaning might be

——— But [to come] to his mother
Mary ——— to [come next to ſpeak
of] his mother. Sanctius obſerves,
that all languages delight in bre-
vity. Milton certainly is fond of
it in ours. His ſtile is exceedingly
elleiptical, and ſometimes crampt
by an unnatural conciſeneſs. This
might be the caſe here ; but I
would rather believe, that the poet
dictated

But O ! his mother Mary, ———

See the happy effect of a very ſmall
alteration ! The tranſition to the
great mother is freed from an auk-
ward elleipſis ; and the poet brings
her upon the ſcene, with a com-
paſſionate

O what avails me now that honour high   66
To have conceiv'd of God, or that falute
Hail highly favor'd, among women bleft!
While I to forrows am no lefs advanc'd,
And fears as eminent, above the lot   70
Of other women, by the birth I bore,
In fuch a feafon born when fcarce a fhed
Could be obtain'd to fhelter him or me
From the bleak air ; a ftable was our warmth,
A manger his ; yet foon enforc'd to fly   75
Thence into Egypt, till the murd'rous king
Were dead, who fought his life, and mifling fill'd
With infant blood the ftreets of Bethlehem ;

                           From

paffionate feeling of her grief. If this reading was but poffeffed of the editions, nothing could be objected to it.   *Calton.*
I am no friend to alterations of the text, unlefs they are abfolutely neceffary. The conftruction is ——— *But to his mother* ——— *within her breaft* ——— *motherly cares and fears got head, and rais'd fome troubled thoughts :* and if the words were brought thus near together, there would not perhaps be thought that difficulty and perplexity in the fyntax.
   63. *Within her breaft, though calm, her breaft though pure, Motherly cares and fears got head,*]

A fentiment much of the fame kind with that in the Paradife Loft, where upon the fall of our firft parents it is faid X. 23.

   —dim fadnefs did not fpare
  That time celeftial vifages, yet
    mix'd
  With pity, violated not their
   blifs :

and may alfo ferve to confirm what has been obferv'd in the note upon that place. How much more dignity and amiablenefs in this character than in that of a Stoical indifference and freedom from all perturbation as they term it ?   *Thyer.*
  79. —*it*

From Egypt home return'd, in Nazareth
Hath been our dwelling many years ; his life   80
Private, unactive, calm, contemplative,
Little fufpicious to any king ; but now
Full grown to man, acknowledg'd, as I hear,
By John the Baptift, and in public fhown,
Son own'd from Heaven by his father's voice ;   85
I look'd for fome great change ; to honor ? no,
But trouble, as old Simeon plain foretold,
That to the fall and rifing he fhould be
Of many in Ifrael, and to a fign
Spoken againft, that through my very foul   90
A fword fhall pierce ; this is my favor'd lot,
My exaltation to afflictions high ;
Afflicted I may be, it feems, and bleft ;

I

79.   —— in Nazareth
Hath been our dwelling many years ;]
She mentions this as part of their
diftrefs, becaufe the country of Ga-
lilee, whereof Nazareth was a city,
was the moft defpifed part of Pa-
leftine, defpifed by the Jews them-
felves : and therefore Nathaniel
afketh Philip John I. 46. Can
there any good thing come out of Na-
zareth ?

93. Afflicted I may be, it feems,
and bleft ;

I will not argue that, nor will re-
pine.
But where delays he now ? fome
great intent
Conceals him :] How charmingly
does Milton here verify the cha-
racter he had before given of the
bleffed Virgin in the lines above ?

Within her breaft though calm,
her breaft though pure,
Motherly cares and fears got
head.

We fee at one view the piety of
the

I will not argue that, nor will repine.

But where delays he now? fome great intent   95
Conceals him : when twelve years he fcarce had feen,
I loft him, but fo found, as well I faw
He could not lofe himfelf ; but went about
His Father's bufinefs ; what he meant I mus'd,
Since underftand ; much more his abfence now   100
Thus long to fome great purpofe he obfcures.
But I to wait with patience am inur'd ;
My heart hath been a ftore-houfe long of things
And fay'ings laid up, portending ftrange events.

Thus Mary pond'ring oft, and oft to mind   105
Recalling what remarkably had pafs'd
Since firft her falutation heard, with thoughts
Meekly compos'd awaited the fulfilling :

The

the faint, and the tendernefs of the
mother ; and I think ...thing can
be conceiv'd more beautiful and
moving than that fudden ftart of
fond impatience in the third line,
But where delays he now? breaking
in fo abruptly upon the compos'd
refignation expefs'd in the two
preceding ones the fame beauty
is continued in the fuddenly check-
ing herfelf, and refuming her calm
and refign'd character again in thefe
we great intent conceals
him

103. *My heart hath been a ftore-
houfe long of things
And fayings laid up,* ——
Thus Mary pond'ring oft.] Allud-
ing to what is faid of her, Luke
II. 19. *But Mary kept all thofe
things, and tender'd them in her heart* :
and again, ver. 51. *but his mother
kept all thofe fayings in her heart* :
fo confiftent is the part that fhe
acts here with her character in
Scripture.

110:——with

The while her fon tracing the defert wild,
Sole but with holieft meditations fed,   110
Into himfelf defcended, and at once
All his great work to come before him fet;
How to begin, how to accomplifh beft
His end of being on earth, and miffion high :
For Satan with fly preface to return   115
Had left him vacant, and with fpeed was gone
Up to the middle region of thick air,
Where all his potentates in council fat ;
There without fign of boaft, or fign of joy,

                                    Solicitous

110. —— *with holieft meditations
fed,*] An expreffion very figni-
ficant, and the fame with that in
Paradife Loft. III. 37.

     Then *fied on thoughts* &c.
                  Thyer.

111. *Into himfelf defcended.*] In
fefe defcendere. Perfius Sat. IV. 23.

115. —— *with fly preface to return*]
Mr. Sympfon propofes to read,

   —— with fly *purpofe* to return :

but *preface* is better, alluding to
what Satan had faid I. 483,

     —— permit me
To hear thee when I come, &c.

Satan's concluding fpeech at their
firft meeting was a preface to their
meeting again.

122.   —— *from th' element
Each of his reign allotted, rightlier
call'd
Pow'rs of fire, air, water, and
   earth beneath,*] It was a notion
among the Ancients, efpecially
among the Platonifts, that there
were Demons in each element,
fome vifible, others invifible, in
the æther, and fire, and air, and
water, fo that no part of the world
was devoid of foul : ειϲι δε και
αλλοι δαιμονες, ἑϲ και καλλοιη αν
τιϲ γεννηϲ θεϲϲ, καθ' εκαϲον
των ϲοιχειων, οἱ μεν ὁρατοι, οἱ δε
αορατοι, εν τε αιθερι, και πυρι,
αερι τε, και ὑδατι, ὡς μηδεν κοϲ-
μϗ μερϴ- ψυχηϲ αμοιϱον ειναι, as
Alcinous in his fummary of the
Platonic doctrine fays cap. 5. Mi-
chael Pfellus. in his dialogue con-
cerning the operation of Demons,
                          from

Solicitous and blank he thus began

    Princes, Heav'n's ancient Sons, ethereal Thrones,
Demonian Spirits now from th' element
Each of his reign allotted, rightlier call'd
Pow'rs of fire, air, water, and earth beneath,
So may we hold our place, and thefe mild feats 125
Without new trouble ; fuch an enemy
Is rifen to invade us, who no lefs
Threatens than our expulfion down to Hell ;
I, as I undertook, and with the vote
Confenting in full frequence was impower'd,   130

                                    Have

from whenceMilton borrow'd fome of his notions of fpirits, (as we obferved in a note upon the Paradife Loſt I. 423.) fpeaks to the fame purpofe, that there are many kinds of Demons, and of all forts of forms and bodies, fo that the air above us and around us is full, the earth and the fea are full, and the inmoſt and deepeſt receffes: πολλα δαιμοιων γενη, και παντοδαπα τας ιδιας και τα σωματα· ως ειναι πληρη μεν τον αερα, τον τε υπερθεν εμων και τον περι ημα:· πληρη δε γαιαν και θαλατιαν, και τας μυχαιτατας και βυθιας [βυθιας] τοπας, p. 41. and he divides them into fix kinds, the fiery, the aery, the earthy, the watry, the fubterraneous, and the lucifugous : το διαπυρον, το αεριον, το χθονιον, το υδραιον τε

και εναλιον, το υποχθονιον, το μισοφαες και δυσαισθητον. p. 45. Edit. Lutet. Parif. 1615. But the Demons not only refided in the elements, and partook of their nature, but alfo prefided and ruled over them, as Jupiter in the air, Vulcan in the fire, Neptune in the water, Cybele in the earth, and Pluto under the earth.

130. —— in full frequence] Milton, in his Hiſtory of England, has faid, The affembly was *full and frequent :* and in Paradife Loſt I. 797. the council of Devils was *frequent and full.* Here the adjective is converted into a fubſtantive, and in I. 128 : and Shakefpear ufes it in the fame manner. Timon Act 5. Sc. 3.

                                    Tell

Have found him, view'd him, tasted him, but find
Far other labor to be undergone
Than when I dealt with Adam first of men,
Though Adam by his wife's allurement fell,
However to this man inferior far,   135
If he be man by mother's side at least,
With more than human gifts from Heav'n adorn'd,
Perfections absolute, graces divine,
And amplitude of mind to greatest deeds.
Therefore I am return'd, left confidence   140
Of my success with Eve in Paradise

Deceive

Tell Athens in the *frequence* of degree.
From high to low throughout.

136. *If he be man by mother's side at least*,] The Tempter had no doubt of Christ's being a *man by the mother's side:* but the want of a comma in its due place after *man*, hath puzzled both the sense and the construction. *He is* must be understood at the end of the verse, to support the syntax.

If he be man, by mother's side at least [he is]. *Calton.*

We have still preserved the pointing of Milton's own edition; for some perhaps may choose to join the whole together, and understand it thus. Satan had heard him de-

clar'd from Heaven, and knew him to be the Son of God ; and now after the trial that he had made of him, he questions whether he be man *even* by the mother's side,

If he be man by mother's side at least.

And it is the purport of Satan in this speech not to say any thing to the evil Spirits that may lessen, but every thing that may raise their idea of his antagonist.

139. *And amplitude of mind to greatest deeds.*] There is a great deal of dignity as well as significancy in this expression, and none certainly could have been better selected to express the idea which the poet intended to convey. He borrow'd it very probably from
the

Deceive ye to perfuafion over-fure
Of like fucceeding here ; I fummon all
Rather to be in readinefs, with hand
Or council to affift ; left I who erft   145
Thought none my equal, now be over-match'd.

So fpake th' old Serpent doubting, and from all
With clamor was affur'd their utmoft aid
At his command ; when from amidft them rofe
Belial, the diffoluteft Spi'rit that fell,   150
The fenfualleft, and after Afmodai
The flefhlieft Incubus, and thus advis'd.

Set

the following paffage in Tully's Tufc. Difp. II. 25. Hoc igitur tibi propone, *amplitudinem et quafi quandam exaggerationem quam altiffimam animi*, quæ maxime eminet contemnendis et defpiciendis doloribus, unam effe omnium rem pulcherrimam. Milton had a very happy talent in the choice of words, and indeed it is a very confiderable part of the poet's art. Let the reader but try to fubftitute any other word of the fame fignification in the place of *amplitude* in this verfe, and he will foon be convinc'd, that none can be found to fill it up with equal beauty and propriety.
Thyer.
150. *Belial, the diffoluteft* &c] I have heard thefe three lines ob-

jected to as harfh and inharmonious, but in my opinion the very objection points out a remarkable beauty in them. It is true, they don't run very fmoothly off the tongue, but then they are with much better judgment fo contriv'd, that the reader is oblig'd to lay a particular emphafis, and to dwell as it were for fome time upon that word in each verfe which moft ftrongly expreffes the character defcrib'd, viz. *diffolutoft, fenfualleft, flefhlieft.* This has a very good effect by impreffing the idea more ftrongly upon the mind, and contributes even in fome meafure to increafe our averfion to the odious character of Belial by giving an air of deteftation to the
very

Set women in his eye, and in his walk,
Among daughters of men the faireft found;
Many are in each region paffing fair   155
As the noon fky; more like to Goddeffes
Than mortal creatures, graceful and difcreet,
Expert in amorous arts, inchanting tongues
Perfuafive, virgin majefty with mild
And fweet allay'd, yet terrible t' approach,   160

Skill'd

very tone of voice with which thefe verfes muft neceffarily be read.
Thyer.

153. *Set women in his eye*, &c.] As this temptation is not mention'd, nor any hint given of it in the gofpels, it could not fo well have been propofed to our Saviour, it is much more fitly made the fubject of debate among the wicked Spirits themfelves. All that can be faid in commendation of the power of beauty, and all that can be alledged to depreciate it, is here fumm'd up with greater force and elegance, than I ever remember to have feen it in any other author. And the character of *Belial* in the Paradife Loft, and the part that he fuftains there, fufficiently fhow how properly he is introduced upon the prefent occafion. He is faid to be *the flefhlieft Incubus after Afmodai*, or *Afmadai* as it is written Paradife Loft VI 365, or *Afmodius* IV. 168. the luftful Angel, who loved Sarah the daughter of

Raguel, and deftroyed her feven hufbands, as we read in the book of Tobit.

155. ——*paffing fair*] Our author had feveral times met with this phrafe in his beloved Spenfer and Shakefpear; and particularly in Romeo's commendations of his miftrefs. Act 1. Scene 2.

Show me a miftrefs, that is *paffing fair*;
What doth her beauty ferve, but as a note,
Where I may read who pafs'd that *paffing fair?*

161. *Skill'd to retire, and in retiring draw*
Hearts after them] In the fame manner Milton in his defcription of Eve. Paradife Loft. VIII. 504.

Not obvious, not obtrufive, but retir'd,
The more defirable.

Hearts after them tangled in amorous nets. Milton feems to ufe the word *amorous*

Skil'd to retire, and in retiring draw
Hearts after them tangled in amorous nets.
Such object hath the pow'r to soft'n and tame
Severest temper, smooth the rugged'st brow,
Enerve, and with voluptuous hope dissolve,   165
Draw out with credulous desire, and lead
At will the manliest, resolutest breast,
As the magnetic hardest iron draws.

                                        Women,

amorous rather in the sense of the Italian *amoroso*, which is applied to any thing relating to the passion of love, than in its common English acceptation, in which it generally expresses something of the passion itself.   *Thyer.*

166. *Draw out with credulous desire,*] This beautiful expression was form'd partly upon the *spes animi credula mutui* of Horace. Od. IV. I. 30.

— fond hope of mutual fire,
The still-believing, still-renew'd
desire,

as Mr. Pope paraphrases it. And as Mr. Thyer thinks, it is partly an allusion to Terence. Andria. IV. I. 23.

— Non tibi satis esse hoc visum
solidum est gaudium
Nisi me lactasses amantem, et
falsa spe produceres.

168. *As the magnetic hardest iron draws.*] Lucian hath this si-
V o l. I.

mile in his Imagines Vol. 2. p. 2. Ed. Græv. Ει δε κακεινη προσ-Ϭλειψει σε, τις εται μηχανη απο-ϛηναι αυτης ; απαξει γαρ σε ανα-δησαμειη ενθα αν εθελη, οπερ και η λιθ⊙· η ηρακλεια δρα τον σιδη-ρον. But if the fair one once look upon you, what is it that can get you from her ? She will draw you after her at pleasure, bound hand and foot, just as the loadstone draws iron. We may observe that Milton, by restraining the comparison to the power of beauty over the wisest men and the most stoical tempers, hath given it a propriety, which is lost in a more general application. See a little poem of Claudian's on the *Magnet.* It is the 5th of his Eidyllia.   *Calton.*
As the magnetic, It should be the *magnet,* or the *magnetic stone :* but Milton often converts the adjective, and uses it as the substantive. Mr. Thyer wishes some authority could be found to justify the omitting of this line, which in his opinion is
F   very

Women, when nothing elſe, beguil'd the heart

Of wiſeſt Solomon, and made him build,   170

And made him bow to the Gods of his wives.

   To whom quick anſwer Satan thus return'd.

Belial, in much uneven ſcale thou weigh'ſt

All others by thyſelf ; becauſe of old

Thou thyſelf doat'dſt on womankind, admiring 175

Their ſhape, their color, and attractive grace,

None are, thou think'ſt, but taken with ſuch toys.

Before the flood thou with thy luſty crew,

                                    Falſe

veᴚy low and mean ; and appears too the more ſo, as it immediately follows ſome of the fineſt and moſt maſterly verſes in the whole poem. The ſimile is in itſelf trite and common, and the conceit implied in the word *hardeſt* boyiſh to the laſt degree. This ſhows that all Milton's learning and genius could not entirely preſerve him from being infected with that fanciful ſort of wit, which too much prevailed in the age in which he firſt formed his taſte.

   117. *None are, thou think'ſt, but taken with ſuch toys.*] The line would be clearer, if it run thus,

   None are, thou think'ſt, *taken but*
   with ſuch toys.   *Sympſon.*

   178. *Before the flood* &c] It is to be lamented that our author has ſo often adopted the vulgar notion of

the Angels having commerce with women, founded upon that miſtaken text of Scripture, Gen. VI. 2. *The ſons of God ſaw the daughters of men, that they were fair ; and they took them wives of all which they choſe.* See Paradiſe Loſt III. 463. and V. 447. But tho' he ſeems to favour that opinion, as we may ſuppoſe, to embelliſh his poetry, yet he ſhows elſewhere that he underſtood the text rightly, of the ſons of Seth, who were the worſhippers of the true God, intermarrying with the daughters of wicked Cain. Paradiſe Loſt XI. 621.

   To theſe that ſober race of men,
      whoſe lives
   Religious titled them the ſons of
      God,
   Shall yield up all their virtue,
      all their fame
                        Ignobly,

Falfe titled fons of God, roaming the earth

Caft wanton eyes on the daughters of men,   180

And coupled with them, and begot a race.

Have we not feen, or by relation heard,

In courts and regal chambers how thou lurk'ft,

In wood or grove by moffy fountain fide,

In valley or green meadow, to way-lay   185

Some beauty rare, Califto, Clymene,

Daphne, or Semele, Antiopa,

Or Amymone, Syrinx, many more

Too

Ignobly, to the trains and to the fmiles
Of thefe fair atheifts.

180. *Caft wanton eyes on the daughters of men,*] In Pfellus's Dialogue De Oper. Dæm. thefe fenfualities feem to be confin'd to the three loweft orders of evil Demons : [p. 39. Ed. Gaulm. Lut. Par. 1615.] and Afmodai in the Greek of Tobit is called only a ·Demon or an evil Demon ; tho' the Talmudifts, Grotius fays, [not. ad Tobiam] fet him at the head of all the Demons. In our poet's time it was ferioufly believed by very learned men of our own, addicted to the Platonic philofophy, that the Devil had carnal commerce with witches. See More's Antidote againft atheifm. B. 3. chap. 12.   *Calton.*

182. —— *or by relation heard,*] Here Milton forgot himfelf. It is a Devil who fpeaks; yet the words can only fuit the poet. *Warburton.*

188.   *many more*
Too long,] A concife way of fpeaking for *many more too long to mention.* The author had ufed it before. Paradife Loft III. 473. And indeed more would have been *too long,* and it would have been better, if he had not enumerated fo many of the loves of the Gods. *Califto, Semele, Antiopa* were miftreffes to *Jupiter* ; *Climene,* and *Daphne* to *Apollo* ; *Amymone* to *Neptune,* and *Syrinx* to *Pan.* Thefe things are known to every fchoolboy, but add no dignity to a divine poem : and in my opinion are not the moft pleafing fubjects in painting any more than in poetry, tho' wrought by the hand of a Ti-

tian

Too long, then lay'ſt thy ſcapes on names ador'd,

Apollo, Neptune, Jupiter, or Pan,   190

Satir, or Faun, or Sylvan ? But theſe haunts

Delight not all ; among the ſons of men,

How many have with a ſmile made ſmall account

Of beauty and her lures, eaſily ſcorn'd

All

tian or a Julio Romano. But our author makes ample amends in what follows.

190 *Apollo, Neptune,* &c] Both here and elſewhere Milton conſiders the Gods of the Heathens as Demons, or Devils. Παιτες ἱ θεοι των εθιων δαιμονια. Pſal. XCV. 5. And the notion of the Demons having commerce with women in the ſhape of the Heathen Gods is very ancient, and is expreſly aſſerted by Juſtin Martyr, from whom probably our author borrow'd it. ειρησεται γαρ τ' αληθες· επει το παλαιον δαιμοσις φαιλοι επιφανεια; ποιησαμενοι, και γυναικας εμοιχευσαν, κ. τ. λ. For verily I muſt tell you, that heretofore theſe impure Spirits under various apparitions went into the daughters of men, and defiled boys, and dreſs'd up ſuch ſcenes of horror, that ſuch as enter'd not into the reaſon of things, but judg'd by appearance only, ſtood aghaſt at the ſpecters, and being ſhrunk up with fear and amazement, and never imagining 'em to be Devils call'd 'em Gods, and invok'd 'em by ſuch titles, as every Devil was

pleas'd to nick-name himſelf by. And again. But far be it from men of ſenſe to harbour ſuch opinions of the Gods, namely that their Jove the ſupreme, and Father of all the Gods, ſhould be a parricide, and the ſon of a parricide, and be captivated by the vileſt luſts, and deſcend upon Ganimede, and a crew of notorious adultereſſes, and beget children after his own likeneſs. But as I have ſaid, theſe were the actions of wicked Spirits. αλλ', ὡς προεφημεν, οι δαιμονες ταυτα επραξαν. Apol. I. p. 10 & 33. Edit. Thirlbii.

196. *Remember that Pellean conqueror,* &c] Alexander the great, who was born at *Pella* in Macedonia : and his continence and clemency to Darius's queen, and daughters, and the other Perſian ladies whom he took captive after the battle at Iſſus, are commended by the hiſtorians. Tum quidem ita ſe geſſit, ut omnes ante eum reges et continentia et clementia vincerentur. Virgines enim regias excellentis formæ tam ſanctè habuit, quam ſi eodem quo ipſe parente genitæ forent : conjugem ejuſdem,

All her affaults, on worthier things intent ? 195
Remember that Pellean conqueror,
A youth, how all the beauties of the eaft
He flightly view'd, and flightly overpafs'd ;
How he firnam'd of Africa difmifs'd
In his prime youth the fair Iberian maid. 200

For

ejufdem, quam nulla ætatis fuæ pulchritudine corporis vicit, adeo ipfe non violavit, ut fummam adhibuerit curam, ne quis captivo corpori illuderet &c. Quint. Curt. Lib. 3. cap. 9. And this is the more extraordinary, as he was then a young conqueror of about 23 years of age, *a youth*, as Milton expreffes it. It would have been happy, if he had behaved with the fame moderation in other inftances afterwards.

199. *How he firnam'd of Africa* &c.] The continence of *Scipio Africanus* at the age of 24, and his generofity in reftoring a handfome Spanifh lady to her hufband and friends, are celebrated by Polybius Lib. 10. and after him by Livy Lib. 26. cap. 50. and Valerius Maximus Lib. 4. cap. 3. and various other authors. And yet, notwithftanding thefe teftimonies, a *noble* author hath lately called in queftion the truth of the fact. and the character of Scipio. " Now " the reputation of the firft Scipio " was not fo clear and uncontro- " verted in *private* as in publiic " life ; nor was he allowed by all

" to be a man of fuch fevere vir- " tue as he affefted, and as that " age required. Nævius was " thought to mean him in fome " verfes Gellius has preferved. " And Valerius Antias made no " fcruple to affert, that far from " reftoring the fair Spaniard to " her family, he debauched and " kept her. See *the Idea of a pa- " triot king* p 204. We hope this is faid only for the fake of a particular application to a particular character, and fhould be forry to have the world deprived of fo fhining an example of virtue, upon no better authority. For as an excellent writer has obferved upon the occafion, " the words of Næ- " vius are thefe,

Etiam qui res magnas manu fæpe gefit gloriofe,
Cujus facta viva nunc vigent,qui apud gentes folus
Præftat ; eum fuus pater cum pallio uno ab amica abduxit.

" Thefe obfcure verfes were in " Gellius's opinion, the fole foun- " dation of Antias's calumny a- " gainft the univerfal concurrence
F 3 " of

For Solomon, he liv'd at eafe, and full
Of honor, wealth, high fare, aim'd not beyond
Higher defign than to enjoy his ftate ;
Thence to the bait of women lay expos'd :
But he whom we attempt is wifer far   205
Than Solomon, of more exalted mind,
Made and fet wholly on th' accomplifhment
Of greateft things ; what woman will you find,

                                        Though

" of hiftorians. His ego verfibus
" credo adductum Valerium An-
" tiatem adverfum cæteros omnes
" fcriptores de Scipionis moribus
" fenfiffe. Lib. 6. cap. 8. And
" what he thought of this hifto-
" rian's modefty and truth, we
" may collect from what he tells
" us of him in another place,
" where having quoted two tribu-
" nicial decrees, which he fays he
" tranfcribed from records, (ex
" annalium monumentis) he adds,
" that Valerius Antias made no
" fcruple to give the lie to them
" in public. Valerius autem An-
" tias, contra hanc decretorum
" memoriam contraque auctori-
" tates veterum annalium &c Lib.
" 7. cap. 19. And Livy in his
" 36th book, quoting this Antias
" for the particulars of a victory,
" fubjoins, concerning the num-
" ber of the flain, fcriptori pa-
" rum fidei fit, quia in eo augen-
" do non alius intemperantior eft.
" And he that will amplify on

" one occafion, will diminifh on
" another ; for it is the fame in-
" temperate paffion that carries
" him indifferently to either." See
a Letter to the Editor of the Idea of
a patriot king &c. p. 25, 26.
    210. On whom his leifure will
vouchfafe an eye
Of fond defire ?] This eye of fond
defire is very beautifully expreffed
by Æfchylus, whom our author
perhaps had in view. Suppl. ver.
1011.

Και παρθενων χλιδαισιν ευμορ-
    φοις επι
Πας τις παρελθων ομματ©· θελκ-
    τηριον
Τοξευμ' επεμψεν, ιμερε νικωμεν©·.
                                Thyer.

    214. — as the zone of Venus once
W'rought that effect on Jove, fo
    fables tell ;] Alluding to the
famous ftory in Homer, of Juno's
borrowing the girdle of Venus, and
thereby deceiving Jupiter. Iliad.
XIV. 214.

                                H,

Though of this age the wonder and the fame,
On whom his leifure will vouchfafe an eye   210
Of fond defire? or fhould fhe confident,
As fitting queen ador'd on beauty's throne,
Defcend with all her winning charms begirt
T' enamour, as the zone of Venus once
Wrought that effect on Jove, fo fables tell;   215
How would one look from his majeftic brow

                                                    Seated

Η, και απο ϛηθεσφιν ελευσατο
κεϛον ιμαϑα,

Ποικιλον· ειθα δε οι ϑελχϑηρια παν-
ϑα τετυχϑο·

Ειθ' ενι μεν φιλοτης, εν δ' ιμερ☾,
εν δ' οαριϛυς,

Παρφασις, η τ' εκλεψε νοον ϖυκα
περ φρονεοντων.

She faid. With awe divine the queen of love
Obey'd the fifter and the wife of Jove:
And from her fragrant breaft the zone unbrac'd,
With various fkill and high embroid'ry grac'd.
In this was every art, and every charm,
To win the wifeft, and the coldeft warm:
Fond love, the gentle vow, the gay defire,
The kind deceit, the ftill-reviving fire,

Perfuafive fpeech, and more perfuafive fighs,
Silence that fpoke, and eloquence of eyes.   Pope.

But the words *fo fables tell* look as if the poet had forgot himfelf, and fpoke in his own perfon rather than in the character of Satan.

216. — *from his majeftic brow Seated as on the top of virtue's hill,*] Here is the conftruction that we often meet with in Milton: from his majeftic brow, that is from the majeftic brow *of him* feated as on the top of virtue's hill: and the expreffion of *virtue's hill* was probably in allufion to the rocky eminence on which the virtues are plac'd in the table of Cebes, or the arduous afcent up the hill to which virtue is reprefented pointing in the beft defigns of *the judgment of Hercules,* particularly that by Annibal Caracci in the palace Farnefe at Rome, as well as that

F 4   by

Seated as on the top of virtue's hill,
Difcount'nance her defpis'd, and put to rout
All her array; her female pride dejeƈt,
Or turn to reverent awe ? for beauty ſtands   220
In th' admiration only of weak minds
Led captive; ceaſe to' admire, and all her plumes
Fall flat and ſhrink into a trivial toy,
At every ſudden ſlighting quite abaſh'd :
Therefore with manlier objeƈts we muſt try   225
His conſtancy, with fuch as have more ſhow
Of worth, of honor, glory', and popular praiſe ;
Rocks whereon greateſt men have ofteſt wreck'd ;
Or that which only ſeems to fatisfy
Lawful defires of nature, not beyond ;   230
And now I know he hungers where no food
Is to be found, in the wide wildernefs ;
The reſt commit to me, I ſhall let pafs

                                        No'

by Paolo Matthæi, painted by the direƈtion of Lord Shaftsbury ; but the firſt thought of ſeating virtue on a hill was borrowed from old Heſiod. Oper. & Dier. I. 288.

— μακρ᷎⌾ δε και ορθ.⌾ οιμ⌾ ιπ' αυτην,

Και τρηχυς το πρωτον· επην δ' εις ακρον ικηαι,
'Ρηιδιη δηπειτα πελει, χαλεπη περ ιεσα.

228. —— have ofteſt wreck'd ;] We read according to Milton's own edition ofteſt, which is better than often in the others.
232.—wide

No' advantage, and his ſtrength as oft aſſay.   234

  He ceas'd, and heard their grant in loud acclame ;
Then forthwith to him takes a choſen band
Of Spirits likeſt to himſelf in guile
To be at hand, and at his beck appear,
If cauſe were to unfold ſome active ſcene
Of various perſons each to know his part ;   240
Then to the deſert takes with theſe his flight ;
Where ſtill from ſhade to ſhade the Son of God
After forty days faſting had remain'd,
Now hungring firſt, and to himſelf thus ſaid.   244

  Where will this end ? four times ten days I've paſs'd
Wand'ring this woody maze, and human food
Nor taſted, nor had appetite ; that faſt
To virtue I impute not, or count part
Of what I ſuffer here ; if nature need not,
Or God ſupport nature without repaſt   250
                                         Though

232. —— *wide wilderneſs* ;] In
moſt of the editions it is falſely
printed *wild wilderneſs*.

244. *Now hungring firſt,*] There
ſeems, I think, to be a little inac-
curacy in this place. It is plain by
the Scripture account, that our Sa-
viour *hungred* before the Devil firſt
tempted him by propoſing to him
his making ſtones into bread, and
Milton's own account in the firſt
book is conſiſtent with this: is there
not therefore a ſeeming impro-
priety in ſaying that he *now firſt
hungred,* eſpecially conſidering the
time that muſt have neceſſarily
elapſed during Satan's convening
                                    and

Though needing, what praife is it to indure ?
But now I feel I hunger, which declares
Nature hath need of what fhe afks ; yet God
Can fatisfy that need fome other way,
Though hunger ftill remain : fo it remain   255
Without this body's wafting, I content me,
And from the fting of famin fear no harm,
Nor mind it, fed with better thoughts that feed
Me hungring more to do my father's will.

It was the hour of night, when thus the Son 260
Commun'd in filent walk, then laid him down
Under the hofpitable covert nigh

Of

and confulting with his compa-
nions ?   *Thyer.*

259. *Me hungring more to do my
Father's will.*] In allufion to
our Saviour's words John IV. 34.
*My meat is to do the will of him that
fent me, and to finifh his work.*

261. *Commun'd in filent walk,
then laid him down*] Agreeable
to what we find in the Pfalms. IV.
4. *Commune with your own heart
upon your bed, and be ftill.*

264. *And dream'd, as appetite is
wont to dream,
Of meats and drinks,*]To this pur-
pofe Lucretius with great ftrength
and elegance. IV. 1018.

Flumen item fitiens, aut fontem
propter amænum

Adfidet, et totum prope faucibus
occupat amnem.

266. *Him thought, &c.*] We fay
now, and more juftly, *he thought* ;
but *him thought* is of the fame con-
ftruction as *me thought*, and is ufed
by our old writers, as by Fairfax
Cant. 13. St. 40.

Him thought he heard the foftly
whiftling wind.

He by the brook of Cherith ftood &c.
Alluding to the account of Elijah.
1 Kings XVII. 5, 6. *He went and
dwelt by the brook Cherith, that is
before Jordan : And the ravens
brought him bread and flefh in the
morning, and bread and fifh in the
evening.* As what follows, *He faw
the*

Of trees thick interwoven ; there he flept,

And dream'd, as appetite is wont to dream, 264

Of meats and drinks, nature's refrefhment fweet ;

Him thought, he by the brook of Cherith ftood,

And faw the ravens with their horny beaks

Food to Elijah bringing ev'n and morn, [brought :

Though ravenous, taught t' abftain from what they

He faw the prophet alfo how he fled 270

Into the defert, and how there he flept

Under a juniper ; then how awak'd,

He found his fupper on the coals prepar'd,

And by the Angel was bid rife and eat,

And

the prophet alfo &c, is in allufion to 1 Kings XIX. 4. &c. *But he him-felf went a day's journey into the wildernefs, and came and fat down under a juniper-tree —— And as he lay and flept under a juniper-tree, behold then, an Angel touched him, and faid unto him, Arife and eat. And he looked, and behold there was a cake baken on the coals, and a crufe of water at his head ; and he did eat and drink, and laid him down again. And the Angel of the Lord came again the fecond time, and touched him, and faid, Arife and eat, becaufe the journey is too great for thee. And he arofe, and did eat and drink, and went in the ftrength of that meat forty days and forty nights, unto Horeb the mount of God.* And

Daniel's living upon *pulfe and wa-ter* rather than the portion of the king's meat and drink is celebrated Dan. I. So that, as our dreams are often compofed of the matter of our waking thoughts, our Sa-viour is with great propriety fup-pofed to dream of facred perfons and fubjects. Lucretius IV. 959.

Et quoi quifque ferè ftudio de-
    vinctus adhæret,
Aut quibus in rebus multum fu-
    mus antè morati,
Atque in qua ratione fuit conten-
    ta magis mens,
In fomnis eadem plerumque vi-
    demur obire.

His very dreams are rightly made to fhow our Saviour to have me-
    ditated

And eat the fecond time after repofe,   275

The ftrength whereof fuffic'd him forty days ;

Sometimes that with Elijah he partook,

Or as a gueft with Daniel at his pulfe.

Thus wore out night, and now the herald lark

Left his ground neft, high tow'ring to defcry   280

The morn's approach, and greet her with his fong :

As lightly from his graffy couch up rofe

Our Saviour, and found all was but a dream,

Fafting he went to fleep, and fafting wak'd.

Up to a hill anon his fteps he rear'd,   285

From whofe high top to ken the profpect round,

If

---

ditated much on the word of God.

278. *Or as a gueft with Daniel at his pulfe.*] Mr. Sympfon propofes to read, Or *was a gueft* &c.

279.—*and now the herald lark*] This is a beautiful thought, which modern wit hath added to the ftock of antiquity. We may fee it rifing tho' out of a low hint of Theocritus, like the bird from his *thatch'd pallat.* Idyll. X. 50.

Αρχισθαι δ᾽ αμωιλας, εγειρομεν κορυδαλλω.

Chaucer leads the way to the Englifh poets, in four of the fineft lines in all his works.   Knight's Tale. 1493.

The merry lark, meffengere of the day,
Salewith in her fong the morow gray,
And firy Phebus ryfith up fo bright,
That all the Orient laughith at the fight.

Faery Queen B. 1. Cant. 11. St. 51.

— when Una her did mark
Climb to her chaiet, all with flowers fpread,
From Heaven high to chace the chearlefs dark,
With merry note her loud falutes the mounting lark,   *Calton.*

To

If cottage were in view, fheep-cote or herd ;

But cottage, herd, or fheep-cote none he faw,

Only' in a bottom faw a pleafant grove,

With chaunt of tuneful birds refounding loud ; 290

Thither he bent his way, determin'd there

To reft at noon, and enter'd foon the fhade

High rooft, and walks beneath, and alleys brown,

That open'd in the midft a woody fcene ;

Nature's own work it feem'd (nature taught art) 295

And to a fuperftitious eye the haunt
[round,

Of Wood-Gods and Wood-Nymphs; he view'd it

When fuddenly a man before him ftood,

Not

To thefe inftances we may proper-
ly add from Shakefpear, Rom. &
Jul. Act 3. Sc. 7.

It was the lark, the *herald* of the
morn.

And the lark not only furnifhes our
author with a moft beautiful de-
fcription, but alfo with a moft exact
fimilitude.

As lightly from his graffy couch
up rofe
Our Saviour.

282. *As lightly from his graffy
couch*] the fame expreffion
he ufes in the Paradife Loft. IV.
600.

—— for beaft and bird,
They to their *graffy couch.*
Thyer.

293. —— *and alleys brown,*] This
idea our author derived from Italy
and the Italian poets. He had ex-
preffed it before, Paradife Loft IX.
1088.

—— where higheft woods impe-
netrable
To ftar or fun-light, fpread their
umbrage broad
And *brown* as evening.

And the reader may fee the word
explain'd in Mr. Thyer's note upon
Paradife Loft IV. 246. *Imbrown'd
the noontide bow'rs.*

299. Not

Not ruſtic as before, but ſeemlier clad,

As one in city', or court, or palace bred,   300

And with fair ſpeech theſe words to him addreſs'd.

With granted leave officious I return,

But much more wonder that the Son of God

In this wild ſolitude ſo long ſhould bide

Of all things deſtitute, and well I know,   305

Not without hunger.   Others of ſome note,

As ſtory tells, have trod this wilderneſs ;

The

299. *Not ruſtic as before, but ſeemlier clad*,] The Tempter is very properly made to change his appearance and habit with the temptation. In the former book, when he came to tempt our Saviour to turn the ſtones into bread to ſatisfy their hunger, he appeared as a poor old man *in rural weeds* ; but now when he comes to offer a magnificent entertainment, he is *ſeemlier clad*, and appears as a wealthy citizen, or a courtier : and here *with fair ſpeech* he addreſſes his words, there it was only *with words thus utter'd ſpake*. Theſe leſſer particulars have a grace and propriety in them, which is well worthy of the reader's obſervation.

302. *With granted leave*] It is true that Satan at parting, in the concluſion of the former book, had aſked leave to come again, but all the anſwer that our Saviour returned was

Thy coming hither, though I
  know thy ſcope,
I bid not or forbid ; do as thou
  find'ſt
Permiſſion from above.

But as the Tempter muſt needs have been a moſt impudent being, it was perfectly in character to repreſent him as taking *permiſſion* for *granted leave.*

308. *The fugitive bond-woman&c*] Hagar, who fled from the face of her miſtreſs, Gen. XVI. 6. and is therefore called a *fugitive* ; and her name by interpretation (ſays Ainſworth) is a *fugitive* or *ſtranger* : but her ſon was not a fugitive. but an *out-caſt* ; ſo exact was our author in the uſe of his epithets. But then what ſhall we ſay to the words following, *Out-caſt Nebaioth ?* For as Mr. Meadowcourt and others have obſerved, Nebaioth was the eldeſt ſon of Iſhmael, (Gen. XXV. 13.) and grandſon of Abraham and Hagar.

The fugitive bond-woman with her fon
Out-caſt Nebaioth, yet found here relief
By a providing angel ; all the race   310
Of Iſrael here had famiſh'd, had not God
Rain'd from Heav'n Manna ; and that Prophet bold
Native of Thebez wand'ring here was fed
Twice by a voice inviting him to eat :
Of thee theſe forty days none hath regard,   315
Forty and more deſerted here indeed.

To

Hagar.   He ſeems here to be put by miſtake for Iſhmael. At leaſt it is not uſual to call the father by the name of the ſon.

313. _Native of Thebez_] In the firſt edition it was falſely printed _Thebes_, but Thebes (ſays Mr. Meadowcourt) was the birth-place of no prophet except blind Tireſias. However this reading hath prevailed throughout the editions, though in the table of Errata at the end of the firſt edition we are deſired to correct and read _Thebez_, the ſame as _Thiſbe_, or _Thiſbe_, or _Tiſhbe_, the birth-place of the prophet Elijah. There is a _Thebez_ mentioned, Judges IX. 50. where Abimelech was ſlain : and it looks as if our author took that and this to be the ſame place. He had before called Elijah _the great Thiſbite_ ver. 16. and he might here more conſiſtently have ſaid _Native of Thiſbe_ : but he ſeems to write ſometimes, as if he had a mind

to make work for commentators.
313. —_wand'ring here was fed_] It appears that Milton conceived the wilderneſs, where Hagar wander'd with her ſon, and where the Iſraelites were fed with Manna, and where Elijah retreated from the rage of Jezebel, to be the ſame with the wilderneſs, where our Saviour was tempted. And yet it is certain that they were very different places, for the wilderneſs, where Hagar wander'd, was _the wilderneſs of Beer-ſheba_ Gen. XXI. 14. and where the Iſraelites were fed with Manna was _the wilderneſs of Sin_ Exod. XVI. 1. and where Elijah retreated was _in the wilderneſs, a day's journey from Beer-ſheba_ 1 Kings XIX. 4. and where our Saviour was tempted, was _the wilderneſs near Jordan_ : but our author conſiders all that tract of country as one and the ſame wilderneſs, though diſtinguiſh'd by different names from the different places adjoining.
319. _How_

To whom thus Jesus. What conclud'st thou hence?
They all had need, I as thou seest have none.
   How hast thou hunger then ? Satan reply'd.
Tell me if food were now before thee set,   320
Would'st thou not eat ? Thereafter as I like
The giver, answer'd Jesus.   Why should that
Cause thy refusal ? said the subtle Fiend.
Hast thou not right to all created things ?
Owe not all creatures by just right to thee   325
Duty and service, not to stay till bid,
But tender all their pow'r ? nor mention I

Meats

319. *How haſt thou hunger then?*]
Thefe words feem to be wrong,
they being neither an anfwer to
the words preceding,

> They all had need, I as thou
> feeſt have none ;

nor correfponding to the words of
Satan himfelf juſt after,

> Tell me if food were now before
> thee fet &c.

What if we read therefore,

> *Doſt thou not* hunger then ?
>   *Symtſon.*

There feems to be no occaſion for
any alteration. Satan could not
doubt, whether our Saviour was
hungry, for he knew very well
that he was fo, ver. 231.

And now I know he hungers
    where no food
Is to be found, in the wide wil-
    dernefs :

and ver. 305.

> Of all things deftitute, and well
>   I know,
> Not without hunger.

But our Saviour had faid

> They all had need, I as thou
> feeſt have none ;

and to this Satan replies directly
and properly, *How haſt thou hunger
then* without having need ?

    325. *Owe not all creatures by juſt
      right to thee*
Duty and ſervice, &c.] The
Tempter is got into the fame cant-
ing, diſſembling ftrain as before
                     I.

Meats by the Law unclean, or offer'd firſt

To idols, thoſe young Daniel could refuſe;

Nor proffer'd by an enemy, though who   330

Would ſcruple that, with want oppreſs'd? Behold

Nature aſham'd, or better to expreſs,

Troubled that thou ſhould'ſt hunger, hath purvey'd

From all the elements her choiceſt ſtore

To treat thee as beſeems, and as her Lord   335

With honor, only deign to ſit and eat,

   He ſpake no dream, for as his words had end,

Our Saviour lifting up his eyes beheld

In

I. 475. Chriſt is *Lord of nature* ver. 335 of this book, and all creatures owe him duty and ſervice, and that *by right.* This could not be true, but on the ſuppoſition of his being the *Eternal Word*; and to what purpoſe could the temptation be continued, if the Devil had been really convinced that he was ſo?   *Calton.* This part of the Tempter's ſpeech alludes to that heavenly declaration which he had heard at Jordan, *This is my beloved Son,* &c. One may obſerve too, that it is much the ſame ſort of flattering addreſs with that which he had before made uſe of to ſeduce Eve. Paradiſe Loſt. IX. 539.
   Thee all things living gaze on, all things thine
   By gift &c.   *Thyer.*

329—*thoſe young Daniel could re-fuſe;*] Dan. I. 8 *But Daniel purpoſed in his heart that he would not defile himſelf with the portion of the king's meat, nor with the wine which he drank:* and the reaſon aſſign'd by commentators is, becauſe in thoſe and moſt other countries they uſed to offer ſome part of what they eat and drank to their Gods; and therefore Daniel refuſed to partake of the proviſions from the king's table, as of meats offered to idols, and conſequently unclean. The poet had before mention'd *Daniel at his pulſe* ver. 278: and Moſes in the mount, and Elijah in the wilderneſs are brought in ſeveral times, as hiſtory affords no inſtances of abſtinence ſo like our Saviour's.

337 *He ſpake no dream.*] This

In ample fpace under the broadeft fhade
A table richly fpread, in regal mode,   340
With difhes pil'd, and meats of nobleft fort
And favor, beafts of chafe, or fowl of game,

                                                        In

was no dream as before ver. 264.
but a reality. And the ban-
quet here furnifh'd by Satan is
like that prepared by Armida for
her lovers. Taffo Cant. 10. St.
64.

Appreftar sù l'herbetta, ou' è
   più denfa
L' ombra, e vicino al fuon de
   l' acque chiare
Fece difculti vafi altera menfa,
E ricca di vivande elette, e
   care.
Era qui ciò, ch' ogni ftagion dif-
   penfa ;
Ciò che dona la terra, ò manda
   il mare :
Ciò che l' arte condifce, e cento
   belle
Servivano al convito accorte an-
   celle.

Under the curtain of the green-
   wood fhade,
Befide the brook, upon the vel-
   vet grafs,
In maffy veffel of pure filver
   made,
A banquet rich and coftly fur-
   nifh'd was ;
All beafts, all birds beguil'd by
   fowler's trade,
All fifh were there in floods or
   feas that pafs,

All dainties made by art, and at
   the table
An hundred virgins ferv'd, for
   hufbands able.   Fairfax.

340. A table richly fpread, &c.]
This temptation is not recorded in
Scripture, but is however invented
with great confiftency, and very
aptly fitted to the prefent condition
of our Saviour. This way of em-
bellifhing his fubject is a privilege
which every poet has a juft right
to, provided he obferves harmony
and decorum in his hero's charac-
ter; and one may further add, that
Milton had in this particular place
ftill a ftronger claim to an indul-
gence of this kind, fince it was a
pretty general opinion among the
Fathers, that our Saviour under-
went many more temptations than
thofe which are mentioned by the
Evangelifts ; nay Origen goes fo far
as to fay, that he was every day,
whilft he continued in the wilder-
nefs, attacked by a frefh one. The
beauties of this defcription are too
obvious to efcape any reader of
tafte. It is copious, and yet ex-
prefs'd with a very elegant concife-
nefs. Every proper circumftance
is mentioned, and yet it is not at
all clogg'd or incumber'd, as is of-
ten the cafe, with too tedious a de-
                                          tail

In paſtry buiłt, or from the ſpit, or boil'd,
Gris-amber-ſteam'd ; all fiſh from ſea or ſhore,
Freſhet, or purling brook, of ſhell or fin,　　345
And exquiſiteſt name, for which was drain'd

　　　　　　　　　　　　　　　Pontus

tail of particulars. It was a ſcene entirely freſh to our author's imagination, and nothing like it had before occurr'd in his Paradiſe Loſt, for which reaſon he has been the more diffuſe, and labor'd it with greater care, with the ſame good judgment that makes him in other places avoid expatiating on ſcenes which he had before deſcrib'd. See the note on his ſhort deſcription of night at the end of the firſt book. In a word, it is in my opinion work'd up with great art and beauty, and plainly ſhows the crudity of that notion which ſo much prevails among ſuperficial readers, that Milton's genius was upon the decay when he wrote his Paradiſe Regain'd.　　*Thyer.*

344. *Gris-amber-ſteam'd* ;] Ambergris or grey amber is eſteemed the beſt, and uſed in perfumes and cordials. A curious lady communicated the following remarks upon this paſſage to Mr. Peck, which we will here tranſcribe. " *Grey am-*
" ber is the amber our author heie
" ſpeaks of, and melts like butter.
" It was formerly a main ingre-
" dient in every conceit for a ban-
" quet ; viz. to fume the meat
" with, and that whether boiled,
" roaſted, or baked ; laid often on
" the top of a baked pudding ;

" which laſt I have eat of at an
" old courtier's table. And I re-
" member, in an old chronicle
" there is much complaint of the
" nobilities being made ſick at
" Cardinal Wolſey's banquets, with
" rich ſcnted cates and diſhes moſt
" coſtly dreſſed with ambergris. I
" alſo recollect I once ſaw a little
" book writ by a gentlewoman of
" Queen Elizabeth's court, where
" ambergris is mention'd as the
" haut-gout of that age. I fancy
" Milton tranſpoſed the word for
" the ſake of his verſe ; to make
" it read more poetically." So far this curious Lady. And Beaumont and Fletcher in the Cuſtom of the Country. Act III. Scene 2.

　　Be ſure
The wines be luſty, high, and
　　full of ſpirit,
And *amber'd* all.

346. *And exquiſiteſt name,*] He alludes here to that ſpecies of Roman luxury, which gave *exquiſite names* to fiſh of exquiſite taſte, ſuch as that they called *cerebrum Jovis.* They extended this even to a very capacious diſh as that they called *clypeum Minervæ.* The modern Italians fall into the ſame wantonneſs of luxurious impiety, as when they call their exquiſite wines by

　　　　　　　　　　　　the

Pontus, and Lucrine bay, and Afric coaſt.

Alas how ſimple, to theſe cates compar'd,

Was that crude apple that diverted Eve!

And at a ſtately ſide-board by the wine   350

That fragrant ſmell diffus'd, in order ſtood

Tall ſtripling youths rich clad, of fairer hue

Than

the names of *lacrymæ Chriſti* and *lac Virginis.*   Warburton.

347. *Pontus and Lucrine bay, and Afric coaſt.*] The fiſh are brought to furniſh this banquet from all the different parts of the world then known ; from *Pontus* or the Euxine ſea in Aſia, from the *Lucrine bay* in Europe in Italy, and from the *coaſt of Africa.* And all theſe places are celebrated for different kinds of fiſh by the authors of antiquity. It would be almoſt endleſs to quote the paſſages. Of the *Lucrine lake* in particular many derive the name *à lucro,* from the abundance of fiſh there taken.

349. —— *that diverted Eve!*] It is uſed, as he uſes many words according to their proper ſignification in Latin. *Diverto,* to turn aſide. We ſhould rather ſay *perverted.*

350. *And at a ſtately ſide-board &c*] As the ſcene of this entertainment lay in the eaſt. Milton has with great judgment thrown in this and the following particulars to give it an air of eaſtern grandeur, in which part of the world it is

well known a great part of the pomp and ſplendor of their feaſts conſiſts in their having a great number of beautiful ſlaves of both ſexes to attend and divert the gueſts with muſic and ſinging.   *Thyer.*

352. —— *of fairer hue Than Ganymed or Hylas* ;] Theſe were two moſt beautiful youths, and belov'd the one by Jupiter, and the other by Hercules. Ganymed was cup-bearer to Jupiter, and Hylas drew water for Hercules, and therefore they are both properly mentioned upon this occaſion.

355. —— *and Naiades*] Milton is not to be blamed for writing as others did in his time. But ſince the critics have determin d to write *Naides* in three ſyllables, or *Naïades* in four, it is time for the Engliſh poets to call theſe nymphs *Naïds,* and not *Naïads.*   Jortin.

356. —— *from Amalthea's horn.*] The ſame as the cornu copiæ ; the horn of plenty. Amalthea was, as ſome ſay, a Naid, the nurſe of Jupiter, who nouriſh'd him with the milk of a goat, whoſe horn was afterwards made the horn of plenty ; others

Than Ganymed or Hylas ; diftant more
Under the trees now tripp'd, now folemn ftood
Nymphs of Diana's train, and Naiades   355
With fruits and flow'rs from Amalthea's horn,
And ladies of th' Hefperides, that feem'd
Fairer than feign'd of old, or fabled fince

Of

others fay, that Amalthea was the name of the goat.

357. *And ladies of th' Hefperides,*] If we compare this with what the Devil fays a little lower, ver. 374.

All thefe are Spirits of air and woods and fprings,

we fhall find that they do not tally each to the other, for the Hefperides were neither ladies of woods nor fprings.   *Sympfon.*
What are the Hefperides famous for but the gardens and orchards which they had bearing golden fruit in the weftern iles of Africa ? They may therefore not improperly be rank'd, they and their ladies with the Spirits of woods and fprings.

357. *And ladies of th' Hefperides, that feem'd* &c.] This is the pointing of the firft, and all the editions ; but I take it to be wrong. The Demons *feem'd* (or were like) nymphs of Diana's train &c, but they were really fairer than thofe nymphs, &c, were feign'd to be. This I take to be the poet's thought, and therefore the comma fhould be put after *feem'd.*   *Calton.*

This is very good fenfe, but it may be queftion'd whether *that feem'd* may be referred fo far back as to *nymphs of Diana's train*; and if thefe Spirits were fome *nymphs of Diana's train*, and fome *Naiades*, others might as well be faid to be *ladies of th' Hefperides* ; and then *that feem'd* will be join'd in conftruction, as it is plac'd, with what follows,

Fairer than feign'd of old, or fabled fince
Of faery damfels &c.

But here feems to be fome defect in the fyntax, as if the poet had meant to fay *Fairer than feign'd of old, or* what has been *fabled fince of faery damfels met in foreft wide by knights*, &c, of whom he had read in his romances, where it is not fo eafy to trace him, but the name of Sir *Pelleas* occurs in the Faery Queen B. 6. Cant. 12. St. 39.

358. —— *or fabled fince* &c.] Some readers may perhaps in this paffage think our author a little too fond of fhowing his great reading, a fault which he is indeed fometimes guilty of : but thofe who are converfant in romance-writers, and
know

Of faery damfels met in foreft wide
By knights of Logres, or of Lyones,   360
Lancelot, or Pelleas, or Pellenore :
And all the while harmonious airs were heard
Of chiming ftrings, or charming pipes, and winds
Of gentleft gale Arabian odors fann'd
From their foft wings, and Flora's earlieft fmells. 365
Such was the fplendor, and the Tempter now
His invitation earneftly renew'd.

    What doubts the Son of God to fit and eat?
Thefe are not fruits forbidden ; no interdict
Defends the touching of thefe viands pure ;   370
                          Their

know how lavifh they are in the praifes of their beauties, will I doubt not difcover great propriety in this allufion.   *Thyer.*

363. *Of chiming ftrings, or charming pipes,*] So Spenfer hath ufed the verb *charms.* Faery Queen, B. 4. Cant. 9. St. 13.

    Like as the fowler on his guileful pipe
    Charms to the birds full many a pleafant lay.   *Calton.*

363. —— *and winds*
Of gentleft gale Arabian odors fann'd
From their foft wings, and Flora's earlieft fmells.] Milton, I fancy, introduc'd this circumftance in allu-

fion to the eaftern cuftom of ufing perfumes at their entertainments, for the reafon alledged in the note on ver. 350. He has exprefs'd the very fame idea in the Paradife Loft in the following lines IV. 156.

    —— now gentle gales
Fanning their odoriferous wings difpenfe
Native perfumes, and whifper whence they ftole
Thofe balmy fpoils :

and by this little fpecimen one may fee, as I obferv'd before, that our poet's imagination did not flag in the latter part of his life, and that there is no difference in the Paradife Loft and Paradife Regain'd, but

Their tafte no knowledge works at leaft of evil,
But life preferves, deftroys life's enemy,
Hunger, with fweet reftorative delight.
All thefe are Spi'rits of air, and woods, and fprings,
Thy gentle minifters, who come to pay   375
Thee homage, and acknowledge thee their Lord :
What doubt'ft thou Son of God ? fit down and eat.
     To whom thus Jefus temp'rately reply'd.
Said'ft thou not that to all things I had right ?
And who withholds my pow'r that right to ufe ? 380
Shall I receive by gift what of my own,
When and where likes me beft, I can command ?

                                                 I

but fuch as was occafioned by the different fubjects.   *Thyer.*

368. *What doubts the Son of God to fit and eat ?*] *What* feems to be ufed here much like the Latin *quid*, which fignifies both what and why, as we obferved in Paradife Loft. II. 329.

    What fit we then [projecting peace and war ?

370. *Defends the touching*] Forbids, prohibits, hinders, as the word is ufed in Paradife Loft XI. 86. XII. 207. where the reader may fee other inftances.

379. *Saidft thou not &c*] If Chrift was really the *eternal living Word of God*, the Tempter knew the certainty of the confequence, that he muft *of right* be *Lord of all things :* and Chrift by admitting the laft to be a truth, (as he doth here) confequentially afferts the principle ; for one cannot hold without the other.

    Saidft thou not that to all things I had right ?

The *right* of the Son of God being founded on his *power*, his *power* muft needs be fully adequate to his *right.* He therefore adds,

    And who withholds my pow'r that right to ufe ?

In the two next lines Chrift's *ftrict natural propriety* is diftinguifh'd from a *right by gift.*

                    G 4   Shall

I can at will, doubt not, as foon as thou,
Command a table in this wildernefs,
And call fwift flights of Angels miniftrant   385
Array'd in glory on my cup to' attend :
Why fhouldft thou then obtrude this diligence,
In vain, where no acceptance it can find ?
And with my hunger what haft thou to do ?
Thy pompous delicacies I contemn,   390
And count thy fpecious gifts no gifts but guiles.

   To whom thus anfwer'd Satan malecontent.

That I have alfo pow'r to give thou feeft ;

                       If

Shall I receive by gift what of *my own,*
When and where likes me beft,
I can command ?   *Calton.*

385. ———— *flights of angels*] An expreffion likewife in Shakefpear. Hamlet, Act 5. Sc. 6.

And *flights of angels* fing thee to thy reft.

391. ———— *thy gifts no gifts*] Exprefs'd from the Greek proverb. Sophocles. Ajax 675.

Εχθρων αδωρα δωρα, κ' εκ ονησιμα.

401. ———— *the far fet fpoil.*] *Fet* is much fofter than *fetch'd,* and it is ufed by Chaucer, Squire's Tale 296.

This ftrangir knight is *fet* to him full fone ;

and by Spenfer, Faery Queen B. 3. Cant. 1. St. 8.

Whom ftrange adventure did from Britain *fet :*

and Muiopotmos,

Not Bilbo fteel, nor brafs from Corinth *fet :*

and by Johnfon, Prol. to Silent Woman,

Though there be none *far fet :*

and in profe as well as in verfe by Sir Philip Sidney, Arcad. p. 360. Therewith he told her a *far fet* tale: Defence of Poetry p. 551. and much lefs with *far fet* maxims of philofophy : as if our old writers had

If of that pow'r I bring thee voluntary
What I might have beftow'd on whom I pleas'd, 395
And rather opportunely in this place
Chofe to impart to thy apparent need,
Why fhouldft thou not accept it ? but I fee
What I can do or offer is fufpeƈt ;
Of thefe things others quickly will difpofe,   400
Whofe pains have earn'd the far fet fpoil. With that
Both table and provifion vanifh'd quite
With found of harpies wings, and talons heard ;
Only th' impórtune Tempter ftill remain'd,

And

had a better ear, and ftudied the beauties of found more than the moderns.

401. —— *With that* &c] The breaking off fhort of the verfe admirably expreffes the fudden and abrupt manner, wherein

> Both table and provifion vanifh'd quite
> With found of harpies wings, and talons heard ;

in which the author has imitated Virgil Æn. III. 225.

> At fubitæ horrifico lapfu de montibus adfunt
> Harpyiæ, et magnis quatiunt clangoribus alas,
> Diripiuntque dapes.

When from the mountain-tops, with hideous cry,
And clatt'ring wings, the hungry harpies fly ;
They fnatch the meat. *Dryden.*

And we have a like fcene in Skakefpear, in the Tempeft Aƈt III. where *feveral ftrange fhapes bring in a banquet,* and afterwards *enters Ariel like a harpy, claps his wings upon the table, and with a quaint device the banquet vanifhes.*

404. *Only th' impórtune Tempter ftill remain'd,*] The word *impórtune* is often pronounced with this accent by our old writers, as Spenfer Faery Queen B. 1. Cant. 12. St. 16.

> And often blame the too *impòrtune* fate :

and

And with thefe words his temptation purfu'd.

By hunger, that each other creature tames,
Thou art not to be harm'd, therefore not mov'd ;
Thy temperance invincible befides,
For no allurement yields to appetite,
And all thy heart is fet on high defigns,   410
High actions ; but wherewith to be achiev'd ?
Great acts require great means of enterprife ;
Thou art unknown, unfriended, low of birth,

A

and B. 2. Cant. 8. St. 38.
  The which dividing with *impór-
  tune* fway :
and Cant. 11. St. 7.
  With greedy malice and *impór-
  tune* toil :
whereas now, I think, we com-
monly pronounce it with the ac-
cent upon the laft fyllable in the
adjective, and always in the verb,
importúne.
  419. *What followers, what re-
  tinue canft thou gain,
  Or at thy heels the dizzy multitude,*
&c] This is a ftrange paffage ! I
read
  Or at thy heels *what* dizzy mul-
  titude,
but it does not pleafe me.
                         Sympfon.
There are two words unhappily
loft in the fecond line by the negli-

gence of the poet's amanuenfis or
printer, which may be reftor'd, I
think, with certainty cnough. Be-
hold them, Reader, in the place
they feem to me to have a right
to; confider and judge.

  Or at thy heels *how keep* the
  dizzy multitude.

One may almoft venture to deter-
min on the fide of thefe claimants,
from what our bleffed Saviour faith,
in the beginning of his reply to this
fpeech of the Tempter.

  Yet wealth without thefe three
  is impotent
  To *gain* dominion, or to *keep* it
  gain'd.

Milton's verfes are not always to
be meafur'd by counting fyllables
on the fingers ends. There are ex-
amples enow in him, and other
poets, in blank verfe efpecially, of
thefe *Hypercataleclic* verfes, as one
may

A carpenter thy father known, thyfelf
Bred up in poverty and ftraits at home,   415
Loft in a defert here and hunger-bit :
Which way or from what hope doft thou afpire
To greatnefs? whence authority deriv'ft ?
What followers, what retinue canft thou gain ?
Or at thy heels the dizzy multitude,   420
Longer than thou canft feed them on thy coft ?
Money brings honor, friends, conqueft, and realms :

                                        What

may call them ; where the two laft fyllables are redundant. One or two from Milton will be fufficient.

> Extolling patience as the trueft fortitude Samf. Ag. ver. 655.

But this is from the Chorus. Take another from a fpeech of Dalila's, ver. 870.

> Private refpects muft yield; with grave | authority.

But an inftance of it from Paradife Loft will be moft to the purpofe, IX. 249.

> For fol | itude | fometimes | is beft | fōcīĕtȳ.   *Calton.*

This reading makes very good fenfe, and clears the fyntax : but moft readers, I imagin, rather than admit fuch a *Hypercataleƈtic* verfe, will underftand *the dizzy multitude* as the accufative cafe after the verb *gain,* making favorable allowances for a little inaccuracy of expreffion.

422. *Money brings honor, friends, conqueft, and realms :*] Mammon in the Faery Queen attempts the virtue of Sir Guyon with the fame pretences. B. 2. Cant. 7. St. 11.

> Vain-glorious Elf, faid he, doft thou not weet,
> That money can thy wants. at will fupply ?
> Shields, fteeds, and arms, and all things for thee meet
> It can purvey in twinkling of an eye ;
> And crowns and kingdoms to thee multiply.
> Do I not kings create, and throw the crown
> Sometimes to him that low in duft doth lie ?

                                        And

What rais'd Antipater the Edomite,

And his fon Herod plac'd on Juda's throne,   424

(Thy throne) but gold that got him puiffant friends?

Therefore, if at great things thou would'ft arrive,

Get riches firft, get wealth, and treafure heap,

Not difficult if thou hearken to me ;

Riches are mine, fortune is in my hand ;

They whom I favor thrive in wealth amain,   430

While virtue, valor, wifdom fit in want.

　　To whom thus Jefus patiently reply'd.

Yet wealth without thefe three is impotent

　　　　　　　　　　　　　　　　　　　To

And him that reign'd into his room thruft down,
And whom I luft do heap with glory and renown?   *Calton.*

423. *What rais'd Antipater the Edomite,* &c.] This appears to be the faĉt from hiftory. When Jofephus introduces Antipater upon the ftage, he fpeaks of him as a-bounding with great riches. Φιλⲟⲥ δε τι; Ύρκαⲛⲁ Ιδⲟⲙⲁ ⲟⲥ, Αѵⲧⲓⲡⲁ-τρⲟⲥ λεγⲟⲙενⲟⲥ, ⲡⲟλλⲱν μεν εⲩ-ⲡⲟρⲱν χρηⲙⲁⲧⲱν, κ. τ. λ. Antiq. Lib. XIV. Cap. 1. And his fon Herod was declared king of Judea by the favor of Mark Antony, partly for the fake of the Money which he promifed to give him———τα δε και ὑπο χρηⲙⲁⲧⲱν ⲱν αυⲧⲱ Ηρⲱ-δης ὑⲡⲓⲥχεⲧⲟ δⲱⲥειν ει γενⲟιⲧⲟ βαⲥι-λιυς. Ibid. Cap. 14.

427. *Get riches firft,*] Quærenda pecunia primùm. Hor. Ep. l. l. 53.
429. *Riches are mine,* &c.] This temptation we alfo owe to our au-thor's invention, and 'tis very hap-pily contriv'd, not only as it leads the reader gradually on to thofe ftronger ones in the following book, but as it is fo juftly fitted to the charaĉter of the Tempter, the prince of Hell, who was fuppofed by all antiquity to be the king and difpofer of riches. Hence was he ftil'd Pluto from ⲡλⲉⲧⲟⲥ divitiæ. Spenfer much in the fame tafte places *the delve of Mammon* clofe by the entrance into Hell. Faery Queen B. 2. Cant. 7. St. 24.
　　Betwixt them both was but a little ftride,
　　That did the houfe of riches from Hell-mouth divide.   *Thyer.*
432. *To*

To gain dominion, or to keep it gain'd.

Witnefs thofe ancient empires of the earth,   435

In highth of all their flowing wealth diffolv'd :

But men indued with thefe have oft attain'd

In loweft poverty to higheft deeds ;

Gideon, and Jephtha, and the fhepherd lad,

Whofe ofspring on the throne of Judah fat   440

So many ages, and fhall yet regain

That feat, and reign in Ifrael without end.

Among the Heathen, (for throughout the world

To me is not unknown what hath been done

Worthy'

432. *To whom thus Jefus* &c.] When our Saviour, a little before, refufed to partake of the banquet, to which Satan had invited him, the line run thus, ver. 378,

> To whom thus Jefus *temp'rately* reply'd.

But now when Satan has reproached him with his poverty and low circumftances, the word is fitly altered, and the verfe runs thus,

> To whom thus Jefus *patiently* reply'd.

439. *Gideon, and Jephtha, and the fhepherd lad,*] Our Saviour is rightly made to cite his firft inftances from Scripture, and of his own nation, which was certainly the beft known to him ; but it is with great art that the poet alfo

fuppofes him not to be unacquainted with Heathen hiftory, for the fake of introducing a greater variety of examples. Gideon faith of himfelf, *O my Lord, wherewith fhall I fave Ifrael ? behold my family is poor in Manaffeh, and I am the leaft in my father's houfe.* Judges VI. 15. And Jephtha *was the fon of an harlot,* and his brethren *thruft him out, and faid unto him, Thou fhalt not inherit in our father's houfe, for thou art the fon of a ftrange woman.* Judges XI. 1, 2. And the exaltation of David from a fheephook to a fcepter is very well known. *He chofe David alfo his fervant and took him from the fheep-folds. From following the ewes great with young, he brought him to feed Jacob his people, and Ifrael his inheritance.* Pfal. LXXVIII. 70, 71.

446. *Quin-*

Worthy' of memorial) canft thou not remember 445
Quintius, Fabricius, Curius, Regulus ?
For I efteem thofe names of men fo poor
Who could do mighty things, and could contemn
Riches though offer'd from the hand of kings.
And what in me feems wanting, but that I   450
May alfo in this poverty as foon

Accomplifh

446. *Quintius, Fabricius, Curius, Regulus ?*] *Quintius* (not *Quintus*, as it is in moft of the editions befides the firft) Cincinnatus was twice invited from following the plough to be conful and dictator of Rome ; and after he had fubdued the enemy, when the fenate would have enriched him with public lands and private contributions, he rejected all thefe offers, and retired again to his cottage and old courfe of life. *Fabricius* could not be bribed by all the large offers of king Pyrrhus to aid him in negociating a peace with the Romans: and yet he lived and died fo poor, that he was buried at the public expenfe, and his daughters fortunes were paid out of the treafury. *Curius* Dentatus would not accept of the lands which the fenate had affign'd him for the reward of his victories : and when the embaffadors of the Samnites offer'd him a large fum of money as he was fitting at the fire and roafting turnips with his own hands, he nobly refufed to take it, faying that it was his ambition not

to be rich, but to command thofe who were fo. And *Regulus*, after performing many great exploits, was taken prifoner by the Carthaginians, and fent with the embaffadors to Rome to treat of peace, upon oath to return to Carthage, if no peace or exchange of prifoners fhould be agreed upon : but Regulus was himfelf the firft to diffuade a peace, and chofe to leave his country, family, friends, every thing, and return a glorious captive to certain tortures and death, rather than fuffer the fenate to conclude a difhonorable treaty. Our Saviour cites thefe inftances of noble Romans in order of time, as he did thofe of his own nation : And as Mr Calton obferves, the Romans in the moft degenerate times were fond of thefe (and fome other like) examples of ancient virtue ; and their writers of all forts delight to introduce them : but the greateft honor that poetry ever did them, is here, by the praife of the Son of God.

447. *For I efteem &c*] The author

Accomplifh what they did, perhaps and more ?

Extol not riches then, the toil of fools,

The wife man's cumbrance if not fnare, more apt

To flacken virtue, and abate her edge,   455

Than prompt her to do ought may merit praife.

What if with like averfion I reject

Riches and realms ; yet not for that a crown,

Golden

thor had here plainly Claudian in mind. De IV. Conf Honor. 412.

> Difcitur hinc quantum paupertas
> fobria poffit :
> Pauper erat Curius cum reges
> vinceret armis :
> Pauper Fabricius, Pyrrhi cum
> fperneret aurum :
> Sordida Serranus flexit Dictator
> aratra : &c.

And again In Rufinum I. 200.

> Semper inops, quicunque cupit.
> contentus honefto
> Fabricius parvo fpernebat mune-
> ra regum,
> Sudabatque gravi Conful Serra-
> nus aratro,
> Et cafa pugnaces Curios angufta
> tegebat.
> Hæc mihi paupertas opulentior.

And it is probable that he remem-ber'd here fome of his beloved re-publicans,

> —thofe names of men fo poor
> Who could do mighty things—

and it is poffible that he might alfo think of himfelf, who

——— could contemn Riches though offer'd from the hand of kings,

if that ftory be true of his having been offer'd to be Latin fecretary to Charles the 2d, and of his re-fufing it.

453. *Extol not riches then*, &c.] Milton concludes this book and our Saviour's reply to Satan with a fe-ries of thoughts as noble and juft, or, to fay all in one word, as worthy of the fpeaker as can pof-fibly be imagined : and I think one may venture to affirm, that as the Paradife Regain'd is a poem en-tirely moral and religious, the ex-cellency of which does not confift fo much in bold figures and ftrong images as in deep and virtuous fen-timents exprefs'd with a becoming gravity, and a certain decent ma-jefty, this is as true an inftance of the fublime as the battles of the Angels in the Paradife Loft.

Thyer.

458 —*yet not for that a crown,*] I reject them, yet not for that rea-fon becaufe a crown &c : and in fetting

Golden in fhow, is but a wreath of thorns,
Brings dangers, troubles, cares, and fleeplefs nights
To him who wears the regal diadem,   461
When on his fhoulders each man's burden lies ;
For therein ftands the office of a king,
His honor, virtue, merit, and chief praife,
That for the public all this weight he bears.   465
Yet he who reigns within himfelf, and rules
Paffions, defires, and fears, is more a king ;
Which every wife and virtuous man attains :
And who attains not, ill afpires to rule
Cities of men, or headftrong multitudes,   470
Subject himfelf to anarchy within,
Or lawlefs paffions in him which he ferves.
But to guide nations in the way of truth

By

fetting forth the duty and office of
a king, let the friends of the houfe
of Stuart confider, whether he in-
tended any compliment to the king
then reigning.

466. *Yet he who reigns within
himfelf,* &c] Such fentiments
are inculcated not only by the phi-
lofophers, but alfo by the poets, as
Hor. Od. II. II. 9.

Latius regnes avidum domando
Spiritum &c.

and Sat. II. VII. 83.

Quifnam igitur liber ? Sapiens ;
fibi qui imperiofus, &c.

473. *But to guide nations* &c.] In
this fpeech concerning riches and
realms, our poet has cull'd all the
choiceft, fineft flowers out of the
heathen poets and philofophers
who have written upon thefe fub-
jects ; it is not fo much their words,
as their fubftance fublimated and
improv'd : but here he foars above
them, and nothing could have given
him fo complete an idea of a divine
teacher,

By faving doctrin, and from error lead
To know, and knowing worfhip God aright,   475
Is yet more kingly ; this attracts the foul,
Governs the inner man, the nobler part ;
That other o'er the body only reigns,
And oft by force, which to a generous mind
So reigning can be no fincere delight.   480
Befides to give a kingdom hath been thought
Greater and nobler done, and to lay down
Far more magnanimous, than to affume.
Riches are needlefs then, both for themfelves,
And for thy reafon why they fhould be fought,   485
To gain a fcepter, ofteft better mifs'd.

teacher, as the life and character of
our bleffed Saviour.

   481.*Befides to give a kingdom* &c]
So Hephæftion to thofe who tranf-
ferred the kingdom of Sidon from
themfelves to another. Quint. Curt.
IV. 1. Vos quidem macti virtute,
inquit, eftote, qui primi intellexi-
ftis, quanto majus effet, regnum

faftidire quam accipere &c. Dio-
cletian, Charles V, and others who
have refign'd the crown, were no
doubt in our author's thoughts upon
this occafion. For as Seneca fays,
Thyeft. III. 529.

   Habere regnum, cafus eft : vir-
tus, dare.

The end of the Second Book.

THE

THIRD BOOK

OF

PARADISE REGAIN'D.

PARADISE REGAIN'D.

B O O K III.

S O fpake the Son of God, and Satan ftood
A while as mute confounded what to fay,
What to reply, confuted and convinc'd
Of his weak arguing, and fallacious drift ;
At length colleting all his ferpent wiles,   5
With foothing words renew'd, him thus accofts.
I fee thou know'ft what is of ufe to know,
What beft to fay canft fay, to do canft do ;
Thy actions to thy words accord, thy words
To thy large heart give utterance due, thy heart 10

                           Contains

10,   —— *thy heart*
Contains of good, wife, juft, the
   perfect fhape.] Milton, no
doubt, by the word *fhape* intended
to exprefs the meaning of the Greek
term ιδια, but in my opinion it
does not at all come up to it, and
feems rather harfh and inelegant.
There are words in all languages,
which cannot well be tranflated
without lofing much of their beau-
ty, and even fome of their mean-
ing ; of this fort I take the word
idea to be. Tully renders it by the

word *fpecies* with as little fuccefs in
my opinion as Milton has done
here by his Englifh *fhape*. *Thyer.*
Of good, wife, juft, the perfect fhape.
I fhould rather think it exprefs'd
from the *perfecta forma honeftatis,*
and the *forma ipfa honefti* of Ci-
cero. De Fin. II. 15. Habes undi-
que expletam et *perfectam*, Tor-
quate, *formam honeftatis*, &c. De
Off. I. 5. *Formam* quidem *ipfam,*
Marce fili, et tanquam faciem *ho-*
nefti vides ; quæ fi oculis cernere-
tur &c. And the more, becaufe
       H 3   he

Contains of good, wife, juft, the perfect fhape.

Should kings and nations from thy mouth confult,

Thy counfel would be as the oracle

Urim and Thummim, thofe oraculous gems

On Aaron's breaft; or tongue of feers old   15

Infallible: or wert thou fought to deeds

That might require th' array of war, thy fkill

Of conduct would be fuch, that all the world

Could not fuftain thy prowefs, or fubfift

In

he renders *firma* by *fhape* in the Paradife Loft. IV. 848.

Virtue in her *fhape* how lovely.

13.   —— *as the oracle Urim and Thummim, thofe oraculous gems On Aaron's breaft; &c.*] Aaron's breaft-plate was a piece of cloth doubled, of a fpan fquare, in which were fet in fockets of gold twelve precious ftones bearing the names of the twelve tribes of Ifrael ingraven on them, which being fixed to the ephod, or upper veftment of the high-prieft's robes, was worn by him on his breaft on all folemn occafions. In this breaft-plate the *Urim and Thummim*, fay the Scriptures, were put. And the learned Prideaux, after giving fome account of the various opinions conerning *Urim and Thummim*, fays it will be fafeft to hold, that the words *Urim and Thummim* meant only the divine virtue and power, given to the breaft-plate in its confecration, of obtaining an oraculous anfwer from God, whenever counfel was afked of him by the high-prieft with it on, in fuch manner as his word did direct; and that the names of *Urim and Thummim* were given hereto only to denote the clearnefs and perfection, which thofe oracular anfwers always carried with them. For *Urim* fignifieth *light*, and *Thummim* perfection. But Milton by adding

—— thofe oraculous gems
On Aaron's breaft——

feems to have been of the common received opinion among the Jews, that the anfwer was given by the precious ftones, that it was by the fhining and protuberating of the letters in the names of the twelve tribes graven on the twelve ftones in the breaft-plate of the high-prieft, and that in them he did read the anfwer. But as Dr.

In battel, though againſt thy few in arms.　20
Theſe God-like virtues wherefore doſt thou hide,
Affecting private life, or more obſcure
In ſavage wilderneſs? wherefore deprive
All earth her wonder at thy acts, thyſelf
The fame and glory, glory the reward　25
That ſole excites to high attempts, the flame
Of moſt erected ſpi'rits, moſt temper'd pure
Ethereal, who all pleaſures elſe deſpiſe,

All

Dr. Prideaux ſays, it appears plain from Scripture, that when the high-prieſt appear'd before the veil to aſk counſel of God, the anſwer was given him by an audible voice from the mercy-ſeat, which was within behind the veil.

— or tongue of ſeers old ·
Infallible :

The poet by mentioning this after *Urim and Thummim* ſeems to allude to another opinion of the Jews, that the Holy Spirit ſpake to the children of Iſrael during the tabernacle by *Urim and Thummim*, and under the firſt temple by the *prophets*. See Prideaux Connect. Part I. Book III.

17.　—— *thy ſkill*
Of conduct would be ſuch,] The meaning is, thy ſkill in conducting an army would be ſuch, that &c: ſo that there is no occaſion for reading, as Mr. Meadowcourt has propos'd, *thy ſkill And conduct,*

which would be an alteration for the worſe, the commendation in this place not being of his *ſkill* in general, but of his *ſkill of conduct* in particular.

25 —— *glory the reward*] Our Saviour having withſtood the allurement of riches, Satan attacks him in the next place with the charms of glory. I have ſometimes thought, that Milton might poſſibly take the hint of thus connecting theſe two temptations from Spenſer, who in his ſecond book of the Faery Queen repreſenting the virtue of temperance under the character of Guyon, and leading him through various trials of his conſtancy, brings him to the houſe of riches or *Mammon's delve* as he terms it, and immediately after it to the palace of glory, which he deſcribes in his allegorical manner under the figure of a beautiful woman called *Philotimè*.　Thyer.

27. *Of moſt erected ſpirits,*] The
H 4　author

All treafures and all gain efteem as drofs,

And dignities and pow'rs all but the higheft ?   30

Thy years are ripe, and over-ripe ; the fon

Of Macedonian Philip had ere thefe

Won Afia, and the throne of Cyrus held

At his difpofe ; young Scipio had brought down

The Carthaginian pride ; young Pompey quell'd 35

The Pontic king, and in triumph had rode.

Yet

author here remember'd Cicero. Pro Archia. Trahimur omnes laudis ftudio, et optimus quifque maxime gloria ducitur. De Off. l. 8. In maximis animis fplendidiffimifque ingeniis plerumque exfiftunt honoris, imperii, potentiæ, gloriæ cupiditates.

31. *Thy years are ripe, and over-ripe* ;] Our Saviour's temptation was foon after his baptifm, and he was baptized when he was about *thirty years of age.* Luke III. 23. And *the fon of Macedonian Philip,* Alexander the great, *had ere thefe,* before thefe years, *won Afia and the throne of Cyrus,* the Perfian empire founded by Cyrus, *held at his difpofe* ; for Alexander was but 20 when he began to reign, and in a few years overturned the Perfian empire, and died in the 33d year of his age. *Young Scipio had brought down the Carthaginian pride* ; for Scipio Africanus was no more than 24 years old, when he was fent proconful into

Spain, and was only between 28 and 29, when he was chofen conful before the ufual time, and transferr'd the war into Africa. *Young Pompey quell'd the Pontic king, and in triumph had rode.* In this inftance our author is not fo exact as in the reft, for when Pompey was fent to command the war in Afia againft Mithridates king of Pontus, he was above 40, but had fignalized himfelf by many extraordinary actions in his younger years, and had obtained the honor of two triumphs before that time. Pompey and Cicero were born in the fame year ; and the Manilian law, which gave the command in Afia to Pompey, was propofed when Cicero was in the 41ft year of his age. But no wonder that Milton was miftaken in point of time, when feveral of the Ancients were, and Plutarch himfelf, who fpeaking of Pompey's three memorable triumphs over the three parts of the world, his firft over Africa, his
fecond

Yet years, and to ripe years judgment mature,
Quench not the thirſt of glory, but augment.
Great Julius, whom now all the world admires,
The more he grew in years, the more inflam'd   40
With glory, wept that he had liv'd ſo long
Inglorious : but thou yet art not too late.
   To whom our Saviour calmly thus reply'd.
Thou neither doſt perſuade me to ſeek wealth

                     For

ſecond over Europe, and this laſt over Aſia, ſays that as for his age, thoſe who affect to make the parallel exact in all things betwixt him and Alexander the great, would not allow him to be quite 34, whereas in truth at this time he was near 40. ἡλικια δε τοτε ην (ὡς μιν οἱ κατα παντα τω Aλιξανδρω παραβαλλοντις αυτον και προσοιβαζονʇε; αξιεσι) νεωτερ۞ των τριακονʇα και τεʇʇαρων, αληθεια δε τοις τεʇʇαρακονʇα προσηγιν. Plut. Vit. Pompeii.

41. —wept that he had liv'd ſo long Inglorious :] Alluding to a ſtory related of Julius Cæſar, that one day reading the hiſtory of Alexander, he ſat a great while very thoughtful, and at laſt burſt into tears, and his friends wondring at the reaſon of it, Do you not think, ſaid he, I have juſt cauſe to weep, when I conſider that Alexander at my age had conquer'd ſo many nations, and I have all this time done nothing that is memorable ?

See Plutarch's Life of Cæſar. Others ſay, it was at the ſight of an image of Alexander the great— animadverſa apud Herculis templum magni Alexandri imagine ingemuit ; et quaſi pertæſus ignaviam ſuam, quod nihil dum à ſe memorabile actum eſſet in ætate qua jam Alexander orbem terrarum ſubegiſſet, &c. Suetonii Jul. Cæſ. cap. 7.

44. Thou neither doſt perſuade me &c] How admirably does Milton in this ſpeech expoſe the emptineſs and uncertainty of a popular character, and found true glory upon its only ſure baſis, the approbation of the God of truth ? There is a remarkable dignity of ſentiment runs quite through it, and I think it will be no extravagance at all to aſſert, that he has compris'd in this ſhort compaſs the ſubſtance and quinteſſence of a ſubject which has exerciſed the pens of the greateſt moraliſts in all ages.   Thyer.
The juſtneſs of this remark will
              appear

appear to geater advantage by the learned collection out of the Heathen moralists in the following note of Mr. Jortin.

47. *For what is glory* &c] The love of glory is a passion deeply rooted in us, and difficultly kept under. Τ~ν κενοδοξιαν, ὡς τελευταιον χιτωια, ἡ ψυχη πεφυκεν αποτιθεσθαι, says Plato. Helvidius Priscus, as Tacitus relates, was possessed of all the virtues which make a great and a good man. He was a Stoic into the bargain, and therefore bound by the principles of his philosophy to set a small value upon the τα εκ εφ' ημιν· yet erant quibus appetentior famæ videretur: quando etiam sapientibus cupido gloriæ novissima exuitur. Hist. IV. 5. As at Rome and in Greece a spear, a crown of oak or laurel, a statue, a public commendation, was esteemed an ample recompense for many brave actions ; so it is as true, that not a few of their great men were over fond of fame, and mere slaves to the love of it. Let us see what the philosophers have said concerning a greedy desire of glory, such a desire of it as leads men to make it the ruling principle of their actions, and incites them to do well only, or chiefly in order to be admired. We shall find them condemning it, and saying things agreeable enough to what Milton

puts into the mouth of our Saviour. Illud autem te admoneo, ne eorum more, qui non proficere sed conspici volunt, facias aliqua. Seneca, Epist. V. Qui virtutem suam publicari vult, non virtuti laborat, sed gloriæ. Id. Epist. CXIII. Cavenda est gloriæ cupiditas, is a lesson delivered by one who in that particular did not practice what he taught. De Officiis I.

Laudis amore tumes ? sunt certa
   piacula, quæ te
Ter pure lecto poterunt recreare
   libello.   Hor. Epist. I. 1.

An quidquam stultius, quam quos singulos, sicut operarios barbarosque contemnas, eos esse aliquid putare universos ? Cicero, Tusc. Disp. V. 36. where Dr. Davies : Egregium hoc monitum Socrati debetur, qui Alcibiadem, in concionem populi prodire veritum, ita excitavit : Ου καταφρονει: (ειπε Σωκρατης) εκεινε τε σκυτοτιμε ; το ονομα ειπων αυτε· φησαιθ- δε τε Αλκιβιαδε, ιπολαβων παλιν ὁ Σωκρατης. ετι δε εκεινε τε εν τοις κυκλοις κηρυτλονθ- ; η εκεινε τε σκηνορραφε ; ὁμολογενθ- δε τε Κλεινε μειρακιε, εκ ε, εφη ὁ Σωκρατης, ὁ δημθ- Αθηναιων εκ τετων ηθροισαι ; και ει των καθ' εια καταφροιητεον, αρα και των ηθροισμενων. Epictetus, Enchir. XLV. says : Σημεια προκοπλονθ-· εδεια ψεγει, εδεια επαινει, εδεια
               μεμ

For what is glory but the blaze of fame,

The peoples praife, if always praife unmix'd ?

And

μεμφεται, ϧδεν εἰκαλει, ϧδεν σε-
ρι ἑαυτε λεγει, —— καν τις αυτον
επαινη, καταγελα τε επαινϧντϲ·
αυτϲ· σαρ᾽ ἑαυτω· καν ψεγη, ϧκ
απολογειται. Signa proficientis
funt : neminem vituperat, nemi-
nem laudat, de nemine queritur,
neminem incufat, nihil de feipfo
dicit,——et fi quis ipfum laudet,
ridet laudantem ipfe fecum ; et fi
vituperet, non fe purgat. Idem
apud Stobæum : Ουδεις φιλοχρη-
ματϲ·, και φιληδονϲ·, και φιλο-
δοξϲ·, και φιλαιθρωπϲ· αλλα
μονϲ· ὁ φιλοκαλϲ·. Nemo pecu-
niæ amans, et voluptatis, et glo-
riæ fimul homines amat; fed folus
honefti amans. So Plato De Re-
pub. I. fays, that a fondnefs of
glory is as mean a vice as a fond-
nefs of money. Many fuch like
paffages might be added, particu-
larly from Marcus Aurelius, and
other Stoical writers. The Stoics,
tho' they refufed to give fame and
glory a place amongft good things,
yet I think did not flight the efteem
of good men : they diftinguifh be-
tween gloria and claritas. Gloria
multorum judiciis conftat, claritas
bonorum. — [Sed claritas] poteft
unius boni viri judicio effe conten-
ta. Seneca, Epift. CII. I cannot
forbear inferting here a paffage
from Seneca, which I believe will
pleafe the reader as much as it
does me : it relates to that fond
hope which we writers, good, bad,
and indifferent, are apt to enter-

tain, that our name and labors
fhall be immortal, and it tells us
as elegantly as truly what we have
to expeft. Profunda fupra nos al-
titudo temporis veniet, pauca in-
genia caput exferent, et in idem
quandoque filentium abitura obli-
vioni refiftent, ac fe diu viudica-
bunt. Epift. XXI. We expeft that
Time fhould take the charge of
our writings, and deliver them
fafe to the lateft pofterity : but
he is as furly and whimfical as
Charon :

Stabant orantes primi tranfmit-
    tere curfum,
Tendebantque manus ripæ ulte-
    rioris amore.
Navita fed triftis nunc hos, nunc
    accipit illos,
Aft alios longe fummotos arcet
    arena.

If we have the mortification to fee
our works die before us, we may
comfort ourfelves with the confi-
deration, which Seneca fuggefts to
us, that a time will come when the
moft excellent and admired com-
pofitions fhall perifh. Nor is the
confolation much fmaller, which
offers itfelf to us, when we look
back and confider how many good
authors there muft needs have been,
of whom no memorial is left, and
how many of whom nothing but
the bare name furvives, and how
many books are extant indeed, but
never read.

Aufer

And what the people but a herd confus'd, 49
A miscellaneous rabble, who extol
[praise?
Things vulgar, and well weigh'd, scarce worth the
They praise, and they admire they know not what,
And know not whom, but as one leads the other;
And what delight to be by such extoll'd,
To live upon their tongues and be their talk, 55
Of whom to be disprais'd were no small praise?
His lot who dares be singularly good.
Th' intelligent among them and the wise

Are

Auferabhinc lacrimas, Barathro,
& compesce querelas;
Lumina iis oculis etiam bonus
Ancus reliquit,
Qui melior multis, quam tu,
fuit, improbe, rebus.

To these motives of contentment
under such circumstances, I need
not add what every neglected au-
thor says to himself, that the age
he lives in has no taste.   *Jortin.*

56. *Of whom to be disprais'd were
no small praise?*] So it is in
Milton's own edition, *disprais'd*;
in most of the others it is *despis'd*,

Of whom to be *despis'd* were no
small praise:

but we have restor'd the first read-
ing for very obvious reasons.
57. *His lot who dares be singularly
good.*] A glorious example of
this *singular goodness* is exhibited in

the character and behaviour of the
Seraph Abdiel in the Paradise Lost.
And perhaps the poet might think
it likewise his own case, and at this
time was not without a pleasing
reflection upon himself, who *dar'd*
to be as singular in his opinions
and in his conduct, as any man
whatever.
59. —*and glory scarce a few is
rais'd.*] Seneca would prove
in his 102d Epistle, that the judg-
ment of *one* good man is sufficient
to constitute this *glory* or *clarity*, as
he calls it: for *glory* according to
him is the judgment of the many,
clarity of the good. If one good
man, says he, thinks well of me,
it is the same as if all good men
thought well of me, because if
they all knew me, they would all
think as he doth; so that the judg-
ment of all is really included in
that of one.   Quia si de me bene
vir

Are few, and glory fcarce of few is rais'd.

This is true glory and renown, when God   60
Looking on th' earth, with approbation marks
The juft man, and divulges him through Heaven
To all his Angels, who with true applaufe
Recount his praifes : thus he did to Job,   64
When to extend his fame through Heav'n and Earth,
As thou to thy reproach may'ft well remember,
He afk'd thee, Haft thou feen my fervant Job ?
Famous he was in Heav'n, on Earth lefs known ;

Where

vir bonus fentit, eodem loco fum, quo, fi omnes boni idem fentirent; omnes enim, fi me cognoverint, idem fentient. Par illis idemque judicium eft. *Calton.*

60. *This is true glory and renown, when God &c*] Here is a glory that is folid and fubftantial, expreffa (as Tully fays) non adumbrata ; and that will indure, when all the records and memorials of human pride are perifhed. There is a pretty paffage near the end of the laft book of Hieronymus Oforius's treatife De Gloria, where the author is confidering that honor, which confifts in the approbation and applaufe of God and Angels, as a reward of virtue in the life to come. Nam fi laudatoris amplitudo ad dignitatis amplificationem pertinet, quid effe poteft Chrifti majeftate magnificentius ? Si verum judicium in certa gloriæ ra-

tione requirimus, Deus folus intimos hominum fenfus perfpectos habet. Si laudantis conftantiam attendimus, divina mens nullam in omni æternitate poteft habere mutationem. Si lucem et celebritatem confideres, tunc clarorum hominum laudes coram omnibus angelis et hominibus illuftrabuntur. Si ad diuturnitatem *animum advertas,* [in my edition it is *animadvertas*] nullum finem funt ullis unquam fæculis habituræ. Quid igitur illa gloria divinius, quam mentes caftæ in illa cœlefti regione confequentur ? Eft enim dignitate laudatoris immenfa, fpectatorum celebritate clariffima, diuturnitate temporis infinita. *Calton.*

67. *He afk'd thee, Haft thou feen my fervant Job ?*] Job I. 8. *And the Lord faid unto Satan, Haft thou confidered my fervant Job, that there is none like him in the earth,*

a

Where glory is falſe glory, attributed
To things not glorious, men not worthy' of fame.
They err who count it glorious to ſubdue   71
By conqueſt far and wide, to over-run
Large countries, and in field great battels win,
Great cities by aſſault : what do theſe worthies,
But rob and ſpoil, burn, ſlaughter, and inſlave   75
                                        Peaceable

a perfeſt and an upright man, one that feareth God, and eſcheweth evil. See too II. 3.

69. *Where glory is falſe glory, attributed To things not glorious, men not worthy of fame.*] True glory (Tully ſays) is the praiſe of good men, the echo of virtue : but that ape of glory, the random injudicious applauſe of the multitude, is often beſtowed upon the worſt of actions. Eſt enim gloria ſolida quædam res et expreſſa, non adumbrata: ea eſt conſentiens laus bonorum, incorrupta vox bene judicantium de excellente virtute : ea virtuti reſonat tanquam imago: — illa autem, quæ ſe ejus imitatricem eſſe volt, temeraria atque inconſiderata et plerumque peccatorum vitiorumque laudatrix, fama popularis, ſimulatione honeſtatis formam ejus pulchritudinemque corrumpit. Qua cæcitate homines, cum quædam etiam præclara cuperent, eaque neſcirent nec ubi nec qualia eſſent, funditus alii everte-

runt ſuas civitates, alii ipſi occiderunt. Tuſc. Diſp. III. 2.   When Tully wrote his Tuſculan Diſputations, Julius Cæſar had overturned the conſtitution of his country, and was then in the highth of his power ; and Pompey had loſt his life in the ſame purſuit of glory. Of him the alii ipſi occiderunt— may very well be underſtood.
                        Calton.

71. *They err who count it glorious &c*] From hence to ver. 88. we have a juſt and complete character of the great conquerors of the world, who inſtead of being, as they have too often been, the idols of mankind, ought rather to be the principal objects of their utmoſt averſation   The character is general, but yet not without particular alluſions ; as when it is ſaid

—— muſt be titled Gods,
Great Benefactors of mankind,
    Deliverers,

it is in alluſion to the titles of *Theus, Euergetes,* and *Soter,* which have often been aſcrib'd by their ſycophants

Peaceable nations, neighb'ring, or remote,
Made captive, yet deferving freedom more
Than thofe their conquerors, who leave behind
Nothing but ruin wherefoe'er they rove,
And all the florifhing works of peace deftroy,   8o
Then fwell with pride, and muft be titled Gods,
Great Benefactors of mankind, Deliverers,

                                            Worfhipt

phants and flatterers to the worft
of tyrants : and when it is faid

> One is the fon of Jove, of Mars
> the other,

Alexander is particularly intended
by the one, and Romulus by the
other, who tho' better than Alex-
ander, yet it muft be faid founded
his empire in the blood of his bro-
ther, and for his overgrown ty-
ranny was at laft deftroy'd by his
own fenate. And certainly the
method that Milton has here ta-
ken is the beft method that can
be taken of drawing general cha-
racters, by felecting the particulars
here and there, and then adjufting
and incorporating them together ;
as Apelles from the different beau-
ties of feveral nymphs of Greece
drew his portrait of Venus, the
Goddefs of beauty.

74. — *What do thefe worthies*
But rob and fpoil, burn, flaughter,
   and inflave
Peaceable nations, neighb'ring, or
   remote, &c] Milton faith not

a word directly of the exploits of
thofe heroes, who in purfuit of
falfe glory had done what Cæfar
did. He was unwilling perhaps to
give his readers occafion to reflect,
that there was a Cæfar in his own
time and country, whom he had
prais'd, admir'd, and ferv'd.
                                    Calton.

81. *Then fwell with pride, and*
   muft be titled Gods, &c] The
fecond Antiochus king of Syria
was called Antiochus Θεὸ- or *the*
God : and the learned author De
Epoch. Syro-Macedonum p. 151.
fpeaks of a coin of Epiphanes in-
fcrib'd Θεε Επιφανης. The Athe-
nians gave Demetrius Poliorcetes,
and his father Antigonus the titles
of Ευεργεται *Benefactors*, and Σω-
τηρες *Deliverers*. The laft was a
divine title ; [See Suidas in voce
Σωτηρ] and they finifh'd the com-
pliment by calling their Head-ma-
giftrate, inftead of *Archon*, Ιερευς
Σωτηρων, *Prieft of the Deliverers*.
Plut. in vita Demetrii.   *Calton.*

                           96. *Poor*

Worſhipt with temple, prieſt and ſacrifice;

One is the ſon of Jove, of Mars the other;

Till conqu'ror Death diſcover them ſcarce men,   85

Rolling in brutiſh vices, and deform'd,

Violent or ſhameful death their due reward.

But if there be in glory ought of good,

It may by means far different be attain'd

Without ambition, war, or violence;   90

By deeds of peace, by wiſdom eminent,

By patience, temperance : I mention ſtill

Him whom thy wrongs with ſaintly patience borne

Made famous in a land and times obſcure;

Who names not now with honor patient Job?   95

Poor

---

96. *Poor Socrates (who next more memorable?)* &c.] Milton here does not ſcruple with Eraſmus to place Socrates in the foremoſt rank of Saints; an opinion more amiable at leaſt, and agreeable to that ſpirit of love which breathes in the Goſpel, than the ſevere orthodoxy of thoſe rigid textuaries, who are unwilling to allow ſalvation to the moral virtues of the Heathen. *Thyer.*

98. ———— *lives now Equal in fame to proudeſt conquerors.*] And therefore the very ingenious author of the viſion of the Table of Fame has given him a place there with Alexander, and Cæſar, and the moſt celebrated heroes of antiquity. See the Tatler N° 81 by Mr. Addiſon. And the no leſs ingenious author of the Temple of Fame has made him the principal figure among the better ſort of heroes.

Much-ſuff'ring heroes next their honors clame,
Thoſe of leſs noiſy, and leſs guilty fame,
Fair Virtue's ſilent train : ſupreme of theſe
Here ever ſhines the godlike Socrates.

And if Mr. Addiſon had completed his

Poor Socrates (who next more memorable?)
By what he taught and fuffer'd for fo doing,
For truth's fake fuffering death unjuft, lives now
Equal in fame to proudeft conquerors.
Yet if for fame and glory ought be done,   100
Ought fuffer'd ; if young African for fame
His wafted country freed from Punic rage,
The deed becomes unprais'd, the man at leaft,
And lofes, though but verbal, his reward.
Shall I feek glory then, as vain men feek,   105
Oft not deferv'd? I feek not mine, but his
Who fent me', and thereby witnefs whence I am.
To whom the Tempter murm'ring thus reply'd.

Think

his defign of writing a tragedy of Socrates, his fuccefs in all probability would have been greater, as the fubject would have been better than that of Cato.

101. —— *if young African for fame His wafted country freed from Punic rage,*] This fhows plainly that he had fpoken before of the elder Scipio Africanus ; for he only can be faid with propriety to have *freed his wafted country from Punic rage,* by transferring the war into Spain and Africa after the ravages which Hannibal had committed in Italy during the fecond Punic war.

106. —— *I feek not mine, but his Who fent me', and thereby witnefs whence I am.*] I honor my Father, *I feek not mine own glory,* fays our Saviour in St. John's Gofpel VIII. 49, 50 : and this he urgeth as a proof of his divine miffion, VII. 18. *He that fpeaketh of himfelf, feeketh his own glory : but he that feeketh his glory that fent him, the fame is true, and no unrighteoufnefs is in him.*

Think not fo flight of glory ; therein leaft

Refembling thy great Father : he feeks glory,   110

And for his glory all things made, all things

Orders and governs; nor content in Heaven

By all his Angels g'orify'd, requires

Glory from men, from all men good or bad,

Wife or unwife, no difference, no exemption;   115

Above all facrifice, or hallow'd gift

Glory' he requires, and glory he receives

Promifcuous from all nations, Jew, or Greek,

Or barbarous, nor exception hath declar'd ;

From

109. *Think not fo flight of glory* ;
&c] There is nothing throughout
the whole poem more expreffive of
the true character of the Tempter
than this reply.   There is in it all
the real falfhood of *the father of
lies*, and the glozing fubtlety of an
infidious deceiver.   The argument
is falfe and unfound, and yet it is
veil'd over with a certain plaufible
air of truth.   The poet has alfo
by introducing this furnifh'd him-
felf with an opportunity of ex-
plaining that great queftion in di-
vinity, why God created the world,
and what is meant by that glory
which he expects from his crea-
tures.   This may be no improper
place to obferve to the reader the
author's great art in weaving in-
to the body of fo fhort a work fo

many grand points of the Chriftian
theology and morality.   *Thyer.*

118. *Premifcuous from all nations,*]
The poet puts here into the mouth
of the Devil the abfurd notions of
the apologifts for Paganifm.   See
Themiftius Orat. XII. de Relig.
Valent. Imp. ταυτα νομιζε γινεσθαι
&c. p. 160.   *Warburton.*

121. *To whom our Saviour fer-
vently reply'd.*] As this poem
confifts chiefly of a dialogue be-
tween the Tempter and our Sa-
viour, the poet muft have labor'd
under fome difficulty in compofing
a fufficient variety of introductory
lines to the feveral fpeeches, and
it required great art and judgment
to vary and adapt them fo properly
as he hath done to the fubject in
hand.   We took notice of a beauty
of

From us his foes pronounc'd glory' he exacts.   120
　To whom our Saviour fervently reply'd.
And reason ; since his word all things produc'd,
Though chiefly not for glory as prime end,
But to show forth his goodness, and impart
His good communicable to every soul   125
Freely ; of whom what could he less expect
Than glory' and benediction, that is thanks,
The slightest, easiest, readiest recompense
From them who could return him nothing else,
And not returning that would likeliest render   130

Contempt

of this kind in a note upon II. 432 : and here we have another instance not unworthy of our observation. When the Tempter had proposed to our Saviour the baits and allurements of glory, he was nothing mov'd, but reply'd with great calmness and composure of mind. ver. 43.

　To whom our Saviour *calmly* thus reply'd :

but now the Tempter reflects upon the glory of God, our Saviour is warm'd upon the occasion, and answers with some eagerness and fervor.

　To whom our Saviour *fervently* reply'd.

And this is perfectly just, and a-greeable to the true character of our Saviour, who was all meekness and forbearance in every thing that related to himself, but where God's honour was concern'd, was warm and zealous ; as when he drove the buyers and sellers out of the temple, infomuch that the disciples apply'd to him the saying of the Psalmist, *The zeal of thine house hath eaten me up.* John II. 17.

　128. *The slightest, easiest, readiest recompense!* The same sentiment in the Paradise Lost. IV. 46.

What could be less than to afford
　him praise.
The easiest recompense, and pay
　him thanks,
How due !

　130. *And not returning that*] We
　I 2　　　　　　　　　　　　have

Contempt inftead, difhonor, obloquy ?

Hard recompenfe, unfuitable return

For fo much good, fo much beneficence.

But why fhould man feek glory, who' of his own

Hath nothing, and to whom nothing belongs   135

But condemnation, ignominy', and fhame ?

Who for fo many benefits receiv'd

Turn'd recreant to God, ingrate and falfe,

And fo of all true good himfelf defpoil'd,

Yet, facrilegious, to himfelf would take   140

That which to God alone of right belongs ;

Yet fo much bounty is in God, fuch grace,

That who advance his glory, not their own,

Them he himfelf to glory will advance.

    So fpake the Son of God ; and here again   145

                       Satan

---

have replac'd the reading of the firft edition : moft of the later editions have it

    And not returning *what*

which fpoils the fenfe of the paffage. I had correcfed it in my own book before I had feen the firft edition, and Mr. Thyer had done the fame.

    151. *Worth or not worth the feeking*,] In all the editions which I have feen except the firft, it is printed

Worth or not worth *their* feeking, but not knowing to whom *their* could refer, I imagin'd it fhould be

Worth or not worth *thy* feeking, but the firft edition exhibits this reading

Worth or not worth *the* feeking, as Mr. Sympfon propofed to read by conjecture.

    158. *Reduc'd a province under Roman yoke*,] Judæa was reduced

                to

Satan had not to anfwer, but ftood ftruck
With guilt of his own fin, for he himfelf
Infatiable of glory had loft all,
Yet of another plea bethought him foon.

Of glory, as thou wilt, faid he, fo deem,   150
Worth or not worth the feeking, let it pafs :
But to a kingdom thou art born, ordain'd
To fit upon thy father David's throne ;
By mother's fide thy father ; though thy right
Be now in pow'rful hands, that will not part   155
Eafily from poffeffion won with arms :
Judæa now and all the promis'd land,
Reduc'd a province under Roman yoke,
Obeys Tiberius ; nor is always rul'd
With temp'rate fway ; oft have they violated   160

The

to the form of a Roman province, in the reign of Auguftus, by Quirinius or Cyrenius then governor of Syria; and Coponius a Roman of the equeftrian order was appointed to govern it under the title of Procurator of Judæa ; our Saviour being then (as Dean Prideaux fays) in the 12th year of his age, but according to the vulgar æra, which begins four years later than the true time, it was A. D. 8. *Nor is always rul'd with temp'rate fway :* and indeed the Roman government was not always the moft temperate. At this time Pontius Pilate was procurator of Judæa ; and if hiftory be true, he was a moft corrupt, and flagitious governor. See particularly Philo de Legatione ad Caium.

160. —— *oft have they violated The temple, &c*] As Pompey did particularly with feveral of his officers, who enter'd not only into the holy place, but alfo penetrated into the holy of holies, where none were permitted by the law to en-

The temple, oft the law with foul affronts,
Abominations rather, as did once
Antiochus : and think'ft thou to regain
Thy right by fitting ftill or thus retiring ?
So did not Maccabeus : he indeed   165
Retir'd unto the defert, but with arms ;
And o'er a mighty king fo oft prevail'd,
That by ftrong hand his family obtain'd,   [ufurp'd,
Though priefts, the crown, and David's throne
With Modin and her fuburbs once content.   170
If kingdom move thee not, let move thee zeal
And duty ; zeal and duty are not flow ;
But on occafion's forelock watchful wait.
They themfelves rather are occafion beft,
Zeal of thy father's houfe, duty to free   175
Thy country from her heathen fervitude ;

                                                        So

ter, except the high-prieft alone once in a year, on the great day of expiation. And this profanation of the temple might well remind the author of a former one by Antiochus Epiphanes. See 2 Macab. V.

165. *So did not Maccabeus :*] The Tempter had compar'd the profanation of the temple by the Romans to that by Antiochus Epiphanes, king of Syria ; and now

he would infer that Jefus was to blame for not vindicating his country againft the one, as *Judas Maccabeus* had done againft the other. He fled indeed into the wildernefs from the perfecutions of Antiochus, but there he took up arms againft him, and obtained fo many victories over his forces, that he recovered the city and fanctuary out of their hands, and his family was in his brother Jonathan advanced

So fhalt thou beft fulfil, beft verify
The prophets old, who fung thy endlefs reign ;
The happier reign the fooner it begins ;   179
Reign then ; what canft thou better do the while ?

To whom our Saviour anfwer thus return'd.
All things are beft fulfill'd in their due time,
And time there is for all things, Truth hath faid :
If of my reign prophetic Writ hath told,
That it fhall never end, fo when begin   185
The Father in his purpofe hath decreed,
He in whofe hand all times and feafons roll.
What if he hath decreed that I fhall firft   .
Be try'd in humble ftate, and things adverfe,
By tribulations, injuries, infults,   190
Contempts, and fcorns, and fnares, and violence,
Suffering, abftaining, quietly expecting,

Without

vanced to the high priefthood, and in his brother Simon to the principality, and fo they continued for feveral defcents fovran pontiffs and fovran princes of the Jewifh nation till the time of Herod the great : tho' their father Mattathias (the fon of John, the fon of Simon, the fon of Afmonæus, from whom the family had the name of Afmonæans) was no more than a prieft of the courfe of Joarib, and dwelt at *Modin*, which is famous for nothing fo much as being the country of the Maccabees. See 1. Maccab. Jofephus, Prideaux &c.

183 *And time there is for all things, Truth hath faid :*] Ecclef. III. 1. *To every thing there is a feafon, and a time to every purpofe under the Heaven.*

187. *He in whofe hand all times and feafons roll.*] Alluding to Acts I. 7. *It is not for you to know*

the

Without diftruft or doubt, that he may know
What I can fuffer, how obey ? who beft
Can fuffer, beft can do; beft reign, who firft   195
Well hath obey'd ; juft trial ere I merit
My exaltation without change or end.
But what concerns it thee when I begin
My everlafting kingdom, why art thou
Solicitous, what moves thy inquifition?   200
Know'ft thou not that my rifing is thy fall,
And my promotion will be thy deftruction ?

    To whom the Tempter inly rack'd reply'd.
Let that come when it comes ; all hope is loft
Of my reception into grace ; what worfe ?   205
For where no hope is left, is left no fear :
If there be worfe, the expectation more
Of worfe torments me than the feeling can.

I would

---

the times or the feafons, which the
Father hath put in his own power.

195. —— beft reign, who firft
Well hath obey'd;] Here probably
the author remember'd Cicero. De
Legib. III. 2. Qui bene imperat,
paruerit aliquando necefle eft ; et
qui modefte paret, videtur, qui ali-
quando imperet, dignus effe. The
fame fentiment occurs in Ariftotle,
Polit. III. 4.VII. 14. and in Plato,

De Legg. VI. as Urfinus and Da-
vies have noted.

206. For where no hope is left, is
left no fear : &c.] Milton in
this and the five following verfes
plainly alludes to thefe lines in that
fine foliloquy of Satan's in the be-
ginning of the 4th book of Para-
dife Loft. ver. 108.

    So farewel hope, and with hope
    farewel fear,

Farewel

I would be at the worſt ; worſt is my port,

My harbour, and my ultimate repoſe,   210

The end I would attain, my final good.

My error was my error, and my crime

My crime ; whatever for itſelf condemn'd,

And will alike be puniſh'd, whether thou

Reign or reign not ; though to that gentle brow 215

Willingly I could fly, and hope thy reign,

From that placid aſpéct and meek regard,

Rather than aggravate my evil ſtate,

Would ſtand between me and thy Father's ire

(Whoſe ire I dread more than the fire of Hell)   220

A ſhelter and a kind of ſhading cool

Interpoſition, as a ſummer's cloud.

If I then to the worſt that can be haſte,

Why move thy feet ſo ſlow to what is beſt,

Happieſt

Farewel remorſe : all good to
  me is loſt ;
Evil be thou my good. ⸺
                    Thyer.

212.   ⸺ *and my crime*
My crime ; *whatever for itſelf*
  condemn'd,] This is the point-
ing in Milton's own edition, and
I conceive the expreſſion to be el-
leiptical, and this to be the mean-
ing, *My error was my error, and my*
crime my crime ; *whatever* it be, it
is *for itſelf condemn'd, and will alike*
be puniſh'd &c : and I do not ſee
how the paſſage is emended, or the
ſenſe improv'd by placing the ſe-
micolon after *my crime whatever,*
as Mr. Sympſon preſcribes ; or by
blotting out the ſemicolon after
crime, and putting a comma at
whatever, as Mr. Meadowcourt
directs.

234. And

Happieſt both to thyſelf and all the world,   225

That thou who worthieſt art ſhould'ſt be their king ?

Perhaps thou linger'ſt in deep thoughts detain'd

Of th' enterpriſe ſo hazardous and high ;

No wonder, for though in thee be united

What of perfection can in man be found,   230

Or human nature can receive, conſider

Thy life hath yet been private, moſt part ſpent

At home, ſcarce view'd the Galilean towns,

And once a year Jeruſalem, few days   234

Short ſojourn; and what thence could'ſt thou obſerve ?

The world thou haſt not ſeen, much leſs her glory,

Empires, and monarchs, and their radiant courts,

Beſt ſchool of beſt experience, quickeſt inſight

In all things that to greateſt actions lead.

                                            The

234. *And once a year Jeruſalem,* &c] At the feaſt of the paſſover, Luke II. 41.

238.   —— *quickeſt inſight In all things that to greateſt actions lead.*] In all the editions, and indeed in Milton's own, it is printed

          —— quickeſt *in fight* In all things &c ;

but we cannot but think it an error of the writer or printer, and pre-fer the emendation, which Mr. Theobald, Mr. Meadowcourt, and Mr. Thyer have, unknown to each other, propoſed,

          quickeſt *inſight* &c :

and it was eaſy for Milton's amanuenſis (his wife moſt probably) or his printer to miſtake the one for the other. Thoſe are the beſt and moſt probable emendations, which conſiſt in ſuch ſmall alterations. When other words are ſubſtituted,

                                            we

The wifeft, unexperienc'd, will be ever   240
Timorous and loath, with novice modefty,
(As he who feeking affes found a kingdom)
Irrefolute, unhardy, unadventrous :
But I will bring thee where thou foon fhalt quit
Thofe rudiments, and fee before thine eyes   245
The monarchies of th' earth, their pomp and ftate,
Sufficient introduction to inform
Thee, of thyfelf fo apt, in regal arts,
And regal myfteries, that thou may'ft know
How beft their oppofition to withftand.   250
    With that (fuch pow'r was giv'n him then) he took
The Son of God up to a mountain high.
It was a mountain at whofe verdant feet
A fpacious plain out-ftretch'd in circuit wide

                                        Lay

we ought to have fome better au-
thority than conjecture.
    242. *As he who feeking affes found
      a kingdom*] Saul, who feeking
his father's loft affes, came to Sa-
muel, and by him was annointed
king. The ftory is related in
1 Sam. IX.
    253. *It was a mountain* &c] All
that the Scripture faith, is that the
Devil took our Saviour up into *a
high mountain,* Luke IV. 5. *an ex-
ceeding high mountain,* Mat. IV. 8.

and commentators generally fup-
pofe it to be one of the mountains
in the neighbourhood of Jerufa-
lem, Jerufalem being furrounded
by mountains, or fome mountain
near the wildernefs, near the place
where our Saviour was tempted.
The Ancients fpeak little concern-
ing it, but the Moderns conceive
it to be the mountain Quarantania,
as it is now call'd. That inge-
nious traveler, Mr. Maundrel in
his Journey from Aleppo to Jeru-
                              falem,

Lay pleaſant ; from his ſide two rivers flow'd,   255
Th' one winding, th' other ſtrait, and left between
Fair champain with leſs rivers intervein'd,
Then meeting join'd their tribute to the ſea :
Fertil of corn the glebe, of oil and wine ;   259
With herds the paſtures throng'd, with flocks the hills;
Huge cities and high towr'd, that well might ſeem
The ſeats of mightieſt monarchs, and ſo large

The

ſalem, mentioning the plain of Je-
richo, ſays that (Mat. 29.) " we
" deſcended into it, after about
" five hours march from Jeruſa-
" lem.   As ſoon as we enter'd the
" plain, we turned up on the left
" hand, and going about one hour
" that way, came to the foot of
" the Quarantania ; which they
" ſay is the mountain into which
" the Devil took our bleſſed Sa-
" viour, when he tempted him
" with that viſionary ſcene of all
" the kingdoms and glories of the
" world.   It is, as St. Matthew
" ſtiles it, an exceeding high
" mountain, and in its aſcent not
" only difficult, but dangerous."
But this is all conjecture, for the
Scripture has not ſpecified any par-
ticular place, and the Scripture
having not aſcertained the place,
the poet was at liberty to chooſe
any mountain, that beſt ſuited his
fancy, for the ſcene of this viſion.
And accordingly he ſuppoſes the
Devil *(ſuch pow'r was given him
then)* to carry our Saviour *many a*

league up to a high mountain, of
which he forbears to mention the
name out of reverence to the Scrip-
ture, which hath likewiſe men-
tion'd no name ; but by his de-
ſcription of it he muſt mean mount
Taurus, as Mr. Thyer and Mr. Cal-
ton have concurred with me in ob-
ſerving ; for he deſcribes it exactly
in the ſame manner as Strabo has
deſcribed that part of mount Tau-
rus, which divides the greater Ar-
menia from Meſopotamia, and
contains the ſources of the two
rivers Euphrates and Tigris. Stra-
bo Lib. XI. p. 521. Edit. Amſtel.
Το δ' εν νοτιωτατον (βορειοτατον)
μαλιϛα εϛιν ὁ Ταυρ⌀ ὁριζων την
Αρμενιαν απο της Μεσοποταμιας.
Εντευθεν δ' αμφοτεροι ῥευσιν οἱ
την Μεσοποταμιαν εἰκυκλυμενοι
ποταμοι, και συναπτοντες αλλη-
λοις εἰγυς κατα την Βαβυλωνιαν,
ειτα εκδιδοντες εἰς την κατα Περ-
σας Θαλατίαν, ὁ τε Ευφρατης,
και ὁ Τιγρις.   And the courſe of
the rivers is deſcribed in the ſame
manner by Strabo, the Euphrates
winding,

The profpect was, that here and there was room
For barren defert fountainlefs and dry.   264
To this high mountain top the Tempter brought
Our Saviour, and new train of words began.
Well have we fpeeded, and o'er hill and dale,
Foreft and field and flood, temples and towers,
Cut fhorter many a league ; here thou behold'ft
Affyria and her empire's ancient bounds,   270
                                                  Araxes

winding, and the Tigris *ftrait* and fwift as an arrow. Εςι δε μειζων ὁ Ευφρατης, και πλειω διεξεισι χωραν, σκολιω τω ρειθρω, κ. τ. λ. Dionyfius, and other ancient Geographers give us much the fame defcription : of the Euphrates, he fays ver. 797. Edit. Wells.

'Ος δητοι πρωτ☉ μεν απ' ὐξι☉
  Αρμενιοιο
Μακρ☉ επι νοτον εισι, παλιν δ'
  αἰκωνας ελιξας;
Αυτην πελιοιο, κ. τ. λ.

and for the fame reafon as Lloyd has remarked in his Dictionary, it is called *vagus Euphrates* by Statius, and *flexuofus* by Martianus Capella. Of the Tigris Dionyfius fays

Τον δε μετ' εις αυγας, ποταμων
  ωκις☉ απαιλων
Τιγρις εὐρρειτης φερεται, κ. τ. λ.

And indeed we need only look into the map to be fati fied, that the courfe of thefe rivers anfwers to the defcription here given, and

that afterwards they unite their ftreams, and fall together into the Perfian gulf. And as to the fertility of the country, Milton copies after Dionyfius, but contracts his defcription.

Ου μεν τοι κεινης γε νομ¤ς; ωιοσ-
  σατο Ε¤της,
Ουδ' ὑςις συρ:λγι κερωνυχα Παια
  γεραιρων,
Μηλοις αγραιλοισιν εφεσπεται· ¤δε
  μεν ὑλην
Παντοιην φυτοεργ☉ αιηρ αθεριο-
  σατο καρπων.
Τοιη επι κεινης αροσις πελει, εν μεν
  αιξειν
Ποιην, εν δε νομ¤ς ευανθεας;,
  κ. τ. λ.

261. *Huge cities and high tow'r'd*,] So alfo in the L' Allegro,

Towred cities pleafe us then.

Turritæ urbes is very common amongft the Latin poets.   *Thyer.*
269.   *— here thou behold'ft*
Affyria and her empire's ancient
  bounds,] A fitter fpot could
                                          not

Araxes and the Caſpian lake, thence on
As far as Indus eaſt, Euphrates weſt,
And oft beyond ; to ſouth the Perſian bay,
And inacceſſible th' Arabian drouth :
Here Nineveh, of length within her wall   275
Several days journey, built by Ninus old,
Of that firſt golden monarchy the ſeat,
And ſeat of Salmanaſſar, whoſe ſuccefs

Iſrael

not have been choſen to take a view of the Aſſyriau empire and its ancient bounds, the river *Araxes and the Caſpian lake* to the north, the river *Indus* to the eaſt, the river *Euphrates* to the weſt, *and oft beyond*, as far as to the Mediterranean, and to the ſouth the *Perſian bay* and the deſerts of *Arabia*.

275. *Here Nineveh*, &c] This city was ſituated on the Tigris, *of length*, as Mr. Sympſon ſays he means *of circuit, within her wall ſeveral days journey*, and according to Diodorus Siculus Lib. II. its circuit was 60 of our miles, and in Jonah III. 3. it is ſaid to be *an exceeding great city of three days journey*. 20 miles being the common computation of a day's journey for a foot-traveler : *built by Ninus old*, and after him the city is ſaid to be called *Niniveh ; of that firſt golden monarchy the ſeat*, a capital city of the Aſſyrian empire, which the poet ſtiles *golden monarchy*, probably in alluſion to the *golden head* of

the image in Nebuchadnezzar's dream of the four empires ; *and ſeat of Salmanaſſar*, who in the reign of Hezekiah king of Judah carried the ten tribes captive into Aſſyria 721 years before Chriſt, ſo that it might now be properly called *a long captivity*.

280. *There Babylon*, &c.] As Nineveh was ſituated on the river Tigris, ſo was Babylon on the river Euphrates; *the wonder of all tongues*, for it is reckon'd among the ſeven wonders of the world ; *as ancient* as Nineveh, for ſome ſay it was built by Belus, and others by Semiramis, the one the father, and the other the wife, of Ninus who built Nineveh ; *but rebuilt by him*, whoever built it, it was rebuilt, and inlarged, and beautify'd, and made one of the wonders of the world by Nebuchadnezzar. *(Is not this great Babylon that I have built &c.* Dan. IV. 30.) *who twice Judah led captive*, in the reign of Jehoiachin 2 Kings XXIV. and eleven years after

Ifrael in long captivity ftill mourns ;

There Babylon, the wonder of all tongues,   280

As ancient, but rebuilt by him who twice

Judah and all thy father David's houfe

Led captive, and Jerufalem laid wafte,

Till Cyrus fet them free ; Perfepolis

His city there thou feeft, and Bactra there ;   285

Ecbatana her ftructure vaft there fhows,

                                                     And

after in the reign of Zedekiah, *and laid wafte Jerufalem,* 2 Kings XXV. in which defolate condition it lay many years, *till Cyrus fet them free,* and reftor'd the Jews to their country again. Ezra I. and II.

284. —— *Perfepolis*

His city there thou feeft, &c] The city of Cyrus, if not built by him, yet by him made the capital city of the Perfian empire : *and Bactra there,* the chief city of Bactria, a province of Perfia, famous for its fruitfulnefs. Virg. Georg. II 136.

Sed neque Medorum fylvæ, ditiffima terra,
Nec pulcher Ganges, atque auro turbidus Hermus,
Laudibus Italiæ certent, *non Bactra,* neque Indi &c.

Ecbatana, the metropolis of Media, *her ftructure vaft there fhows,* and the ancient hiftorians fpeak of it as a very large city ; Herodotus compares it to Athens, Lib. I. cap. 98. and Strabo calls it a great

city, μεγαλη πολις Lib. XI. p. 522. and Polybius fays that it greatly excelled other cities in riches and magnificence of buildings. Lib. X. *And Hecatompylos her hundred gates,* the name fignifies a city with an hundred gates, and fo the capital city of Parthia was call'd, Ἑκατομπυλον το των Παρθυαιων βασιλειον, Strabo Lib. XI. p. 514. as was likewife Thebes in Egypt for the fame reafon. *There Sufa,* the Shuſhan of the holy Scriptures, the royal feat of the kings of Perfia, who refided here in the winter and at Ecbatana in the fummer, *by Choafpes,* fituated on the river Choafpes, or Eulæus, or Ulai as it is called in Daniel, or rather on the confluence of thefe two rivers, which meeting at Sufa form one greater river, fometimes called by one name, fometimes by the other, *amber ftream,* fee the fame expreffion and the conclufion of the note on Paradife Loft III. 359. *the drink of none but kings,* of which we will

And Hecatompylos her hundred gates ;
There Sufa by Choafpes, amber ftream,

The

will fay nothing, as it is fo fully dif-
cufs'd in a note by Mr. Jortin.
289. *The drink of none but kings;*]
If we examin it as an hiftorical
problem, whether the kings of Per-
fia alone drank of *Choafpes*, we
fhall find great reafon to determin
in the negative. 1. We have for
that opinion the filence of many
authors, by whom we might have
expected to have found it confirm-
ed, had they known of any fuch
cuftom. Herodotus, Strabo, Ti-
bullus, Aufonius, Maximus, Ty-
rius, Ariftides, Plutarch, Pliny the
elder, Athenæus, Dionyfius Perie-
getes, Euftathius, have mentioned
Choafpes (or Eulæus) as the drink
of the kings of Perfia or Parthia,
or have called it βασιλικον ὑδωρ,
regia lympha, but have not faid that
they alone drank of it. I fay *Cho-
afpes* or *Eulæus*, becaufe fome make
them the fame, and others counted
them different rivers. The filence
of Herodotus ought to be of great
weight, becaufe he is fo particular
in his account of the Perfian af-
fairs; and next to his, the filence
of Pliny, who had read fo many
authors, is confiderable. 2. Though
it can hardly be expected that a
negative fhould be proved any
other way than from the filence of
writers, yet fo it happens that
Ælian, if his authority be admit-
ted, affords us a full proof that
Choafpes might be drunk by the

fubjects of the kings of Perfia.
τατε αλλα εφοδια ειπετο τω Ξερξη
πολυτελειας και αλαζοιειας πε-
πληρωμενα, και ὗ και ὑδωρ ηκο-
λὖθει το εκ τὖ Χοασπὖ. Επει δ' εν
τινι ερημω τοπω εδιψησαν, ὖδι-
πω της θεραπειας ἡκὖσης, εκη-
ρυχθη τω ϛρατοπεδω, ει τις εχει
ὑδωρ εκ τὖ Χοασπὖ, ινα δω βασι-
λει πιειν. Και εὑρεθη τις βραχυ
και σιωπῷ· εχων. Επιεν ὖν τὖ-
το ὁ Ξερξης, και ευεργετην τον
δοντα ειομισεν, ὁτι αν απωλετο τη
διψη, ει μη εκεινο ευρεθη. *In the
carriages which followed Xerxes,
there were abundance of things which
ferved only for pomp and oftentation;
there was alfo the water of* Cho-
afpes. *The army being oppreffed with
thirft in a defert place, and the car-
riages not being yet come up, it was
proclamed, that if any one had of the
water of* Choafpes, *he fhould give
it Xerxes to drink. One was found
who had a little, and that not fweet.
Xerxes drank it, and accounted him
who gave it him a benefactor, be-
caufe he had perifhed with thirft,
if that little had not been found.*
Var. Hift. XII. 40. 3. Mention
is made indeed by Agathocles of a
certain water, which none but Per-
fian kings might drink; and if
any other writers mention it, they
take it from Agathocles. We find
in Athenæus : Αγαθοκλης εν Περ-
σαις φησιν ειναι και χρυσὖν κα-
λὖμενον ὑδωρ· ειναι δε τὖτο λι-
βαδας

The drink of none but kings ; of later fame
Built by Emathian, or by Parthian hands,   290

The

Ϛαδας εϲδομηκοϛτα,   και   μηδινα
ϖ.ιιν ατ' αυτε η μονον βασιλεα
και τον πρεσϲυτατον αυτε των
παιδων· των δε αλλων εαν τις πιη,
Θανατϲ· η ζημια.   *Agathocles
says that there is in Persia a wa-
ter called* golden, *that it is seventy
streams, that none drinks of it ex-
cept the king and his eldest son ;
and that if any other person does,
death is the punishment.* See He-
rodotus, Edit. Gronov. p. 594.
where this passage is to be found.
4. It appears not that the *golden
water*, and *Choaspes* were the same.
Eustathius, transcribing from Aga-
thocles, says : το παρα Περσαις
χρυσεν καλεμενον υδωρ, οπερ ην
διαδες εϲδομηκοϛία, επερ εδις,
φασιν, επινεν οτι μη βασιλευς,
και ο των παιδων αυτη πρεσϲυ-
ταιϲ· των δ' αλλων ει τις πιη,
Θανατϲ η ζημια. —— Ζητητεον
δς ει και το Χοασπειον υδωρ, οπερ
επινε ϛρατευομενϲ ο Περσων βα-
σιλευς, τοιαυτην επιτιμιον κηρα
εφυλαϛετο. *The Persians had a wa-
ter called* golden &c. *Quaere, whe-
ther the water of* Choaspes, *which
the Persian king drank in his expe-
ditions, was forbidden to all others
under the same penalty.* Eustathius
in Homer. Iliad. Υ. p. 1301. Ed.
Basil. 5. It may be granted, and
it is not at all improbable, that
none besides the king might drink
of that water of *Choaspes*, which
was boiled and barrel'd up for

his use in his military expeditions,
6. Solinus indeed. who is a frivo-
lous writer, says *Choaspes* ita dul-
cis est, ut Persici reges quamdiu
intra ripas Persidis fluit, solis sibi
ex eo pocula vendicarint. 7. Mil-
ton, considered as a poet, with
whose purpose the fabulous suited
best, is by no means to be blamed
for what he has advanced ; and
even the authority of Solinus is
sufficient to justify him. Milton,
when he calls *Choaspes amber stream*,
seems to have had in view the *gol-
den water* of Agathocles and of his
transcribers.   *Jortin.*

289. —— *of later fame* &c] Ci-
ties of later date, *built by Ema-
thian*, that is Macedonian, the suc-
cessors of Alexander in Asia, *or
by Parthian hands, the great Seleu-
cia.* built near the river Tigris by
Seleucus Nicator, one of Alexan-
der's captains, and called *great* to
distinguish it from others of the
same name ; *Nisibis*, another city
upon the Tigris, called also An-
tiochia, *Antiochia, quam Nisibin vo-
cant.* Plin. Nat. Hist. Lib. 6. Sect.
16. *Artaxata*, the chief city of
Armenia, seated upon the river
Araxes, *juxta Araxem Artaxata.*
Plin. Lib. 6. Sect 10. *Teredon*,
a city near the Persian bay, below
the confluence of Euphrates and
Tigris, *Teredon infra confluentem
Euphratis et Tigris.* Plin. Lib. 6.
Sect. 32. *Ctesiphon* near Seleucia,

The great Seleucia, Nifibis, and there
Artaxata, Teredon, Ctefiphon,
Turning with eafy eye thou may'ft behold.
All thefe the Parthian, now fome ages paft,
By great Arfaces led, who founded firft   295
That empire, under his dominion holds,
From the luxurious kings of Antioch won.
And juft in time thou com'ft to have a view
Of his great pow'r ; for now the Parthian king

In

the winter refidence of the Par-
thian Kings. Strabo. Lib. 16.
p. 743. *All thefe* cities, which be-
fore belonged to the Seleucidæ or
Syro-Macedonian princes, fome-
times called *kings cf Antioch*, from
their ufual place of refidence, are
now under the dominion of the
Parthians, whofe empire was found-
ed by *Arfaces*, who revolted from
Antiochus Theus according to Pri-
deaux 250 years before Chrift.
This view of the Parthian empire
is much more agreeably and poeti-
cally defcribed than Adam's pro-
fpect of the kingdoms of the
world from the mount of vifion
in the Paradife Loft. XI. 385——
411 : but ftill the anachronifm in
this is worfe than in the other' : in
the former Adam is fuppofed to
take a view of cities many years
before they were built, and in the
latter our Saviour beholds cities,

as Nineveh, Babylon &c. in their
florifhing condition many years
after they were laid in ruins ; but
it was the defign of the former vi-
fion to exhibit what was future, it
was not the defign of the latter to
exhibit what was paft.

298. *And juft in time thou com'ft*
   to have a view
Of his great pow'r ;] Although
Milton in this temptation had no
lefs a fcene at his command than
all the empires of the world, yet
being fenfible how incapable his
fubject was of poetic decoration
in many other parts of it, and
confidering too, very probably,
that a geographic defcription of
kingdoms, however varied in the
manner of expreffion and diverfi-
fied with little circumftances, muft
foon grow tedious, has very judi-
cioufly thrown in this digreffive
                              picture

In Ctefiphon hath gather'd all his hoft   300
Againft the Scythian, whofe incurfions wild
Have wafted Sogdiana ; to her aid
He marches now in hafte ; fee, though from far,
His thoufands, in what martial equipage   304
They iffue forth, fteel bows, and fhafts their arms
Of equal dread in flight, or in purfuit ;
All horfemen, in which fight they moft excel ;
See how in warlike mufter they appear,

In

picture of an army muftering for an expedition, which he has executed in a very mafterly manner. The fame conduct he has obferved in the fubfequent defcription of the Roman empire by introducing into the fcene prætors and proconfuls marching out to their provinces with troops, lictors, rods, and other enfigns of power, and embaffadors making their entrance into that imperial city from all parts of the world. There is great art and defign in this contrivance of the author's, and the more as there is no appearance of any, fo naturally are the parts connected.
Thyer.

299. ——*for now the Parthian king*
In Ctefiphon hath gather'd all his hoft] When Strabo mentions Ctefiphon, Lib. 16. p. 743. which

we quoted before, he fays that the Parthian kings made it their winter refidence to prevent the incurfions of the Scythians ; and he defcribes it as a place able to contain a vaft multitude and all preparations and provifions for them : Ταυτην δ' εποιωντο χειμαδιον οι των Παρθυαιων βασιλεις, Φειδομενοι των Σελευκειων, ἱνα μη καταςαζβμενοιτο ὑπο τυ Σκιθικυ φυλυ και ςρατιωτικυ· διναμει υ, Παρθικη πυλις αιτι κωμης εςι και το μεγεθ☉ τοσυτον γι πληθ☉ διχομειη, και την κατασκευην κ. τ. λ. and therefore the poet might well fuppofe the Scythians at this time to have made an incurfion into *Sogdiana,* which was the province next adjoining to them, and the Parthian king to have affembled a great army at Ctefiphon in order to oppofe them.

K 2   309. *In*

In rhombs and wedges, and half-moons, and wings.

He look'd, and faw what numbers numberlefs

The city gates out-pour'd, light armed troops   311

In coats of mail and military pride ;

In mail their horfes clad, yet fleet and ftrong,

Prauncing their riders bore, the flow'r and choice

Of many provinces from bound to bound ;   315

From Arachofia, from Candaor eaft,

And

309. *In rhombs and wedges,* *Rhombs* is a word formed from the Greek ῥομβ⊙ or Latin *rhombus*, a figure of four fides, which being converted into one of three makes a *wedge*. In re militari etiam transformatum in triquetrum, cuneum feu roftrum vocamus. Rob. Stephens. In Greek it was called ῥομβοίδης φαλαγξ.

310.—*what numbers numberlefs*] A manner of expreffion this, tho' much cenfur'd in our author, very familiar with the beft Greek poets. Æfchyl. Prom. 904.

Απολεμ⊙ ἰδε γ' ὁ πολεμ⊙, απορα Πορίμ⊙.

Perfæ 682.

ιαες αιαες αιαες — πολις απολις. Thyer.

313. *In mail their horfes clad,*] That this was the practice among the Parthians we learn from Juftin XLI. 2. Munimentum ipfis equifque loricæ plumatæ funt, quæ utrumque toto corpore tegunt : and from Appian De Bell. Parth. ὁι δ' ἱπποι καταπεφραγμενοι χαλκοις και σιδηροις σκεπασμασι.

315. *Of many provinces from bound to bound ;*] He had mention'd before the principal cities of the Parthians, and now he recounts feveral of their provinces : *Arachofia* near the river Indus, μεχρι τȣ Ινδε ποταμȣ τεταμενη, Strabo Lib. 11. p. 516. *Candaor* not *Gandaor* as in fome editions, I fuppofe the *Candari* a people of India mention'd by Pliny. Lib. 6. Sect. 18. who are different Father Harduin fays from the *Gandari*. Thefe were provinces to the *eaft*, and to the north *Margiana* and *Hyrcania*, ἁπασαι γαρ ὑιται προσεχεις μεν εισι τη βοιειη πλιιρα τȣ Ταυρȣ Strabo Lib. 2. p. 72. and mount *Caucafus*, and *Iberia*, which is called *dark*, as the country abounded with forefts, Iberi faltuofos locos incolentes. Tacitus Annal. Lib. 6. *Atropatia* lay weft of *Media*, τη δι

5

And Margiana to the Hyrcanian cliffs
Of Caucafus, and dark Iberian dales,
From Atropatia and the neighb'ring plains
Of Adiabene, Media, and the fouth   320
Of Sufiana, to Balfara's haven.
He faw them in their forms of battel rang'd,
How quick they wheel'd, and fly'ing behind them fhot
Sharp fleet of arrowy fhow'rs againft the face
                                                          Of

δε μεγαλη Mηδια προς δυσιν. Strabo Lib. 11. p. 523. *Adiabene* was the weftern part of Babylonia, απο δε δυσιως Αδιαβηνη, and Strabo fays was a *plain* country, της μεν εν Αδιαβηνης η πλεισα πεδιας εςι, Strabo Lib. 16. p. 745. *Sufiana* was on the fouth, extending to the Perfian gulf, η δε χωρα της θαλατης καθηκει, Strabo Lib. 15. p. 728. where was alfo *Balfara's haven*, the fame as *Teredon* beforemention'd. And thus he furveys their provinces *from bound to bound*. And the reader cannot but remark with pleafure how very exact he is in his account of cities and countries, and how well he muft have remember'd, and how faithfully he has copied the ancient geographers and hiftorians.

323.—*and flying behind them fhot Sharp fleet of arrowy fhow'rs*] In the firft edition it was printed *fhow'r* by miftake, and is corrected *fhow'rs* among the Errata, but this notwithftanding the faulty reading

is follow'd in all the editions fince. *Sharp fleet* &c is a metaphor, as Mr. Richardfon has noted, not unlike that in Virgil Æn. XI. 610.

—fundunt fimul undique tela
Crebra *nivis* ritu.

And the cuftom of the Parthians of fhooting their arrows behind them and overcoming by flight is fo celebrated by hiftorians and poets, and is fo well known to every one of the leaft reading, that it is almoft needlefs to bring any authorities to prove it. υπεφευγον γαρ αμα βαλλονλες οι Παρθοι — και σοφωτατοι εςιν, αμυνομενας ετι σωζεσθαι, και της φυγης αφαιρειν το αισχρον. Appian de Bel. Parth. Virg. Georg. III. 31.

Fidentemque fugâ Parthum verfifque fagittis.

Hor. Od. I. XIX. 11.

Et verfis animofum equis
Parthum dicere.

K 3   326. *The*

Of their purfuers, and overcame by flight;   325
The field all iron caft a gleaming brown :
Nor wanted clouds of foot, nor on each horn
Cuiraffiers all in fteel for ftanding fight,
Chariots or elephants indors'd with towers
Of archers, nor of lab'ring pioneers   330
A multitude with fpades and axes arm'd

                                                  To

326. *The field all iron caft a gleaming brown :*] One cannot pafs over this line without taking notice of the particular beauty and expreffivenefs of it. The fenfe contained in it would have ferved a common romance-writer to have fpun out into a paragraph of half a page length.   *Thyer.*
I believe the reader will agree with me that it greatly exceeds Fairfax. Cant. 1. St. 64.

Imbatteled in walls of *iron brown.*

and even Virgil, Æn. XI. 601.

——— tum late *ferreus haftis*
Horret *ager.*

327. *Nor wanted clouds of foot,*] So we have in Homer Iliad. IV. 274. νεφος πεζων, and in Virgil Æn. VII. 793. *nimbus peditum :* but as Mr. Thyer obferves with me, this verfe is not very confiftent with what goes before, ver. 307.

All horfemen, in which fight they moft excel ;

nor with what follows to the fame purpofe ver. 344.

Such and fo numerous was their *chivalry.*

328. *Cuiraffiers all in fteel*] By *cuiraffiers* are to be underftood horfemen armed with cuiraffes, which covered the body quite round from the neck to the wafte. If what Chambers fays in his Dictionary be true, viz. that thefe fort of troops were not introduc'd till the year 1300, Milton has been guilty of a great anachronifm.
                                          Thyer.
But it appears that the Parthians had fuch troops, and particularly from the quotation which we lately made from Juftin ; Munimentum ipfis equifque loricæ plumatæ funt, quæ utrumque toto corpore tegunt. XLI. 2.

329. ——— *elephants indors'd with towers*] That is with towers upon their backs. The reader muft know very little of Milton's ftile, who knoweth not that it is his method to make ufe of words in their
                                          primary

To lay hills plain, fell woods, or valleys fill,

Or where plain was raife hill, or overlay

With bridges rivers proud, as with a yoke ;

Mules after thefe, camels and dromedaries,   335

And waggons fraught with utenfils of war.

Such forces met not, nor fo wide a camp,

When Agrican with all his northern powers

Befieg'd

primary and original meaning, ra-ther than according to their com-mon acceptation.

330. — *nor of lab'ring pioneers A multitude* &c.] *Nor* wanted the verb in ver. 327, *a multitude with fpades and axes arm'd*, very like that in Paradife Loft. I. 675.

—— as when bands
Of pioneers with fpade and pick-ax arm'd &c.

333.   —— *or overlay With bridges rivers proud, as with a yoke* ;] Alluding pro-bably to Æfchylus's defcription of Xerxes's bridge over the Helle-fpont. Perfæ ver. 71.

Πολυγομφον ὁδισμα
Ζυγον αμφιϐαλων αυχενι ποντε.
Thyer.

337. *Such forces met not, nor fo wide a camp,
When Agrican* &c] What Milton here alludes to is related in Boi-ardo's Orlando Inamorato L. 1. Cant. 10. The number of forces faid to be there affembled is in-

credible, and extravagant even be-yond the common extravagancy of romances. Agrican the Tartar king brings into the field no lefs than two millions two hundred thoufand ;

Ventidua centinaia di migliara
Di caualier hauca quel Rè nel campo,
Cofa non mai udita ——

And Sacripante the king of Cir-caffia, who comes to the affiftance of Gallaphrone, three hundred and eighty two thoufand. It muft be acknowledged, I think, by the greateft admirers of Milton, that the impreffion which romances had made upon his imagination in his youth, has in this place led him into a blameable excefs. Not to mention the notorious fabuloufnefs of the fact alluded to, which I doubt fome people will cenfure in a poem of fo grave a turn, the number of the troops of Agrican &c is by far too much difpropor-tion'd to any army, which the Parthian king by any hiftorical

K 4   evidence

Befieg'd Albracca, as romances tell,
The city' of Gallaphrone, from thence to win   340
The faireft of her fex Angelica
His daughter, fought by many proweft knights,
Both Paynim, and the peers of Charlemain.
Such and fo numerous was their chivalry;
At fight whereof the Fiend yet more prefum'd,   345
And to our Saviour thus his words renew'd.

    That thou may'ft know I feek not to engage
Thy virtue, and not every way fecure
On no flight grounds thy fafety; hear, and mark
To what end I have brought thee hither and fhown
All this fair fight: thy kingdom though foretold 351
By Prophet or by Angel, unlefs thou
Endevor, as thy father David did,
Thou never fhalt obtain; prediction ftill
In all things, and all men, fuppofes means,   355
                                    Without

evidence could be fuppofed to bring
into the field.   Thyer.
    341. The faireft of her fex Ange-
    lica &c] This is that Angeli-
ca who afterwards made her ap-
pearance in the fame character in
Ariofto's Orlando Furiofo, which
was intended as a continuation of
the ftory, which Boiardo had be-

gun. As Milton fetches his fimile
from a romance he adopts the
terms ufed by thefe writers, viz.
proweft and Paynim.   Thyer.
    366.—and captive lead away her
    kings
Antigonus, and old Hyrcanus bound,]
Here feems to be a flip of me-
mory in our author. The Par-
                                    thians

Without means us'd, what it predicts revokes.
But fay thou wert poffefs'd of David's throne
By free confent of all, none oppofit,
Samaritan or Jew ; how could'ft thou hope
Long to enjoy it quiet and fecure,   360
Between two fuch inclofing enemies
Roman and Parthian ? therefore one of thefe
Thou muft make fure thy own, the Parthian firft
By my advice, as nearer, and of late
Found able by invafion to annoy   365
Thy country', and captive lead away her kings
Antigonus, and old Hyrcanus bound,
Maugre the Roman : it fhall be my tafk
To render thee the Parthian at difpofe ;   369
Choofe which thou wilt by conqueft or by league.
By him thou fhalt regain, without him not,
That which alone can truly reinftall thee

In

thians indeed led *Hyrcanus* away captive to Seleucia, after his eyes were put out, and when he was paft 70 years of age, fo that he might well be called *old Hyrcanus :* but inftead of leading away *Antigonus* captive, they conftituted him king of the Jews, and he was afterwards depriv'd of his kingdom by the Romans. See Jofephus Antiq. Lib. 14. cap. 13. De Bell. Jud. Lib. 1. cap. 13.   But it fhould be confidered that Milton himfelf was old and blind, and compofing from memory he might fall into fuch a miftake, which may be pardon'd among fo many excellences.

376. *In*

In David's royal feat, his true fucceffor,

Deliverance of thy brethren, thofe ten tribes

Whofe ofspring in his territory yet ferve,   375

In Habor, and among the Medes difpers'd ;

Ten fons of Jacob, two of Jofeph loft

Thus long from Ifrael, ferving as of old

Their fathers in the land of Egypt ferv'd,

This offer fets before thee to deliver.   380

Thefe if from fervitude thou fhalt reftore

To their inheritance, then, nor till then,

Thou on the throne of David in full glory,

From Egypt to Euphrates and beyond

Shalt reign, and Rome or Cæfar not need fear. 385

    To whom our Saviour anfwer'd thus unmov'd.

Much oftentation vain of flefhly arm,

And fragil arms, much inftrument of war

                                    Long

---

376. *In Habor, and among the Medes difpers'd* ;] Thefe were the ten tribes, whom Shalmanefer king of Affyria, carried captive unto Affyria, *and put them in Halah and in Habor by the river of Gozan, and in the cities of the Medes.* 2 Kings XVIII. 11. which cities were now under the dominion of the Parthians.

    384. *From Egypt to Euphrates*]

That is the kingdom of Ifrael in its utmoft extent : for thus the land was promis'd to Abraham, Gen. XV. 18. *Unto thy feed have I given this land, from the river of Egypt, unto the great river, the river Euphrates :* and the extent of Solomon's kingdom is thus defcrib'd, 1 Kings IV. 21. *And Solomon reigned over all kingdoms from the river (Euphrates) unto the land of*

Long in preparing, foon to nothing brought,
Before mine eyes thou' haft fet; and in my ear   390
Vented much policy, and projects deep
Of enemies, of aids, battels and leagues,
Plaufible to the world, to me worth nought.
Means I muft ufe, thou fay'ft, prediction elfe
Will unpredict and fail me of the throne: 395
My time I told thee (and that time for thee
Were better fartheft off) is not yet come;
When that comes, think not thou to find me flack
On my part ought endevoring, or to need
Thy politic maxims, or that cumberfome   400
Luggage of war there fhown me, argument
Of human weaknefs rather than of ftrength.
My brethren, as thou call'ft them, thofe ten tribes
I muft deliver, if I mean to reign

David's

of the Philiftines, and unto the border come. VII. 6. My time is not yet come.

394.   —— prediction elfe
Will unpredict] A manner of
fpeaking this, rather too light and
familiar for the dignity of the
fpeaker.   Thyer.

396. My time—is not yet come;]
Agreeable to our Saviour's man-
ner of fpeaking in the Gofpel.
John II. 4. Mine hour is not yet

401   —— argument
Of human weaknefs rather than
of ftrength.] It is a proof of
human weaknefs, as it fhows that
man is obliged to depend upon
fomething extrinfecal to himfelf,
whether he would attack his ene-
my or defend himfelf. It alludes
to the common obfervation, that
nature

David's true heir, and his full fcepter fway   405
To juft extent over all Ifrael's fons ;
But whence to thee this zeal, where was it then
For Ifrael, or for David, or his throne,
When thou ftood'ft up his tempter to the pride
Of numb'ring Ifrael, which coft the lives   410
Of threefcore and ten thoufand Ifraelites
By three days peftilence ? fuch was thy zeal
To Ifrael then, the fame that now to me.
As for thofe captive tribes, themfelves were they
Who wrought their own captivity, fell off   415
From God to worfhip calves, the deities

Of

nature has furnifhed all creatures with weapons of defenfe except man. See Anacreon's ode on this thought.   *Thyer.*

409. *When thou ftood'ft up his tempter* &c] Alluding to 1 Chron. XXI. 1. *And Satan ftood up againft Ifrael, and provoked David to number Ifrael.* Milton, we fee, confiders it not as the advice of any evil counfellor, as fome underftand the word *Satan*, but as the fuggeftion of the firft author of evil : and he expreffes it very properly by *the pride of numb'ring Ifrael* ; for the beft commentators fuppofe the nature of David's offenfe to confift in pride and va-

nity, in making flefh his arm, and confiding in the number of his people. And for this three things were propofed to him by the prophet, three years famin, or three months to be deftroyed before his enemies, or three days peftilence, of which he chofe the latter. *So the Lord fent peftilence upon Ifrael, and there fell of Ifrael feventy thoufand men,* ver. 14.

414. *As for thofe captive tribes,* &c.] The captivity of the ten tribes was a punifhment owing to their own idolatry and wickednefs. *They fell off from God to worfhip calves,* the golden calves which Jeroboam had fet up in Bethel

Of Egypt, Baal next and Aſhtaroth,
And all th' idolatries of Heathen round,
Beſides their other worſe than heath'niſh crimes;
Nor in the land of their captivity   420
Humbled themſelves, or penitent beſought
The God of their forefathers ; but ſo dy'd
Impenitent, and left a race behind
Like to themſelves, diſtinguiſhable ſcarce
From Gentiles, but by circumciſion vain,   425
And God with idols in their worſhip join'd.
Should I of theſe the liberty regard,
Who freed as to their ancient patrimony,

Unhumbled,

thel and in Dan, and which the poet calls *the deities of Egypt*, for it is probable (as ſome learned men have conjectured) that Jeroboam having converſed with the Egyptians ſet up theſe two calves in imitation of the two which the Egyptians worſhipped, the one called Apis at Memphis the metropolis of the upper Egypt, and the other called Mnevis at Hierapolis the metropolis of the lower Egypt. *Baal next and Aſhtaroth.* Ahab built an altar and a temple for *Baal*, 1 Kings XVI. 32. and at the ſame time probably was introduced the worſhip of *Aſhtaroth, the Goddeſs of the Zidonians,* 1 Kings XI 5.   For Jezebel,

Ahab's wife, who prompted him to all evil, was *the daughter of Ethbaal king of the Zidonians,* 1 Kings XVI. 31.   And by *the prophets of the groves* 1 Kings XVIII. 19.   Mr. Selden underſtands the prophets of *Aſhtaroth* or *Aſtarte:* and *the groves under every green tree* 2 Kings XVII. 10. ſhould be tranſlated *Aſhtaroth* under every green tree.   See Selden de Diis Syris Syntag. II. cap. 2. But for the wickedneſs and idolatry of the Iſraelites, and their rejection thereupon, and ſtill continuing impenitent in their captivity, ſee 2 Kings XVII. and the prophets in ſeveral places.

430   *Herod-*

Unhumbled, unrepentant, unreform'd,
Headlong would follow'; and to their Gods perhaps
Of Bethel and of Dan? no, let them ferve   431
Their enemies, who ferve idols with God.
Yet he at length, time to himfelf beft known,
Remembring Abraham, by fome wondrous call
May bring them back repentant and fincere,   435
And at their paffing cleave th' Affyrian flood,

While

430. *Headlong would follow; and to their Gods perhaps Of Bethel and of Dan?*] There is fome difficulty and obfcurity in this paffage; and feveral conjectures and emendations have been offer'd to clear it, but none, I think, entirely to fatisfaction. Mr. Sympfon would read *Headlong would fall off and &c*, or *Headlong would fall, bow and* i. e. *bowing* the A. Sax. participle. But Mr. Calton feems to come nearer the poet's meaning. Whom or what would they follow, fays he? There wants an accufative cafe; and what muft be underftood to complete the fenfe, can never be accounted for by an elleipfis, that any rules or ufe of language will juftify. He therefore fufpects, that by fome ill accident or other a whole line may have been loft; and propofes one, which he fays may ferve for a commentary at leaft, to explain the fenfe, though it can't be allowed for an emendation.

Their fathers in their old iniquities Headlong would follow; &c.

Or is not the conftruction thus, *Headlong would follow as to their ancient patrimony, and to their Gods perhaps &c?*
431. —— *no, let them ferve Their enemies, who ferve idols with God.*] This is agreeable to God's conftant dealing with the Jewifh nation as recorded in the old Teftament. *Thyer.*

436. *And at their paffing cleave th' Affyrian flood, &c*] There are feveral prophecies of the reftoration of Ifrael: but in faying that the Lord would cleave *th' Affyrian flood*, that is the river Euphrates, at their return from Affyria, as he cleft the Red Sea and the river Jordan at their coming from Egypt, the poet feems particularly to allude to Rev. XVI. 12. *And the fixth Angel poured out his vial upon the great river Euphrates; and the water thereof was dried up, that the*

While to their native land with joy they hafte,
As the Red Sea and Jordan once he cleft,
When to the promis'd land their fathers pafs'd;
To his due time and providence I leave them.   440
    So fpake Ifrael's true king, and to the Fiend
Made anfwer meet, that made void all his wiles.
So fares it when with truth falfhood contends.

the way of the kings of the eaft might be prepared: and to Ifa. XI. 15, 16. And the Lord fhall utterly deftroy the tongue of the Egyptian fea, and with his mighty wind fhall he fhake his hand over the river, and fhall fmite it in the feven ftreams, and make men go over dry-fhod: And there fhall be an highway for the remnant of his people, which fhall be left from Affyria, like as it was to Ifrael in the day that he came up out of the land of Egypt.

The end of the Third Book.

THE

FOURTH BOOK

OF

PARADISE REGAIN'D.

PARADISE REGAIN'D.

B O O K IV.

Perplex'd and troubled at his bad ſucceſs
The Tempter ſtood, nor had what to reply,
Diſcover'd in his fraud, thrown from his hope
So oft, and the perſuaſive rhetoric
That ſleek'd his tongue, and won ſo much on Eve, 5
So little here, nay loſt ; but Eve was Eve,
This far his over-match, who ſelf-deceiv'd
And raſh, beforehand had no better weigh'd
The ſtrength he was to cope with, or his own :
But as a man who had been matchleſs held 10

In

---

7. *This far his overmatch, who ſelf-deceiv'd* &c.] An uſual conſtruction in Milton, *This far an over-match* for him, *who ſelf-deceiv'd and raſh, before-hand had no better weigh'd* &c. Neither is this inconſiſtent, as Mr. Thyer conceives it to be, with what Satan had declared in Book II. 131.

Have found him, view'd him, taſted him, but find
Far other labor to be undergone
&c.

He had made ſome trials of his ſtrength, but had not ſufficiently conſidered it *before-hand*; he had weigh'd it, but ſhould have weigh'd it *better* ; if he had been fully appris'd whom he was contending with, he would have ceaſed from the contention.

10. *But as a man* &c] It is the method of Homer to illuſtrate and adorn the ſame ſubject with ſeveral ſimilitudes, as the reader may ſee particularly in the ſecond book of the Iliad before the catalogue of

ſhips

In cunning, over-reach'd where leaſt he thought,

To ſalve his credit, and for very ſpite,

Still will be tempting him who foils him ſtill,

And never ceaſe, though to his ſhame the more;

Or as a ſwarm of flies in vintage time,   15

About the wine-preſs where ſweet muſt is pour'd,

Beat off, returns as oft with humming ſound;

Or ſurging waves againſt a ſolid rock,

Though

ſhips and warriors: and our author here follows his example, and preſents us, as I may ſay, with a ſtring of ſimilitudes together. This fecundity and variety of the two poets can never be ſufficiently admired: but Milton, I think, has the advantage in this reſpect, that in Homer the loweſt compariſon is ſometimes the laſt, whereas here in Milton they riſe in my opinion, and improve one upon another. The firſt has too much ſameneſs with the ſubject it would illuſtrate, and gives us no new ideas. The ſecond is low, but it is the lowneſs of Homer, and at the ſame time is very natural. The third is free from the defects of the other two, and riſes up to Milton's uſual dignity and majeſty Mr. Thyer, who has partly made the ſame obſervations with me, ſays that Milton, as if conſcious of the defects of the two foregoing compariſons, riſes up here to his uſual ſublimity, and preſents to the reader's mind an

image, which not only fills and ſatisfies the imagination, but alſo perfectly expreſſes both the unmov'd ſtedfaſtneſs of our Saviour, and the fruſtrated baffled attempts of Satan.

15. *Or as a ſwarm of flies in vintage time,* &c] The compariſon is very juſt, and alſo in the manner of Homer. Iliad. XVI 641.

'Οι δ' αιει περι νεκρον ομιλεον, ὡς
   ὁτε μυιαι
Σταθμῳ ενι βρομεωσι περιγλαγεας
   κατα πελλας
'Ωρη εν ειαρινῃ, ὁτε τε γλαγος
   αγγεα δευει.

Illi vero aſſidue circa mortuum verſabantur, ut quum muſcæ
In caula ſuſurrant lacte plenas ad mulctras
Tempore in verno, quando lac vaſa rigat.

Iliad. XVII. 570.

Και ἱ μυιης θαρσ⊙ ενι ſηθεσσιν
   ενηκεν,

'Ητε

Though all to ſhivers daſh'd, th' aſſault renew,

Vain batt'ry, and in froth or bubbles end;   20

So Satan, whom repulſe upon repulſe

Met ever, and to ſhameful ſilence brought,

Yet gives not o'er though deſp'rate of ſucceſs,

And his vain importunity purſues.

He brought our Saviour to the weſtern ſide   25

Of that high mountain, whence he might behold

Another

'Ητε και εργοιεν μαλα περ
χρο۞ ειδρομεοιο,
Ισχαναα δακεειν.

Et ei muſcæ audaciam pectoribus
   immiſit,
Quæ licet abacta crebro à cor-
   pore humano,
Appetit mordere.   *Jortin.*

This ſimile is very much in the
ſame taſte with one in the ſecond
Iliad of Homer, where he com-
paꝛes the Greek army to *ſwarms
of flies buzzing about the ſhepherd's
milk pail in the ſpring,* and ſeems
liable to the ſame objection which
is made to that, of being too low
for the grandeur of the ſubject. It
muſt however be allow'd, that no-
thing could better expreſs the teaz-
ing ceaſeleſs importunity of the
Tempter than this does. Mr. Pope
in his note on this paſſage of Ho-
mer obſerves that *Milton who was
a cloſe imitator of him, has often co-
pied him in theſe humble compariſons,*
and inſtances thoſe lines in the end

of the ſixth book of his Paradiſe
Loſt, where the rebel Angels thun-
der-ſtruck by the Meſſiah are com-
pared to *a herd of goats or timorous
flock together throng'd.* The obſer-
vation is juſt, but very far in my
opinion from being verified by the
paſſage produc'd. No image of
terror or conſternation could be too
low for that exhauſted ſpiritleſs
condition, in which thoſe van-
quiſh'd Angels muſt at that inſtant
be ſuppoſed to be, and that abject
timorouſneſs imputed to them, in-
ſtead of leſſening the dignity of
the deſcription rather adds to it, by
exciting in the reader's mind a
greater idea of the tremendous
majeſty of the Son of God. This
compariſon of the flies now before
us would have anſwer'd his pur-
poſe much better.   *Thyer.*
   I cannot entirely agree with my
ingenious friend; for Mr. Pope is
diſcourſing there of low images,
which are preceded by others of a
lofty ſtrain, and on that account

this

Another plain, long but in breadth not wide,
Wafh'd by the fouthern fea, and on the north
To equal length back'd with a ridge of hills,   29
That fcreen'd the fruits of th' earth and feats of men
From cold Septentrion blafts, thence in the midft
Divided by a river, of whofe banks
On each fide an imperial city ftood,
With tow'rs and temples proudly elevate
On fev'n fmall hills, with palaces adorn'd,   35
Porches and theatres, baths, aqueducts,
Statues and trophies, and triumphal arcs,
Gardens and groves prefented to his eyes,
Above the highth of mountains interpos'd :
By what ftrange parallax or optic fkill   40
Of vifion multiply'd through air, or glafs

                                          Of

this comparifon, however fuitable
in other refpects, would not have
been fo proper for his purpofe.

    27. *Another plain*, &c] The
learned reader need not be in-
formed, that the country here
meant is Italy, which indeed is
long but not broad, and is wafh'd
by the Mediterranean on the fouth,
and fcreen'd by the Alps on the
north, and divided in the midft by
the river Tiber.

    35. *On fev'n fmall hills,*] Virgil
Georg. II. 535.

    Septemque una fibi muro cir-
    cumdedit arces.

    40. *By what ftrange parallax or
    optic fkill* &c] The learned
have been very idly bufy in con-
triving the manner in which Satan
fhowed to our Saviour all the king-
doms of the world. Some fup-
pofe it was done by vifion ; others
                                          by

Of telescope, were curious to inquire:
And now the Tempter thus his silence broke.

   The city which thou seest no other deem
Than great and glorious Rome, queen of the earth
So far renown'd, and with the spoils enrich'd   46
Of nations; there the capitol thou seest
Above the rest lifting his stately head
On the Tarpeian rock, her citadel
Impregnable, and there mount Palatine,   50
Th' imperial palace, compass huge, and high
The structure, skill of noblest architects,
With gilded battlements, conspicuous far,
Turrets and terrases, and glitt'ring spires:
Many a fair edifice besides, more like   55
Houses of Gods, (so well I have dispos'd

                                   My

by Satan's creating phantasms or species of different kingdoms, and presenting them to our Saviour's fight, &c. &c. But what Milton here alludes to is a fanciful notion which I find imputed to our famous countryman Hugh Broughton. Cornelius a Lapide in summing up the various opinions upon this subject gives it in these words: Alii subtiliter imaginantur, quod Dæmon per multa specula sibi invicem objecta species regnorum ex uno speculo in aliud et aliud continuo reflexerit, idque fecerit usque ad oculos Christi In locum Matthæi. For want of a proper index I could not find the place in Broughton's works. But Wolfius in his Curæ philologicæ in SS. Evangelia fathers this whim upon him: Alii cum Hugone Broughtono ad instrumenta artis opticæ se recipiunt. Vid. Wolf. in Matt. IV. 8. *Thyer.*

My aery microfcope) thou may'ft behold
Outfide and infide both, pillars and roofs,
Carv'd work, the hand of fam'd artificers
In cedar, marble, ivory or gold.   60
Thence to the gates caft round thine eye, and fee
What conflux iffuing forth, or entring in,
Pretors, proconfuls to their provinces
Hafting, or on return, in robes of ftate ;

Lictors

57. *My aery microfcope*] He had called it *telefcope* before ver. 42. here *microfcope*, being altogether uncertain what fort of glafs it was, or how this vifion was performed : but *microfcope* feems to be the more proper word here, as here our Saviour is prefented with a view of minuter objects.

58. *Outfide and infide both,*] So Menippus, in Lucian's Icaro-Menippus, could fee clearly and diftinctly from the moon cities and men upon the earth, and what they were doing, both *without doors, and within* where they thought themfelves moft fecret. κατακυψας γην ες την γην, εωρων σαφως τας πολεις, τες ανθρωπες, τα γινομενα, και ε τα εν υπαιθρω μοιον, αλλα και οποσα οικοι επρατιον, οιομενοι λανθανειν. Luciani Op. Vol. 2. p. 197. Ed. Græv.
Calton.

59.—*the hand of fam'd artificers*] The *handywork*, as in Virg. Æn. I. 455.

Artificumque manus inter fe operumque laborem
Miratur.

66. —— *turms of horfe*] Troops of horfe. A word coined from the Latin *turma*. Virg. Æn. V. 560. *Equitum turmæ*.

68. —— *on the Appian road,*
Or on th' *Emilian,*] The *Appian* road from Rome led towards the fouth of Italy, and the *Emilian* towards the north ; and the nations on the *Appian* road are included in ver. 69—76 thofe on the *Emilian* in ver. 77—79.

69. —*fome from fartheft fouth,*
Syene, and where the fhadow both way falls,
Meroe Nilotic ile,] *Syene fartheft fouth*. How can that be ? when *Meroe* mention'd in the next line (to fay nothing of other places) was farther fouth. Milton knew it, and thought of it too, as appears from his faying,

—— *where*

Lictors and rods, the enfigns of their pow'r,   65
Legions and cohorts, turms of horfe and wings :
Or embaffies from regions far remote
In various habits on the Appian road,
Or on th' Emilian, fome from fartheft fouth,
Syene', and where the fhadow both way falls,   70
Meroe Nilotic ile, and more to weft,
The realm of Bocchus to the Black-moor fea ;

From

—— *where the fhadow both way*
falls,
Meroe Nilotic ile.

Syene being fituate under the tropic
of Cancer, the fhadow falls there
always one way, except at the
fummer folftice, when the fun is
vertical, and then at noon the fha-
dow falls no way :

—— umbras nufquam flectente
Syene. Lucan. II. 587.

But in *Meroe* the fhadow falls both
ways at different times of the year,
and therefore Meroe muft be far-
ther fouth than Syene, and nearer
the equator. To this I fay that
Milton had in view what he had
read in Pliny and other authors,
that *Syene* was the limit of the Ro-
man empire, and the remoteft
place to the fouth that belonged
to it ; and to that he alludes. Or
it may be faid, that poets have not
fcrupled to give the epithets *extre-*
mi, ultimi, fartheft, remoteft, to any

people that lived a great way off,
and that poffibly Milton intended
that *fartheft fouth* fhould be fo ap-
plied both to *Syene* and to *Meroe.*
Jortin.
He firft mentions places in *Africa* ;
Syene, a city of Egypt on the con-
fines of Ethiopia ; Ditionis Ægyp-
ti efie incipit a fine Æthiopiæ Sy-
ene : Plin. Lib. 5. Sect. 10. *Meroe,*
an iland and city of Ethiopia in the
river Nile, therefore called *Nilotic*
ile, where the fhadow both way falls;
Rurfus in Meroe (infula hæc ca-
jutque gentis Æthiopum —— in
amne Nilo habitatur) bis anno ab-
fumi umbras ; Plin. Lib. 2. Sect.
75. *The realm of Bocchus,* Mauri-
tania. Then *Afian* nations, among
thefe *the golden Cherfonefe,* Malacca
the moft fouthern promontory of
the Eaft Indies, fee Paradife Loft
XI. 392. *and utmoft Indian ile Ta-*
probane, and therefore Pliny fays
it is extra orbem a natura relegata ;
Lib. 6. Sect. 24. Then the *Euro-*
pean nations as far as to *the Tauric*
pool,

From th' Afian kings and Parthian among thefe,

From India and the golden Cherfonefe,

And utmoft Indian ile Taprobane,   75

Dufk faces with white filken turbants wreath'd ;

From Gallia, Gades, and the Britifh weft,

Germans and Scythians, and Sarmatians north

Beyond Danubius to the Tauric pool.

All nations now to Rome obedience pay,   80

To Rome's great emperor, whofe wide domain

In ample territory, wealth and power,

Civility of manners, arts and arms,

And long renown, thou juftly may'ft prefer

Before the Parthian ; thefe two thrones except,   85

The reft are barb'rous, and fcarce worth the fight,

Shar'd among petty kings too far remov'd ;

Thefe

---

pool, that is the palus Mæotis ; Lacus ipfe Mæotis, Tanain amnem ex Riphæis montibus defluentem accipiens, noviffimum inter Europam Afiamque finem, &c.   Plin. Lib. 4. Sect. 24.

84. — *thou juftly may'ft prefer Before the Parthians* ;] The Tempter had before advifed our Saviour to prefer the Parthian, III. 363.

—— the Parthian firft
By my advice :

but this fhuffling and inconfiftency is very natural and agreeable to the father of lies, and by thefe touches his character is fet in a proper light.

90. *This emp'ror &c*] This account of the emperor Tiberius retiring from Rome to the iland Capreæ, and there enjoying his horrid lufts in private, and in the mean while committing the government to his wicked favorite and minifter Sejanus, together with the

Thefe having fhown thee, I have fhown thee all
The kingdoms of the world, and all their glory.
This emp'ror hath no fon, and now is old, 90
Old and lafcivious, and from Rome retir'd
To Capreæ an iland fmall but ftrong
On the Campanian fhore, with purpofe there
His horrid lufts in private to enjoy,
Committing to a wicked favorite 95
All public cares, and yet of him fufpicious,
Hated of all, and hating ; with what eafe,
Indued with regal virtues as thou art,
Appearing, and beginning noble deeds, 99
Might'ft thou expel this monfter from his throne
Now made a ftye, and in his place afcending
A victor people free from fervile yoke ?

And

the character of this emperor, is perfectly agreeable to the Roman hiftories, and particularly thofe of Suetonius and Tacitus, who have painted this *monfter* (as our author calls him) in fuch colors as he deferved to be defcribed in to pofterity.

101. —*and in his place afcending A victor pe ple free* &c] There fhould be no comma after *victor* according to the author's own correction ; but yet I think all the editors have preferved the firft miftaken pointing,

— and in his place afcending
A victor, people free from fervile yoke *i*

For the meaning is not that our Saviour *afcending a victor might free* &c, but *afcending might free a victor people*, as the Romans are afterwards called ver. 132.

That people victor once &c.

And with my help thou may'ft ; to me the power
Is giv'n, and by that right I give it thee.

Aim therefore at no lefs than all the world,   105
Aim at the high'eft, without the high'eft attain'd
Will be for thee no fitting, or not long,
On David's throne, be prophefy'd what will.

To whom the Son of God unmov'd reply'd.

Nor doth this grandeur and majeftic fhow   110
Of luxury, though call'd magnificence,
More than of arms before, allure mine eye,
Much lefs my mind ; though thou fhould'ft add to tell
Their fumptuous gluttonies, and gorgeous feafts
On citron tables or Atlantic ftone,   115
(For I have alfo heard, perhaps have read)

Their

---

115. *On citron tables or Atlantic ftone,*] Tables made of *citron* wood were in fuch requeft among the Romans, that Pliny calls it *menfarum infania.* They were beautifully vein'd and fpotted. See his account of them Lib. 13. Sect. 29. I do not find that the *Atlantic ftone* or marble was fo celebrated : the *Numidicus lapis* and *Numidicum marmor* are often mention'd in Roman authors.

117. *Their wines of Setia, Cales, and Falerne,*
Chios and Crete,] The three former were Italian, and the two lat-ter were Greek wines, much admired and commended by the Ancients.

119. *Cryftal and myrrhine cups imbofs'd with gems*
And ftuds of pearl,] *Cryftal* and *myrrhine* cups are often join'd together by ancient authors. Murrhina et criftallina ex eadem terra effodimus, quibus precium faceret ipfa fragilitas. Hoc argumentum opum, hæc vera luxuriæ gloria exiftimata eft, habere quod poffet ftatim totum perire. Plin Lib. 33. Sect. 2. We fee that Pliny reckons *myrrhine* cups among foffils ; Scaliger,

Their wines of Setia, Cales, and Falerne,

Chios and Crete, and how they quaff in gold,

Cryſtal and myrrhine cups imbofs'd with gems

And ſtuds of pearl, to me ſhould'ſt tell who thirſt

And hunger ſtill : then embaſſies thou ſhow'ſt   121

From nations far and nigh ; what honor that,

But tedious waſte of time to ſit and hear

So many hollow complements and lies,

Outlandiſh flatt'ries ? then proceed'ſt to talk   125

Of th' emperor, how eaſily ſubdued,

How glorioufly ; I ſhall, thou ſay'ſt expel

A brutiſh monſter : what if I withal

Expel a Devil who firſt made him ſuch ?

Let his tormenter confcience find him out ?   130

For

---

liger, Salmaſius and others contend from this verſe of Propertius IV. V. 26.

> Murrhæque in Parthis pocula coƈta focis,

that they were like our porcelane : but if they were ſo very fragil aş they are repreſented to be, it is not eaſy to conceive how they could be *imbofs'd with gems and ſtuds of pearl.* I ſuppoſe our author af-ſerted it from the words immedi-ately following in Pliny. Nec hoc fuit fatis : turba gemmarum pota-mus, et fmaragdis teximus calices :

ac temulentiæ cauſa tenere Indiam juvat : et aurum jam acceſſio eſt. Or perhaps the words *imbofs'd with gems* &c refer only to *gold* firſt men-tion'd, which is no unuſual con-ſtruƈtion. *They quaff in gold im-bofs'd with gems and ſtuds of pearl.*

130. *Let his tormentor confcience find him out* ;] Milton had in view what Tacitus and Suetonius have related. Tacitus Ann. VI. 6. Inſigne viſum eſt earum Cæſaris litterarum initium ; nam his verbis exorſus eſt : *Quid ſi ibam vobis P C. aut quomodo ſcribam, aut quid omnino non ſcribam hoc tempore ? Dii me*

For him I was not fent, nor yet to free

That people victor once, now vile and bafe,

Deſervedly made vaſſal, who once juſt,

Frugal, and mild, and temp'rate, conquer'd well,

But govern ill the nations under yoke,   135

Peeling their provinces, exhauſted all

By luſt and rapin ; firſt ambitious grown

Of triumph, that inſulting vanity ;

Then cruel, by their ſports to blood inur'd

Of fighting beaſts, and men to beaſts expos'd,   140

Luxurious by their wealth, and greedier ſtill,

And

me Deæque pejus perdant quam perire quotidie ſentio, ſi ſcio. Adeo faci-nora atque flagitia ſua ipſi quoque in ſupplicium verterant.   Sueto-tonius Tiber. 67.   Poſtremo ſemet ipſe pertæſus *talis* epiſtolæ princi-pio tantum non ſummam malorum ſuorum profeſſus eſt : *Quid ſcribam* &c. where perhaps it ſhould be, *tali* epiſtolæ principio.   *Jortin.*

140. *Of fighting beaſts, and men to beaſts expoſ'd.*] The *fighting beaſts* are a poor inſtance of the Roman cruelty in their ſports, in compa-riſon of the gladiators, who might have been introduced ſo naturally, and eaſily here, only by putting the word *gladiators* in place of the other two, that one may very well be ſurpris'd at the poet's omitting them.   See Seneca's 7th epiſtle.
                                   Calton.

145. *Or could of inward ſlaves make outward free ?*] This noble ſentiment Milton explains more fully, and expreſſes more dif-fuſively in his Paradiſe Loſt. XII.90.

— Therefore ſince he permits
Within himſelf unworthy pow'rs to reign
Over free reaſon, God in judg-ment juſt
Subjects him from without to vio-lent lords ; &c. to ver. 101.

So alſo again in his 12th Sonnet,

Licence they mean when they cry Liberty ;
For who loves that muſt firſt be wiſe and good.

No one had ever more refin'd no-tions of true liberty than Milton, and I have often thought that there
never

And from the daily fcene effeminate.
What wife and valiant man would feek to free
Thefe thus degenerate, by themfelves inflav'd,
Or could of inward flaves make outward free ?   145
Know therefore when my feafon comes to fit
On David's throne, it fhall be like a tree
Spreading and overfhadowing all the earth,
Or as a ftone that fhall to pieces dafh
All monarchies befides throughout the world,   150
And of my kingdom there fhall be no end :
Means there fhall be to this, but what the means,

Is

never was a greater proof of the
weaknefs of human nature, than
that he with a head fo clear, and
a heart I really believe perfectly
honeft and difinterefted, fhould con-
cur in fupporting fuch a tyrant and
profefs'd trampler upon the liber-
ties of his country as Cromwell
was.   *Thyer.*

146. *Know therefore when my fea-
fon comes to fit* &c] A particu-
lar manner of expreffion, but fre-
quent in Milton ; as if he had faid,
Know therefore when the feafon
comes for me to fit on David's
throne, *it fhall be like a tree &c.*
For *his feafon* to be *like a tree* fays
Mr. Sympfon is ftrange language,
and therefore reads *I* fhall be like
a tree : but *it* refers to *throne.* The
throne of David fhall then *be like*

a *tree* &c ; alluding to the parable
of the muftard-feed grown into *a
tree, fo that the birds lodge in the
branches thereof,* Matt. XIII. 32.
and to (what that parable alfo re-
fpects) Nebuchadnezzar's dream of
the great *tree whofe highth reached
unto heaven, and the fight thereof to
the end of all the earth,* Dan. IV. 11.
Tertullian alfo compares the king-
dom of Chrift to that of Nebu-
chadnezzar. See Grotius in Matt.
Or as a ftone &c ; alluding to the
ftone in another of Nebuchadnez-
zar's dreams, which brake the
image in pieces, and fo this king-
dom *fhall break in pieces, and con-
fume all thefe kingdoms, and it fhall
ftand for ever.* Dan. II. 44. *And
of my kingdom there fhall be no end :*
the very words of Luke I. 33.
with only the neceffary change of
the

Is not for thee to know, nor me to tell.

    To whom the Tempter impudent reply'd.

I fee all offers made by me how flight   155

Thou valueft, becaufe offer'd, and rejeďt'ft:

Nothing will pleafe the difficult and nice,

Or nothing more than ftill to contradiďt:

On th' other fide know alfo thou, that I

On what I offer fet as high efteem,   160

Nor what I part with mean to give for nought;

All thefe which in a moment thou behold'ft,

The kingdoms of the world to thee I give;

For giv'n to me, I give to whom I pleafe,

No trifle; yet with this referve, not elfe,   165

On this condition, if thou wilt fall down,

And worfhip me as thy fuperior lord,

Eafily done, and hold them all of me;

For what can lefs fo great a gift deferve?

                      Whom

the perfon; *and of his kingdom there fhall be no end.*

    157. *Nothing will pleafe the difficult and nice,*] Mr. Jortin and Mr. Sympfon fay that perhaps we fhould read

    —— *thee* difficult and nice:

but I think the iďtus falls better in the common reading, and the fentence is better as a general obfervation.

    166. *On this condition, if thou wilt fall down,* &c] In my opinion (and Mr. Thyer concurs with me in the fame obfervation) there is not any thing in the difpofition and conduďt of the whole poem fo juftly liable to cenfure as the aukward and prepofterous introduďtion

Whom thus our Saviour anfwer'd with difdain.
I never lik'd thy talk, thy offers lefs,   171
Now both abhor, fince thou haft dar'd to utter
Th' abominable terms, impious condition ;
But I indure the time, till which expir'd,
Thou haft permiffion on me.   It is written   175
The firft of all commandments, Thou fhalt worfhip
The Lord thy God, and only him fhalt ferve ;
And dar'ft thou to the Son of God propound
To worfhip thee accurs'd, now more accurs'd
For this attempt bolder than that on Eve,   180
And more blafphemous ? which expect to rue.
The kingdoms of the world to thee were given,
Permitted rather, and by thee ufurp'd ;
Other donation none thou canft produce :
If giv'n, by whom but by the king of kings,   185
God over all fupreme ? if giv'n to thee,

By

troduction of this incident in this
place. The Tempter fhould have
propofed the condition at the
fame time that he offer'd the
gifts ; as he doth likewife in Scrip-
ture : but after his gifts had been
abfolutely refus'd, to what pur-
pofe was it to propofe the *impious
condition ?*   Could he imagin that
our Saviour would accept the
kingdoms of the world upon *th' a-
bominable terms* of falling down
and worfhipping him, juft after he
had rejected them unclogg'd with
any terms at all ?   Well might the
author fay that Satan *impudent re-
ply'd :* but I think that doth not
entirely folve the objection.

By thee how fairly is the giver now
Repaid? But gratitude in thee is loft
Long fince. Wert thou fo void of fear or fhame,
As offer them to me the Son of God,   190
To me my own, on fuch abhorred pact,
That I fall down and worfhip thee as God?
Get thee behind me; plain thou now appear'ft
That evil one, Satan for ever damn'd.

  To whom the Fiend with fear abafh'd reply'd.
Be not fo fore offended, Son of God,   196
Though fons of God both Angels are and Men,
If I to try whether in higher fort
Than thefe thou bear'ft that title, have propos'd
What both from Men and Angels I receive,   200
Tetrarchs of fire, air, flood, and on the earth
Nations befides from all the quarter'd winds,
God of this world invok'd and world beneath;

            Who

191. *To me my own,*] The right,
which the Demon pretends to,
over the kingdoms of the world,
is by *gift*; but Chrift clames them
as *his own* by nature, and by virtue
of his *Sonfhip.* Ὑιὸς γαρ ων τȣ
Θεȣ, ὁμοιῷ αυτȣ αι ειη· ὁμοιῷ
δε ων, πανlως εςι και κυριῷ και
βασιλευς. For being the Son of
God, he muft of courfe be like
him whofe fon he is; and being
like him, it neceffarily follows. that
he is lord and king. S. Athanaf.
Or. 3. contra Arianos. Op. Vol. I.
p. 387. Edit. Col. *Calton.*

191. ——— *abhorred pact,*] He
ufes the word *pact,* as it is the tech-
nical term for the contracts of for-
cerers with the Devil. *Warburton.*

        203. *God*

Who then thou art, whofe coming is foretold

To me fo fatal, me it moft concerns.   205

The trial hath indamag'd thee no way,

Rather more honor left and more efteem ;

Me nought advantag'd, miffing what I aim'd.

Therefore let pafs, as they are tranfitory,

The kingdoms of this world ; I fhall no more   210

Advife thee ; gain them as thou canft, or not.

And thou thyfelf feem'ft otherwife inclin'd ∙

Than to a worldly crown, addicted more

To contemplation and profound difpute,

As by that early action may be judg'd,   215

When flipping from thy mother's eye thou went'ft

Alone into the temple, there waft found

Amongft the graveft Rabbies difputant

On points and queftions fitting Mofes chair,   219

Teaching not taught ; the childhood fhows the man,

As

203. *God of this world invok'd*] Milton purfues the fame notion, which he had adopted in his Paradife Loft, of the Gods of the Gentiles being the fall'n Angels, and he is fupported in it by the authority of the primitive fathers, who are very unanimous in accufing the Heathens of worfhipping Devils for Deities.   *Thyer.*

217.—— *there waft found*] In Milton's own edition and in moft of the following ones it was printed by miftake *was found* ; but the fyntax plainly requires *waft*, as there is *thou went'ft* in the verfe preceding.

219.—— *fitting Mofes chair,*] *Mofes chair* was the chair, in which the doctors fitting expounded the

As morning fhows the day.   Be famous then
By wifdom; as thy empire muft extend,
So let extend thy mind o'er all the world
In knowledge, all things in it comprehend :
All knowledge is not couch'd in Mofes law,   225
The Pentateuch, or what the Prophets wrote ;
The Gentiles alfo know, and write, and teach
To admiration, led by nature's light ;
And with the Gentiles much thou muft converfe,

Ruling

law either publicly to the people,
or privately to their difciples *The
Scribes and Pharifees fit in Mofes
chair*, επι της Μωσεω; καθεδρας.
Mat. XXIII. 2.
  221.   ―― *Be famous then
By wifdom;*] We are now come
to the laft temptation, properly fo
called ; and it is worth the reader's
while to obferve how well Satan
has purfued the fcheme which he
had propofed in council. II. 225.

  Therefore with manlier objects
  we muft try
  His conftancy, with fuch as have
  more fhow
  Of worth, of honor, glory, and
  popular praife.

The gradation alfo in the feveral
allurements propos'd is very fine ;
and I believe one may juftly fay,
that there never was a more ex-
alted fyftem of morality compris'd
in fo fhort a compafs. Never were
the arguments for vice drefs'd up

in more delufive colors, nor were
they ever anfwer'd with more fo-
lidity of thought or acutenefs of
reafoning.   *Thyer.*

  230. *Ruling them by perfuafion as
  thou mean'ft* ;] Alluding to
thofe charming lines I. 221.

  Yet held it more humane, more
  heav'nly firft
  By willing words to conquer
  willing hearts,
  And make perfuafion do the
  work of fear.

But Satan did not hear this : it was
part of our Saviour's felf-converfe
and private meditation.

  236. ―― *this fpecular mount*] Thi[s]
mount *of fpeculation,* as in Para-
dife Loft. XII. 588, where fee the
note.
  237. *Weftward, much nearer by
  fouthweft,*] This correfponds
exactly to our Saviour's fuppos'd
fituation upon mount Taurus. The
following

5

Ruling them by perſuaſion as thou mean'ſt;   230

Without their learning how wilt thou with them,

Or they with thee hold converſation meet?

How wilt thou reaſon with them, how refute

Their idoliſms, traditions, paradoxes?

Error by his own arms is beſt evinc'd.   235

Look once more e'er we leave this ſpecular mount

Weſtward, much nearer by ſouthweſt, behold

Where on the Ægean ſhore a city ſtands

                                   Built

following deſcription of Athens and its learning is extremely grand and beautiful. Milton's Muſe, as was before obſerved, is too much cramped down by the argumentative caſt of his ſubject, but emerges upon every favorable occaſion, and like the ſun from under a cloud burſts out into the ſame bright vein of poetry, which ſhines out more frequently, tho' not more ſtrongly, in the Paradiſe Loſt. *Thyer.*

238. *Where on the Ægean ſhore a city ſtands*] So Milton cauſed this verſe to be printed, whereby it appears that he would have the word *Ægean* pronounced with the accent upon the firſt ſyllable as in Paradiſe Loſt. l. 746. and as Fairfax often uſes it, as was there remarked. *Built nobly*, and Homer in his time calls it *a well built city*, εὔκτιμενον πτολιεθρον. Iliad. II. 546 *pure the air, and light the ſoil,* Attica being a mountainous country, the ſoil was light and barren,

and the air ſharp and pure, and therefore ſaid to be productive of ſharp wits. την ευκρασιαν των αερων εν αυτῳ κατιδυσα, ὁτι φρονιμωτατυς ανδρας; οισει. Plato in Timæo p. 24. Vol. 3. Edit. Serr. Athenis tenue cœlum, ex quo acutiores etiam putantur Attici. Cicero de Fato. 4. *Athens the eye of Greece,* and ſo Demoſthenes ſomewhere calls it οφθαλμΘ- ἙλλαδΘ-, but I cannot at preſent recollect the place; and in Juſtin it is called one of the two eyes of Greece, Sparta being the other, Lib. 5. cap. 8; and Catullus calls Sirmio the eye of ilands XXXII. 1.

   Peninſularum Sirmio, inſularum-
      que
Ocelle:

but the metaphor is more properly applied to Athens than any other place, as it was the great ſeat of learning.

Built nobly, pure the air, and light the foil,

Athens the eye of Greece, mother of arts   240

And eloquence, native to famous wits

Or hofpitable, in her fweet recefs,

City' or fuburban, ftudious walks and fhades ;

See

239. ―― *pure the air, and light the foil,*] This is from Dio Chryfoftom. See Spanheim on Callimachus. p. 444. De Attica cætorequin dicit Dio Chryfoft. Orat. 7. p. 87. ειαι γαρ την χωραν αραιαν, και τον αερα κεφον, *effe enim regionem tenui folo, ac leveni arrem,* prout una voce λεπτογεως eadem Attica, poft Thucydidem nempe pag. 2. a Galeno dicitur, προτρεπτ. cap. 7. Aeris autem λεπτοτητα eidem tribuit Ariftides, Serm. Sacr. 6. p. 642. Athens was built between two fmall rivers Cephifus and Iliffus ; and hence it is call'd, in the Medea of Euripides, ιερων ποταμων πολις. See the chorus at the end of the 3d Act. The effect of thefe waters upon the air is very poetically reprefented in the fame beautiful chorus.

Καλλιαε τ' επι Κηφιϛε ϛεαις
Ταν Κυπριν κληϊζϛιν αφυ-
σαμειαν χωραν καταπιευϛαι
Μετριας ανεμων
Ἡδυπιους αυρας.

Pulchrifluique ad Cephifi fluenta Venerem ferunt [ex Cephifo] exhauri-
entem, regionem perflaffe,

Mediocres ventorum
Dulce fpirantes auras.   *Calton.*

244. *See there the olive grove of Academe,*
Plato's retirement, &c.] Επανελθων δε εις Αθηνας, διετριβεν εν Ακαδημια. το δ' ιϛι γυμιαϛιον, προαϛειον αλσωδες, απο τιΘ ηρωΘ ειοραϛθεν Ακαδημε, καθα και Ευπολις εν Αϛρατευτοις φηϛιν,

Εν ευϛκιοις δρομοισιν Ακαδημε Θεε.

―― και εταφη εν τη Ακαδημια, ειϐα τον πλειϛον χρειον διετελιϛε φιλοϛοφων. ιθεν και Ακαδημαϊκη προϛηγορευθη ἡ απ' αυτε αιρεϛις. Being return'd to Athens from his journey to Egypt, he fettled himfelf in the Academy, a gymnafium or place of exercife in the fuburbs of that city. befet with woods, taking name from Academus, one of the heroes, as Eupolis,

In facred Academus fhady walks.

―― and he was buried in the Academy, where he continued moft of his time teaching philofophy, whence the fect which fprung from him was called Academic. See Diogenes Laertius, and Stanley in the

See there the olive grove of Academe,
Plato's retirement, where the Attic bird   245
Trills her thick-warbled notes the fummer long;
There flow'ry hill Hymettus with the found
Of bees induftrious murmur oft invites

To

the life of Plato. The Academy is always defcribed as a woody fhady place, as here in Laertius, and in Horace, Ep. II. II. 45.

Atque inter fylvas Academi quæ-
rere verum :

but Milton diftinguifhes it by the particular name of *the olive grove of Academe*, for the olive was particularly cultivated about Athens being facred to Minerva the Goddefs of the city, and he has befides the exprefs authority of Ariftophanes Νεφελαι Act 3. Scene 3.

Αλλ' εις Ακαδημιαν κατιων, ὑπο
ταις μοριαις αποθρεξεις.

Sed in Academiam defcendens, fub facris olivis fpatiaberis.

Where the Attic bird, the nightingale, for Philomela, who according to the fables was changed into a nightingale, was the daughter of Pandion king of Athens, and for the fame reafon the nightingale is called *Atthis* in Latin, quafi Attica avis. Martial Lib. 1. Ep. 46. Edit. Weftm.

Sic, ubi multifona fervet facer
Atthide lucus,

Improba *Cecropias* offendit pica querelas.

Ludovicus de la Cerda in his notes upon Virgil obferves, how often the ancient poets have made ufe of the comparifon of the nightingale; Sophocles has it no lefs than feven times, Homer twice, and Euripides and feveral others : and we obferved upon the Paradife Loft, how much Milton was delighted with the nightingale ; no poet has introduc'd it fo often, or fpoken of it with fuch rapture as he ; and perhaps there never was a verfe more expreffive of the harmony of this fweet bird than the following,

Trills her thick-warbled notes
the fummer long.

So that upon the whole I believe it may be afferted, that Plato's Academy was never more beautifully defcribed than here in a few lines by Milton. Cicero, who has laid the fcene of one of his dialogues there, De Fin. Lib. V. and had been himfelf upon the fpot, has not painted it in more lively colors.

247. *There flow'ry hill Hymettus* &c] And fo Valerius Flaccus calls it *Florea juga Hymetti,* Argonaut.

M 4   V.

To ftudious mufing ; there Iliffus rolls
His whifp'ring ftream : within the walls then view
The fchools of ancient fages ; his who bred   251
Great Alexander to fubdue the world,
Lyceum there, and painted Stoa next :

There

V. 344. and the honey was fo
much efteem'd and celebrated by
the Ancients, that it was reckon'd
the beft of the Attic honey, as the
Attic honey was faid to be the beft
in the world. The poets often
fpeak of the murmur of the bees
as inviting to fleep, Virg. Ecl.
I. 56.

Sæpe levi fomnum fuadebit ini e
fufurro :

but Milton gives a more elegant
turn to it, and fays that it *invites to
ftudious mufing*, which was more
proper indeed for his purpofe, as
he is here defcribing the Attic
learning.

249.   *—— there Iliffus rolls
His whifp'ring ftream :*] Mr. Cal-
ton and Mr. Thyer have obferved
with me, that Plato hath laid the
fcene of his Phædrus on the banks
and at the fpring of this pleafant
river. — χαριετα γυ και καθαρα
και διαφαιη τα υδατια φαινεται,
Nonne hinc aquulæ puræ ac pellu-
cidæ jucundo murmure confluunt ?
Ed. Serr. Vol 3. p. 229. The phi-
lofophical retreat at the fpring-
head is beautifully defcribed by
Plato in the next page, where So-
crates and Phædrus are reprefented

fitting on a green bank fhaded
with a fpreading plantan, of which
Cicero hath faid very prettily, that
it feemeth to have grown not fo
much by the water which is de-
fcribed, as by Plato's eloquence ;
quæ mihi videtur non tam ipfa
aquula, quæ defcribitur, quam Pla-
tonis oratione creviffe. De Orat,
I. 7.

253. *Lyceum there, and painted
Stoa next :*] *Lyceum* was ano-
ther gymnafium of the Athenians,
and was the fchool of Ariftotle,
who had been tutor to Alexander
the great, and was the founder of
the fect of the Peripatetics, fo
call'd απο τυ περιπατειν from his
walking and teaching philofophy.
Stoa was the fchool of Zeno, whofe
difciples from the place had the
name of Stoics ; and this Stoa or
portico, being adorn'd with variety
of paintings, was called in Greek
Ποικιλη or various, and here by
Milton very properly the *painted
Stoa.* See Diogenes Laertius in
the lives of Ariftotle and Zeno.
But there is fome reafon to queftion,
whether the *Lyceum* was *within the
walls*, as Milton afferts. For Sui-
das fays exprefsly, that it was a
place in the fuburbs, built by Pe-
ricles

There thou fhalt hear and learn the fecret power
Of harmony in tones and numbers hit   255
By voice or hand, and various-meafur'd verfe,
Æolian charms and Dorian lyric odes,
And his who gave them breath, but higher fung,
                                                  Blind

ricles for the exercifing of foldiers:
and I find the fcholiaft upon Ari-
ftophanes in the Irene fpeaks of
going into the Lyceum, and going
out of it again, and *returning back
into the city :* ——— τις το Λυκειον ει-
σιονϊες ——— και παλιν εξιονϊες εκ τυ
Λυκειυ, και απιονϊες εις την πολιν.

   257. *Æolian charms and Dorian
      lyric odes,*] *Æolian charms,*
Æolia carmina, verfes fuch as
thofe of Alcæus and Sappho, who
were both of Mitylene in Lefbos,
an iland belonging to the Æolians.
Hor. Od. III. XXX. 13.

   Princeps *Æolium carmen ad Italos*
   Deduxiffe modos.

Od. IV. III. 12.

   Fingent *Æolio carmine* nobilem.

Dorian lyric odes, fuch as thofe of
Pindar, who calls his Δωριαν φορ-
μιῖγα the Dorian harp, Olymp.
I. 26. Δωριω πεδιλω Dorian buf-
kin, Olymp. III. 9. Δωριει κομω
Dorian hymn, Pyth. VIII. 29.

   258. *And his who gave them
      breath,* &c] Our author agrees
with thofe writers, who fpeak of
Homer as the father of all kinds

of poetry. Such wife men as Dio-
nyfius the Halicarnaffean, and Plu-
tarch, have attempted to fhow,
that poetry in all its forms, trage-
dy, comedy, ode, and epitaph,
are included in his works. See
the ingenious author of the *Inquiry
into the life and writings of Homer*
inlarging upon this fubject. Sect. 12.
Blind Melifigenes thence Homer call'd;
our author here follows Herodotus
in his account of the life of Ho-
mer, that he was born near the
river *Meles* from whence he had
the name of *Melefigenes,* τιθεται
ονομα τω παιδ. Μελεσιγενεα, απο
τυ ποταμυ την επωνυμιαν λαβυσα,
and becaufe he was *blind, thence*
he was called *Homer* ὁ μη ὁρων,
εντευθεν δε και τυνομα Ὁμηρ☉ επι-
κρατησε τω Μελησιγενει απο της
συμφορης· οἱ γαρ Κυμαιοι τυς τυ-
φλυς ὁμηρυς λεγυσιν.   *Whofe poem
Phœbus challeng'd for his own,* al-
luding to a Greek epigram in the
firft book of the Anthologia,

   Ηειδον μεν εγων, εχαρασσε δε
      Στ.☉ Ομηρ☉,

which Mr. Fenton has inlarged
and applied to Mr. Pope's Englifh
Iliad.

Blind Melefigenes thence Homer call'd,

Whofe poem Phœbus challeng'd for his own.   260

Thence what the lofty grave tragedians taught

In Chorus or Iambic, teachers beſt

Of moral prudence with delight receiv'd

In brief ſententious precepts, while they treat

Of fate, of chance, and change in human life ;   265

High actions, and high paſſions beſt deſcribing :

Thenc e

262. *In Chorus or Iambic,*] Theſe may be ſaid to be the two conſtituent parts of the ancient tragedy, which was written either in Iambic verſe, or in verſes of various meaſures, whereof the Chorus uſually conſiſted. And the character here given of the ancient Greek tragedy is very juſt and noble ; and the Engliſh reader cannot form a better idea of it in its higheſt beauty and perfection than by reading our author's Sampſon Agoniſtes.

267. *Thence to the famous orators repair,* &c.] How happily does Milton's verſification in this and the following lines concerning the Socratic philoſophy expreſs what he is deſcribing ! In the firſt we feel as it were the nervous rapid eloquence of Demoſthenes, and the latter have all the gentleneſs and ſoftneſs of the humble modeſt character of Socrates.

Thyer.

268. *Thoſe ancient,*] For Milton was of the ſame opinion as Cicero,

who preferred Pericles, Hyperides, Æſchines, Demoſthenes, and the orators of their times to Demetrius Phalereus and thoſe of the ſubſequent ages. See Cicero de claris Oratoribus. And in the judgment of Quintilian Demetrius Phalereus was the firſt who weaken'd eloquence, and the laſt almoſt of the Athenians who can be called an orator : is primus inclinaſſe eloquentiam dicitur— ultimus eſt fere ex Atticis qui dici poſſit orator. De Inſtit. Orat. X. 1.

270. — *and fulmin'd over Greece,*] Alluding (as Mr. Jortin has likewiſe obſerved) to what Ariſtophanes has ſaid of Pericles in his Acharnenſes. Act 2. Scene 5.

Ερξαωλει, εξαʼλα, ξυνεκυκα την Ελλαδα.

Since I have mention'd this paſſage, I will add, that Cicero has alluded to it in his Orator 9, ſpeaking of Pericles.   Qui fi tenui genere

Thence to the famous orators repair,
Thofe ancient, whofe refiftlefs eloquence
Wielded at will that fierce democratie,
Shook th' arfenal and fulmin'd over Greece,   270
To Macedon and Artaxerxes throne :
To fage philofophy next lend thine ear,
From Heav'n defcended to the low-rooft houfe
Of Socrates ; fee there his tenement,

Whom

nere uteretur, nunquam ab Arifto-
phane poeta fulgere, tonare, per-
mifcere Græciam dictus effet. Dio-
dorus Siculus has quoted it like-
wife Lib. 12. and afcribed it to Eu-
polis the poet, the fame who is
mention'd by Horace.

Eupolis, atque Cratinus, Arifto-
phanefque poetæ.

και παλιν εν αλλοις Ευπολις ὁ
ποιητης —— Περικλεης ευλυμπι Ⓖ-
Hραπτ', εξροιτα, συνικυκα την
Ελλαδα. Cicero had at firft fallen
into the fame miftake as Diodorus,
which is often the cafe of writers
who quote by memory ; and there-
fore defires Atticus to correct the
copies, and for Eupolis to put in
Ariftophanes. Cic. ad Att. XII. 6.
mihi erit gratum, fi non modo in
libris tuis, fed etiam in aliorum per
librarios tuos Ariftophanem repo-
fueris pro Eupoli. The miftake
was corrected according to his de-
fire ; at leaft it is fo in all the re-
maining copies and editions.

271. *To Macedon and Artaxerxes
throne :*] As Pericles and others
*fulmin'd over Greece to Artaxerxes
throne* againft the Perfian king, fo
Demofthenes was the orator parti-
cularly, who *fulmin'd over Greece to
Macedon* againft king Philip in his
orations therefore denominated
Philippics.

273. *From Heav'n defcended to the
low-rooft houfe
Of Socrates ;*] Mr. Calton thinks
the author alludes to Juv. Sat.
XI. 27,

—— e cœlo defcendit γνωθι
σεαυτον,

as this famous Delphic precept was
the foundation of Socrates's philo-
fophy, and fo much ufed by him,
that it hath paffed with fome for
his own. Or as Mr. Warburton
and Mr. Thyer conceive, the au-
thor here probably alludes to what
Cicero fays of Socrates, Socrates
autem primus philofophiam devo-
cavit e cœlo, et in urbibus colloca-

vit,

Whom well infpir'd the oracle pronounc'd   275
Wifeft of men ; from whofe mouth iffued forth
Mellifluous ftreams that water'd all the fchools
Of Academics old and new, with thofe
Sirnam'd Peripatetics, and the fect
Epicurean, and the Stoic fevere ;   280
Thefe here revolve, or, as thou lik'ft, at home,
Till time mature thee to a kingdom's weight ;
Thefe rules will render thee a king complete
Within thyfelf, much more with empire join'd.

To

vit, et in domus etiam introduxit.
Tufc. Difp. V. 4. But he has given
a very different fenfe to the words
either by defign or miftake, as
Mr. Warburton obferves. It is
properly call'd *the low-rooft houfe* ;
for I believe, faid Socrates, that
if I could meet with a good pur-
chafer, I might eafily get for my
goods and houfe and all five pounds.
Εγω μεν οιμαι (εφη ὁ Σωκρατης)
ει αγαθυ ωνητη επιτυχοιμι, εὑρειν
αν μοι συν τη οικια και τα οντα
παντα πανυ ῥαδιως πεντε μνας.
Xenophon Oeconomic. five mina's
or Attic pounds were better than
fixteen pounds of our money, a
mina according to Barnard being
three pounds eight fhillings and
nine pence.

275. *Whom well infpir'd the oracle
   pronounc'd*
Wifeft of men ;] The verfe deli-

vered down to us upon this occa-
fion is this,

Ανδρων ἁπαντων Σωκρατης σοφω-
   τατΘ.

Of all men Socrates is the wifeft.
See Diogenes Laertius in vita So-
cratis.   Mr. Calton adds, that the
Tempter defigns here a compli-
ment to himfelf ; for he would be
underftood to be the infpirer.

276.——*from whofe mouth iffued
   forth* &c] Thus Quintilian calls
Socrates *fons philofophorum*, I. 10.
and as the ancients looked upon
Homer as the father of poetry, fo
they efteemed Socrates the father
of moral philofophy. The diffe-
rent fects of philofophers were but
fo many different families, which
all acknowledged him for their
common parent. See Cicero Aca-
demic.

To whom our Saviour fagely thus reply'd,   285
Think not but that I know thefe things, or think
I know them not ; not therefore am I fhort
Of knowing what I ought : he who receives
Light from above, from the fountain of light,
No other doctrin needs, though granted true ;   290
But thefe are falfe, or little elfe but dreams,
Conjectures, fancies, built on nothing firm.
The firft and wifeft of them all profefs'd
To know this only, that he nothing knew;

The

demic. I. 4. Tufc. Difp. V. 4. and particularly De Orat. III, 16, 17. The quotation would be too long to be inferted. See likewife Mr. Warburton's account of the Socratic fchool. B. 3. Sect. 3. of the Divine Legation.

283. *Thefe rules will render thee &c*] Afk *what* rules, and no anfwer can be regularly given : afk *whofe*, and the anfwer is eafy, There is no mention before of rules ; but of poets, orators, philofophers there is. We fhould read therefore,

> *Their* rules will render thee a king complete.   *Calton.*

285. *To whom our Saviour fagely thus reply'd.*] This anfwer of our Saviour is as much to be admired for folid reafoning, and the many fublime truths contain'd in it, as the preceding fpeech of Satan is for that fine vein of poetry which runs through it : and one may obferve in general, that Milton has quite throughout this work thrown the ornaments of poetry on the fide of error, whether it was that he thought great truths beft exprefs'd in a grave unaffected ftile, or intended to fuggeft this fine moral to the reader, that fimple naked truth will always be an overmatch for falfhood though recommended by the gayeft rhetoric, and adorned with the moft bewitching colors.   *Thyer.*

293. *The firft and wifeft of them all*] Socrates *profefs'd to know this only, that he nothing knew.* Hic in omnibus fere fermonibus, qui ab iis, qui illum audierunt, perfcripti varie, copiofe funt, ita difputat, ut nihil adfirmet ipfe, refellat

The next to fabling fell and fmooth conceits ;   295
A third fort doubted all things, though plain fenfe ;
Others in virtue plac'd felicity,
But virtue join'd with riches and long life ;
In corporal pleafure he, and carelefs eafe ;
The Stoic laft in philofophic pride,   300
By him call'd virtue ; and his virtuous man,

Wife,

lat alios : nihil fe fcire dicat, nifi id ipfum : eoque præftare ceteris, quod illi quæ nefciant fcire fe putent ; ipfe, fe nihil fcire, id unum fciat. Cicero Academic. I. 4.

295. *The next to fabling fell and fmooth conceits* ;] See Parker's Free and impartial cenfure of the Platonic philofophy. Oxford 1667. p. 71. " Plato and his followers " have communicated their notions " by emblems, fables, fymbols, " parables, heaps of metaphors, " allegories, and all forts of my- " ftical reprefentations, (as is vul- " garly known.) All which, upon " the account of their obfcurity " and ambiguity, are apparently " the unfitteft figns in the world " to exprefs the train of any man's " thoughts to another : For befides " that they carry in them no in- " telligible affinity to the notices " which they were defign'd to in- " timate, the powers of imagina- " tion are fo great, and the in- " ftances in which one thing may " refemble another are fo many, " that there is fcarce any thing in " nature, in which the fancy can- " not find or make a variety of " fuch fymbolizing refemblances ; " fo that emblems, fables, fym- " bols, allegories, tho' they are " pretty poetic fancies, are infi- " nitely unfit to exprefs philofo- " phical notions and difcoveries of " the natures of things. —— The " end of philofophy is to fearch " into, and difcover the nature of " things ; but I believe you under- " ftand not how the nature of any " thing is at all difcoverered by " making it the theme of allegori- " cal and dark difcourfes."

Calton.

296. *A third fort doubted all things, though plain fenfe* ;] Thefe were the Sceptics or Pyrrhonians the difciples of Pyrrho, who afferted nothing, neither honeft nor dif-honeft, juft nor unjuft, and fo of every thing ; that there is nothing indeed fuch, but that men do all things by law and cuftom ; that in every thing this is not rather than that. This was called the Sceptic philofophy from its continual in-fpeftion,

Wife, perfect in himfelf, and all poffeffing,
Equals to God, oft fhames not to prefer,
As fearing God nor man, contemning all   304
Wealth, pleafure, pain or torment, death and life,
Which when he lifts he leaves, or boafts he can,
For all his tedious talk is but vain boaft,
Or fubtle fhifts conviction to evade.

Alas

fpection, and never finding ; and
Pyrrhonian from Pyrrho. See Stan-
ley's life of Pyrrho, who takes his
account from Diogenes Laertius.

297. *Others in virtue* &c] Thefe
were the old Academics, and the
Peripatetics the fcholars of Ari-
ftotle. Honefte autem vivere, fru-
entem rebus iis, quas primas ho-
mini natura conciliet, et vetus Aca-
demia cenfuit, et Ariftoteles : ejuf-
que amici nunc proxime videntur
accedere. Cicero Academic. II.
42. Ergo nata eft fententia vete-
rum Academicorum et Peripateti-
corum, ut finem bonorum dicerent,
fecundum naturam vivere, id eft,
virtute adhibita, frui primis à na-
tura datis. de Fin. II. 11.

299. *In corporal pleafure he, and
carelefs eafe* ;] Epicurus. Con-
firmat autem illud vel maxime,
quod ipfa natura, ut ait ille, ad-
fcifcat et reprobet, id eft, volupta-
tem et dolorem : ad hæc, et quæ
fequamur et quæ fugiamus, refert
omnia. Cicero de Fin. I. 7.

300. *The Stoic laft* &c] The rea-
fon why Milton reprefents our Sa-

viour taking fuch particular notice
of the Stoics above the reft, was
probably becaufe they made pre-
tenfions to a more refin'd and ex-
alted virtue than any of the other
fects, and were at that time the
moft prevailing party among the
philofophers, and the moft rever'd
and efteem'd for the ftrictnefs of
their morals, and the aufterity of
their lives. The picture of their
virtuous man is perfectly juft, as
might eafily be fhown from many
paffages in Seneca and Antoninus,
and the defects and infufficiency of
their fcheme could not poffibly be
fet in a ftronger light than they
are by our author in the lines fol-
lowing.   *Thyer.*

303. *Equals to God,*] In Milton's
own edition, and all following, it
is *Equal to God :* but I cannot bnt
think this an error of the prefs, the
fenfe is fo much improved by the
addition only of a fingle letter.

Equals to God, oft fhames not
    to prefer,

307. *For all his tedious talk is
    but vain boaft,*

Or-

Alas what can they teach, and not miſlead,

Ignorant of themſelves, of God much more,   310

And how the world began, and how man fell

Degraded by himſelf, on grace depending?

Much of the ſoul they talk, but all awry,

And in themſelves ſeek virtue, and to themſelves

All glory arrogate, to God give none,   315

Rather accuſe him under uſual names,

Fortune and Fate, as one regardleſs quite

Of mortal things. Who therefore ſeeks in theſe

True wiſdom, finds her not, or by deluſion

Far worſe, her falſe reſemblance only meets,   320

An empty cloud. However many books,

Wiſe

Or ſubtle ſhifts] *Vain boaſts* relate to the Stoical paradoxes, and *ſubtle ſhifts* to their dialectic, which this ſect ſo much cultivated, as to be as well known by the name Dialectici as Stoici.   *Warburton.*

313. *Much of the ſoul they talk, but all awry,*] See what Mr. Warburton has ſaid upon this ſubject in the firſt volume of the Divine Legation.

314. *And in themſelves ſeek virtue, and to themſelves All glory arrogate, to God give none,*] Cicero ſpeaks the ſentiments of ancient philoſophy upon this point in the following words : ———— propter virtutem enim jure *laudamur*, et *in virtute recte gloriamur :* quod non contingeret, ſi id donum a Deo, non a nobis haberemus. At vero aut honoribus aucti, aut re familiari, aut ſi aliud quippiam nacti ſumus fortuiti boni, aut depulimus mali, cùm Diis gratias agimus, tum nihil noſtræ laudi aſſumptum arbitramur. Num quis, quòd bonus vir eſſet, gratias Diis egit unquam? At quòd dives, quòd honoratus, quòd incolumis. ——— Ad rem

Wife men have faid, are wearifome ; who reads
Inceffantly, and to his reading brings not
A fpirit and judgment equal or fuperior,
(And what he brings, what needs he elfewhere feek ?)
Uncertain and unfettled ftill remains,   326
Deep vers'd in books and fhallow in himfelf,
Crude or intoxicate, collecting toys,
And trifles for choice matters, worth a fpunge ;
As children gathering pebbles on the fhore.   330
Or if I would delight my private hours
With mufic or with poem, where fo foon
As in our native language can I find
That folace ? All our law and ftory ftrow'd

                                              With

rem autem ut redeam, *judicium hoc
omnium mortalium eft, fortunam à
Deo petendam, à fe ipfo fumendam effe
fapientiam.* De Nat. Deor. III. 36.
                        Warburton.

321. *An empty cloud,*] A me-
taphor taken from the fable of
Ixion, who embrac'd *an empty cloud*
for a Juno.

322. *Wife men have faid.*] Al-
luding to Ecclef. XII. 12. *Of
making many books there is no end,
and much ftudy is a wearinefs of the
flefh.*

322. —— *who reads*
   V o L. I.

Inceffantly, &c] See the fame
juft fentiment in Paradife Loft
VII. 126.

   But knowledge is as food, and
      needs no lefs
   Her temp'rance over appetite,
      &c.   *Thyer.*

325. *And what he brings, what
      needs he elfewhere feek ?*] The
poet makes the old fophifter the
Devil always bufy in his trade.
'Tis pity he fhould make Jefus (as
he does here) ufe the fame arms.
                        Warburton.

                  N   325—*cur*

With hymns, our pfalms with artful terms infcrib'd,

Our Hebrew fongs and harps in Babylon,   336

That pleas'd fo well our victors ear, declare

That rather Greece from us thefe arts deriv'd;

Ill imitated, while they loudeft fing

The vices of their Deities, and their own   340

In fable, hymn, or fong, fo perfonating

Their Gods ridiculous, and themfelves paft fhame.

Remove their fwelling epithets thick laid

As varnifh on a harlot's cheek, the reft,

Thin fown with ought of profit or delight,   345

Will

335. —— *our pfalms with artful terms infcrib'd,*] He means the infcriptions often prefixed to the beginning of feveral pfalms, fuch as To the chief mufician upon Ne-hiloth, To the chief mufician on Neginoth upon Sheminith, Shig-gaion of David, Michtam of Da-vid, &c, to denote the various kinds of pfalms or inftruments.

336. *Our Hebrew fongs and harps in Babylon,*
That pleas'd fo well our victors ear,] This is faid upon the authority of Pfal. CXXXVII. 1 &c. *By the ri-vers of Babylon, there we fat down, yea we wept, when we remembred Sion. We hanged our harps upon the willows in the midft thereof. For there they that carried us away cap-tive, required of us a fong; and they* *that wafted us, required of us mirth, faying, Sing us one of the fongs of Sion.*

338. *That rather Greece from us thefe arts deriv'd;*] This was the fyftem in vogue at that time. It was eftablifhed and fupported with vaft erudition by Bochart. and carried to an extravagant and even ridiculous length by Huetius and Gale.   *Warburton.*

343. ——*fwelling epithets*] Greek compounds.   *Warburton.* The hymns of the Greek poets to their Deities confift of very little more than repeated invocations of them by different names and epi-thets. Our Saviour very probably alluded to thefe, where he cautions his difciples againft vain repetitions and

Will far be found unworthy to compare

With Sion's fongs, to all true taftes excelling,

Where God is prais'd aright, and God-like men,

The Holieft of Holies, and his Saints ;

Such are from God infpir'd, not fuch from thee,　350

Unlefs where moral virtue is exprefs'd

By light of nature not in all quite loft.

Their orators thou then extoll'ft, as thofe

The top of eloquence, ftatifts indeed,

And lovers of their country, as may feem ;　355

But herein to our prophets far beneath,

As

and much fpeaking (βατλολογια) in their prayers, Matt. VI. 7.

Thyer.

346. *Will far be found unworthy to compare*
With Sion's fongs,] He was of this opinion not only in the decline of life, but likewife in his earlier days, as appears from the preface to his fecond book of the *Reafon of Church-Government.*—— " Or if occafion fhall lead to imi- " tate thofe magnific odes and " hymns wherein Pindarus and " Callimachus are in moft things " worthy, fome others in their " frame judicious, in their matter " moft an end faulty. But thofe " frequent fongs throughout the " law and prophets beyond all " thefe, not in their divine argu-

" ment alone, but in the very cri- " tical art of compofition, may " be eafily made appear over all " the kinds of lyric poetry, to be " incomparable "

350. *Such are from God infpir'd,*
not fuch from thee,
Unlefs where moral virtue is ex-
prefs'd &c] The fenfe of thefe lines is obfcure and liable to mif- take. The meaning of them is, poets from thee infpired are not fuch as thefe, unlefs where moral virtue is exprefled &c.

Meadowccurt.

353. —— *as thofe*] I fhould pre- fer — as *though.*　Calton.

354.—— *ftatifts*] Or ftatefmen. A word in more frequent ufe for- merly, as in Shakefpear, Cymbe- line Act 2. Scene 5.

As men divinely taught, and better teaching
The folid rules of civil government
In their majeftic unaffected ftile
Than all th' oratory of Greece and Rome.   360
In them is plaineft taught, and eafieft learnt,
What makes a nation happy', and keeps it fo,
What ruins kingdoms, and lays cities flat;
Thefe only with our law beft form a king.

    So fpake the Son of God ; but Satan now   365
Quite at a lofs, for all his darts were fpent,
Thus to our Saviour with ftern brow reply'd.

    Since neither wealth, nor honor, arms nor arts,
Kingdom nor empire pleafes thee, nor ought
By me propos'd in life contemplative,   370
Or active, tended on by glory', or fame,
What doft thou in this world ? the wildernefs

                                        For

—— I do believe,
(*Statift* though I am none, nor
   like to be ;)

and Hamlet Act 5. Sc. 3.

   I once did hold it, as our *ftatifts*
   do, *&c.*

362.——*makes happy and keeps fo*]
Hor. Epift. 1. VI. 2.

   —— facere et fervare beatum.
                    Richardfon.

380. —— *fulnefs of time,*] Gal.
IV. 4. *When the* fulnefs of the
time *was come, God fent forth his
Son.*

   382.—— *if I read ought in Hea-
ven,* &c] A fatire on Cardan,
who with the boldnefs and impiety
of an atheift and a madman, both
of which he was, caft the nativity
of Jefus Chrift, and found by the
great and illuftrious concourfe of
ftars at his birth, that he muft
                      needs

For thee is fitteft place ; I found thee there,
And thither will return thee ; yet remember
What I foretel thee, foon thou fhalt have caufe 375
To wifh thou never hadft rejected thus
Nicely or cautioufly my offer'd aid,
Which would have fet thee in fhort time with eafe
On David's throne, or throne of all the world,
Now at full age, fulnefs of time, thy feafon,   380
When prophecies of thee are beft fulfill'd.
Now contrary, if I read ought in Heaven,
Or Heav'n write ought of fate, by what the ftars
Voluminous, or fingle characters,
In their conjunction met, give me to fpell,   385
Sorrows, and labors, oppofition, hate
Attends thee, fcorns, reproaches, injuries,
Violence and ftripes, and laftly cruel death ;

A

needs have the fortune which be-fel him, and become the author of a religion, which fhould fpread itfelf far and near for many ages. The great Milton with a juft indignation of this impiety hath fatirized it in a very beautiful manner, by putting thefe reveries into the mouth of the Devil : where it is to be obferved, that the poet thought it not enough to difcredit *judicial aftrology* by making it patro-nifed by the Devil, without fhowing at the fame time the abfurdity of it. He has therefore very judicioufly made him blunder in the expreffion, of *portending a kingdom which was without beginning.* This deftroys all he would infinuate. The poet's conduct is fine and ingenious. See Warburton's Shakefpear Vol. 6. Lear Act 1. Sc. 8.

A kingdom they portend thee, but what kingdom,

Real or allegoric I difcern not,   390

Nor when, eternal fure, as without end,

Without beginning; for no date prefix'd

Directs me in the ftarry rubric fet.

So fay'ing he took (for ftill he knew his power

Not yet expir'd) and to the wildernefs   395

Brought back the Son of God, and left him there,

Feigning to difappear.   Darknefs now rofe,

As day-light funk, and brought in louring night

Her fhadowy ofspring, unfubftantial both,

         Privation

399. — *unfubftantial both*,] His philofophy is here ill placed. It dafhes out the image he had juft been painting.   *Warburton.*

408. ———— *and foon with ugly dreams* &c.] It is remaikable, that the poet made the Devil begin his temptation of Eve by working on her imagination in dreams, and to end his temptation of Jefus in that manner. I leave it to the critics to find out the reafon ; for I will venture to fay he had a very good one.   *Warburton.*

409. — *and either tropic now 'Gan thunder, and both ends of Heav'n, the clouds* &c] Place the ftops thus :

———— and either tropic now

'Gan thunder, and both ends of Heav'n. the clouds &c.

It thunder'd from both tropics, that is perhaps from the right and from the left.   The Ancients had very different opinions concerning the right and the left fide of the world.· Plutarch fays, that Ariftotle, Plato, and Pythagoras were of opinion, that the eaft is the right fide, and the weft the left ; but that Empedocles held that the right fide is towards the fummer tropic, and the left towards the winter tropic. Πυθαγορας, Πλατων, Αριςοτελης, δεξια τȣ κοσμȣ τα αιατολικα μερη, α'φ ωι η αρχη της κιηςεως· αριςερα δε, τα δυτικα. Εμπεδοκλης δεξια μεν τα κατα τον Ξεριιον τροπικον· αριςερα

Privation mere of light and abfent day. 400
Our Saviour meek and with untroubled mind
After his aery jaunt, though hurried fore,
Hungry and cold betook him to his reft,
Wherever, under fome concourfe of fhades,
Whofe branching arms thick intertwin'd might
  fhield 405
From dews and damps of night his fhelter'd head,
But fhelter'd flept in vain, for at his head
The Tempter watch'd, and foon with ugly dreams
Difturb'd his fleep; and either tropic now 409
  'Gan

ρισερα δε τα κατα τον χειμερινοι.
De Placit. Philof. II. 10. Αιγυπ-
τιοι οιονται τα μεν εωα, τω κοσ-
μω προσωπον ειναι, τα δε προ-
βορραν, δεξια, τα δε προ νο-
τον, αριστερα. Id. de Ifid. p. 363.
If by *either tropic* be meant the
right fide and the *left*, by *both ends
of Heav'n* may be underftood, *be-
fore* and *behind*. I know it may be
objected, that the tropics cannot
be the one the right fide, and the
other the left, *to thofe* who are
placed without the tropics : but I
do not think that objection to be
very material. I have another ex-
pofition to offer, which is thus:
It thundered all along the Heav'n,
from the north pole to the tropic
of Cancer, from thence to the tro-
pic of Capricorn, from thence to

the fouth pole. From pole to pole.
The *ends of Heav'n* are the poles.
This is a poetical tempeft, like that
in Virgil Æn. I.

Intonuere poli ——

Id eft extremæ partes cœli —— a
quibus totum cœlum contonuiffe
fignificat. Servius. *Jortin.*
Mr. Sympfon propofes to read and
point the paffage thus ;

—— and either tropic now
'Gan thunder ; *at* both ends of
Heav'n the clouds &c :

Mr. Meadowcourt points it thus ;

—— and either tropic now
'Gan thunder, and both ends of
Heav'n : the clouds &c :

But after all I am ftill for pre-
serving

'Gan thunder, and both ends of Heav'n, the clouds
From many a horrid rift abortive pour'd
Fierce rain with lightning mix'd, water with fire
In ruin reconcil'd : nor flept the winds
Within their ftony caves, but rufh'd abroad
From the four hinges of the world, and fell   415
On the vex'd wildernefs, whofe talleft pines,

Though

serving Milton's own punctuation, unlefs there be very good reafon for departing from it, and I underftand the paffage thus : *and either tropic now 'gan thunder*, it thundered from the north and from the fouth, for this I conceive to be Milton's meaning, tho' the exprefsion is inaccurate, the fituation of our Saviour and Satan being not within the tropics : *and both ends of Heav'n*, that is, and *from* or *at* both ends of Heav'n, the prepofition being omitted, as is frequent in Milton, and feveral inftances were given in the notes on the Paradife Loft. See particularly Dr. Pearce's note on I. 282. *and* from *both ends of Heav'n, the clouds* &c. This ftorm is defcrib'd very much like one in Taffo, which was raifed in the fame manner by evil Spirits. See Canto 7. St. 114, 115. for I would not lengthen this note, too long already, with the quotation.

412.   ―― *water with fire In ruin reconcil'd :*] That is, joining together to do hurt. *Warburton*.

This bold figure our poet has borrow'd from Æfchilus, where he is defcribing the ftorm, which fcatter'd the Grecian fleet. Agamemnon. ver. 659.

Ειιωμοσαν γαρ, οιτες εχθιςοι το-
    πριν,

Πυρ και Θαλασσα, και τα πιςι'
    εδειξατην,

Φθειροιτε τον ουςτιον Αργειων ςα-
    τον.   *Thyer*.

Or perhaps it means only *water and fire falling down both together*, according to Milton's ufage of the word *ruin* in Paradife Loft, I. 46. VI. 868.

415. *From the four hinges of the world*,] That is from the four cardinal points, the word *cardines* fignifying both the one and the other. This, as was obferved before, is a poetical tempeft like that in Virgil. Æn. I. 85.

    Unà Eurufque Notufque ruunt,
        creberque procellis
    Africus.

And as Mr. Thyer adds, tho' fuch
ftorms

Though rooted deep as high, and sturdiest oaks
Bow'd their stiff necks; loaden with stormy blasts,
Or torn up sheer: ill wast thou shrouded then,
O patient Son of God, yet only stood'st   420
Unshaken; nor yet stay'd the terror there,
Infernal ghosts, and Hellish furies, round [shriek'd,
Environ'd thee, some howl'd, some yell'd, some
                                        Some

storms are unknown to us in these parts of the world, yet the accounts we have of hurricanes in the Indies agree pretty much with them.

417. *Though rooted deep as high,*] Virgil Georg. II. 291. Æn. IV. 445.

— quantum vertice ad auras
Æthereas, tantum radice in Tartara tendit.   *Richardson.*

420.   *—— yet only stood'st Unshaken ; &c.*] Milton seems to have raised this scene out of what he found in Eusebius de Dem. Evan. Lib. 9. [Vol. 2, p. 434. Ed. Col.] The learned father observes, that Christ was tempted forty days and the same number of nights —— Και επειδηπερ ημεραις τεσσαρακοντα, και ταις τοσαυταις νιξιν επειραζετο. And to these night temptations he applies what is said in the 91st Psalm, v. 5. and 6. Ου φοβηθηση απο φοβε νυκτερινε, Thou shalt not be afraid for any terror by night, — απο πραγματος εν σκοτει διαπορευομενου,

nor for the danger that walketh in darkness. The first is thus paraphras'd in the Targum, (tho' with a meaning very different from Eusebius's) Non timebis *à timore Dæmonum* qui ambulant in nocte. The Fiends *surround* our Redeemer with their threats and terrors; but they have no effect.

Infernal ghosts, and Hellish furies, round
Environ'd thee,

This too is from Eusebius, [ibid. p. 435.] Επειπερ εν τω πειραζειν δυναμεις πονηραι εκυκλουν αυτον. —— quoniam dum tentabatur, malignæ potestates *illum circumstabant.* And their repulse, it seems, is predicted in the 7th verse of this Psalm : *A thousand shall fall beside thee, and ten thousand at thy right hand, but it shall not come nigh thee.* Calton.

422. *Infernal ghosts,* &c] This taken from the legend or the pictures of St. Anthony's temptation.   *Warburton.*

This description is taken from a print which I have seen of the temptation of St. Anthony. *Jortin.*

Some bent at thee their fiery darts, while thou

Satſt unappall'd in calm and ſinleſs peace.   425

Thus paſs'd the night ſo foul, till morning fair

Came forth with pilgrim ſteps in amice gray,

Who with her radiant finger ſtill'd the roar

Of thunder, chas'd the clouds, and laid the winds,

And griſly ſpectres, which the Fiend had rais'd   430

To tempt the Son of God with terrors dire.

And now the ſun with more effectual beams

Had chear'd the face of earth, and dry'd the wet

From drooping plant, or dropping tree; the birds,

Who all things now behold more freſh and green,

After a night of ſtorm ſo ruinous,   436

Clear'd up their choiceſt notes in buſh and ſpray

To

---

426. —— *till morning fair Came forth* &c] As there is a ſtorm raiſed by evil Spirits in Taſſo as well as in Milton, ſo a fine morning ſucceeds after the one as well as after the other. See Taſſo Cant. 8. St. 1. But there the morning comes *with a forehead of roſe, and with a foot of gold; con la fronte di roſe, e co' piè d'oro* ; here *with pilgrim ſteps in amice gray*, as Milton deſcribes her progreſs more leiſurely, firſt the gray morning, and afterwards the ſun riſing : *with pilgrim ſteps*, with the ſlow ſolemn pace of a pilgrim on a journey of

devotion ; *in amice gray*, in gray cloathing ; *amice*, a proper and ſignificant word, derived from the Latin *amicio* to clothe, and uſed by Spenſer, Faery Queen. B. 1. Cant. 4 St. 18.

> Array'd in habit black, and
> *amice* thin,
> Like to an holy monk, the ſervice to begin.

428. *Who with her radiant finger ſtill'd the roar Of thunder, chas'd the clouds*, &c] This is a very pretty imitation of a paſſage in the firſt Æneid of Virgil,

To gratulate the sweet return of morn ;
Nor yet amidst this joy and brightest morn
Was absent, after all his mischief done,   440
The prince of darkness, glad would also seem
Of this fair change, and to our Saviour came,
Yet with no new device, they all were spent,
Rather by this his last affront resolv'd,
Desp'rate of better course, to vent his rage,   445
And mad despite to be so oft repell'd.
Him walking on a sunny hill he found,
Back'd on the north and west by a thick wood ;
Out of the wood he starts in wonted shape,
And in a careless mood thus to him said.   450
  Fair morning yet betides thee, Son of God,

After

---

gil, where Neptune is reprefented with his trident laying the ftorm which Æolus had raifed. ver. 142.

  Sic ait, et dicto citius tumida
    æquora placat,
  Collectafque fugat nubes, folemque reducit.

There is the greater beauty in the Englifh poet, as the fcene he is defcribing under this charming figure is perfectly confiftent with the courfe of nature, nothing being more common than to fee a ftormy night fucceeded by a pleafant ferene morning.   *Thyer.*

430. *And grifly fpectres,*] Very injudicious to retail this popular fuperftition in this place.
                              Warburton.

432. *And now the fun* &c] There is in this defcription all the bloom of Milton's youthful fancy. See an evening fcene of the fame kind in the Paradife Loft. II. 488.

  As when from mountain tops
    &c.   *Thyer.*

435. *Who all things now behold*] Doth not the fyntax require, that we fhould rather read
  Who all things now *beheld* — ?
                              453. *As*

After a difmal night ; I heard the wrack
As earth and fky would mingle ; but myfelf
Wasdiftant; and thefeflaws, though mortals fear them
As dang'rous to the pillar'd frame of Heaven,   455
Or to the earth's dark bafis underneath,
Are to the main as inconfiderable,
And harmlefs, if not wholefome, as a fneeze
To man's lefs univerfe, and foon are gone ;
Yet as being oft times noxious where they light   460
On man, beaft, plant, wafteful and turbulent,
Like turbulencies in th' affairs of men,
Over whofe heads they roar, and feem to point,
They oft fore-fignify and threaten ill :
This tempeft at this defert moft was bent ;   465
Of men at thee, for only thou here dwell'ft.
Did I not tell thee, if thou didft reject
The perfect feafon offer'd with my aid
To win thy deftin'd feat, but wilt prolong
All to the pufh of fate, purfue thy way   470
                                        Of

453. *As earth and fky would mingle* ;] Virgil Æn. I. 137.

Jam *cælum terramque*, meo fine numine, venti,

Mifcere, et tantas audetis tollere moles ?   *Richardfon.*

455. *As dang'rous to the pillar'd frame of Heaven*,] So alfo in the Mafk

— if

Of gaining David's throne no man knows when,

For both the when and how is no where told,

Thou fhalt be what thou art ordain'd, no doubt;

For angels have proclam'd it, but concealing

The time and means : each act is rightlieft done, 475

Not when it muft, but when it may be beft.

If thou obferve not this, be fure to find,

What I foretold thee, many a hard affay

Of dangers, and adverfities, and pains,

Ere thou of Ifrael's fcepter get faft hold ;   480

Whereof this ominous night that clos'd thee round,

So many terrors, voices, prodigies

May warn thee, as a fure fore-going fign.

　　So talk'd he while the Son of God went on

And ftay'd not, but in brief him anfwer'd thus. 485

　　Me worfe than wet thou find'ft not; other harm

Thofe terrors which thou fpeak'ft of, did me none ;

I never fear'd they could, though noifing loud

And threatning nigh ; what they can do as figns

　　　　　　　　　　　　　　　　　　　Betokening

―― if this fail,
The *pillar'd firmament* is rotten-
nefs.
In both, no doubt, alluding to Job
XXVI. 11. *The* pillars of Heaven

*tremble, and are aftonifh'd at his re-
proof.*　　Thyer.
　　467. *Did I not tell thee,* &c]
This fentence is dark and per-
plex'd, having no proper exit.
　　　　　　　　　　501. *Fer*

Betokening, or ill boding, I contemn   490
As falfe portents, not fent from God, but thee;
Who knowing I fhall reign paft thy preventing,
Obtrud'ft thy offer'd aid, that I accepting
At leaft might feem to hold all pow'r of thee,
Ambitious Spi'rit, and wouldft be thought my God,
And ftorm'ft refus'd, thinking to terrify   496
Me to thy will; defift, thou art difcern'd
And toil'ft in vain, nor me in vain moleft.

    To whom the Fiend now fwoln with rage reply'd.
Then hear, O Son of David, Virgin-born;   500
For Son of God to me is yet in doubt:
Of the Meffiah I have heard foretold
By all the Prophets; of thy birth at length
Announc'd by Gabriel with the firft I knew,
And of th' angelic fong in Bethlehem field,   505
On thy birth-night, that fung thee Saviour born.
From that time feldom have I ceas'd to eye

                                                              Thy

---

501. *For Son of God to me is yet in doubt:*] The Tempter had heard Chrift declar'd to be *Son of God* by a voice from Heaven. He allows him to be *virgin-born*. He hath no fcruples about the annunciation, and the truth of what Ga-briel told the bleffed woman (Luke I. 35. *The Holy Ghoft fhall come upon thee, and the power of the Higheft fhall overfhadow thee; therefore alfo that holy thing which fhall be born of thee fhall be called the Son of God.*) and yet he doubts of his being the
                                 Son

Thy infancy, thy childhood, and thy youth,
Thy manhood laſt, though yet in private bred;
Till at the ford of Jordan whither all   510
Flock'd to the Baptiſt, I among the reſt,
Though not to be baptiz'd, by voice from Heaven
Heard thee pronounc'd the Son of God belov'd.
Thenceforth I thought thee worth my nearer view
And narrower ſcrutiny, that I might learn   515
In what degree or meaning thou art call'd
The Son of God, which bears no ſingle ſenſe;
The Son of God I alſo am, or was,
And if I was, I am; relation ſtands;
All men are Sons of God; yet thee I thought   520
In ſome reſpect far higher ſo declar'd.
Therefore I watch'd thy footſteps from that hour,
And follow'd thee ſtill on to this waſte wild;
Where by all beſt conjectures I collect
Thou art to be my fatal enemy.   525

Good

Son of God notwithſtanding. This is eaſily accounted for. On the terms of the annunciation Chriſt might be the Son of God in a ſenſe very particular, and yet a mere man as to his nature: but the doubt relates to what he was more than man, worth calling Son of God, that is worthy to be called Son of God in that high and proper ſenſe, in which his ſonſhip would infer his divinity.   Calton.

538.—— what

Good reason then, if I before-hand feek

To underftand my adverfary, who

And what he is; his wifdom, pow'r, intent ;

By parl, or compofition, truce, or league

To win him, or win from him what I can.   530

And opportunity I here have had

To try thee, fift thee, and confefs have found thee

Proof againft all temptation, as a rock

Of adamant, and as a center, firm,

To th' utmoft of mere man both wife and good,   535

Not more ; for honors, riches, kingdoms, glory

Have been before contemn'd, and may again :

> Therefore

538 —— *what more thou art than man, Worth naming Son of God by voice from Heaven.*] See Bifhop Pearfon on the Creed. p. 106. " We muft find yet a more pe- " culiar ground of our Saviour's " filiation, totally diftinct from any " which belongs unto the reft of " the Sons of God, that he may " be clearly and fully acknow- " ledged the *only begotten Son.* " For altho' to be born of a vir- " gin be in itfelf miraculous, yet " is it not fo far above the pro- " duction of all mankind, as to " place him in that fingular emi- " nence, which muft be attributed " to the *only-begotten.* . We read

" of *Adam the Son of God* as well " as *Seth the Son of Adam :* Luke " III. 38. and furely the framing " Chrift out of a woman cannot " fo far tranfcend the making " Adam out of the earth, as to " caufe fo great a diftance, as we " muft believe, between the firft " and fecond Adam.   *Calton.*

541.   —— *and without wing Of hippogrif* &c] Here Milton defign'd a reflection upon the Ita- lian poets, and particularly upon Ariofto. An *hippogrif* is an ima- ginary creature, part like an horfe and part like a gryphon. See Orlando Furiofo Cant. 4. St. 18. or 13th Stanza of Harringtch's tranflation.

> Only

Therefore to know what more thou art than man,
Worth naming Son of God by voice from Heaven,
Another method I muſt now begin.   540
  So ſay'ing he caught him up, and without wing
Of hippogrif bore through the air ſublime
Over the wilderneſs and o'er the plain ;
Till underneath them fair Jeruſalem,
The holy city lifted high her towers,   545
And higher yet the glorious temple rear'd
Her pile, far off appearing like a mount
Of alabaſter, topt with golden ſpires :
There on the higheſt pinnacle he ſet

The

Only the beaſt he rode wꝰ not
  of art,
But gotten of a griffeth and a
  mare,
And like a griffeth had the for-
  mer part.
As wings and head, and claws
  that hideous are,
And paſſing ſtrength and force,
  and ventrous heart,
But all the reſt may with a horſe
  compare.
Such beaſts as theſe the hills of
  Ryfee yield,
Though in theſe parts they have
  been ſeen but ſeeld.

Arioſto frequently makes uſe of
this creature to convey his heroes

hither and thither ; but Milton
would inſinuate that he employ'd
no ſuch machinery.

  549. *There on the higheſt pinnacle
  he ſet*

  The Son of God,] He has choſen
to follow the order obſerved by
St. Luke in placing this temptation
laſt, becauſe if he had with St. Mat-
thew introduc'd it in the middle,
it would have broke that fine thred
of moral reaſoning, which is ob-
ſerved in the courſe of the other
temptations.   *Thyer.*
In the Goſpel account of the
temptation no diſcovery is made
of the incarnation ; and this grand
myſtery is as little known to the
Tempter at the end, as at the be-
ginning.

The Son of God, and added thus in fcorn.   550

There ftand, if thou wilt ftand ; to ftand upright
Will aſk thee ſkill ; I to thy Father's houſe
Have brought thee', and higheſt plac'd, higheſt is beſt,
Now ſhow thy progeny ; if not to ftand,
Caſt thyſelf down ; ſafely, if Son of God :   555

For

ginning. But now, according to Milton's ſcheme, the poem was to be clos'd with a full diſcovery of it : there are *three* circumſtances therefore, in which the poet, to ſerve his plan, hath varied from the accounts in the Goſpels. 1. The critics have not been able to aſcertain what the πτερύγιον or *pinnacle* (as we tranſlate it) was, on which Chriſt was ſet by the Demon : but whatever it was, the Evangeliſts make no difficulty of his ſtanding there. This the poet (following the common uſe of the word *pinnacle* in our own language) ſuppoſeth to be ſomething like thoſe on the battlements of our churches, a pointed ſpire, on which Chriſt could not ſtand without a miracle. 2. In the poem, the Tempter bids Chriſt give proof of his pretenſions by ſtanding on the pinnacle, or by caſting himſelf down. In the Goſpels, the laſt only is or could be ſuggeſted. 3. In the Goſpel account the prohibition *Thou ſhalt not tempt the Lord thy God* is alleged only as a reaſon why Chriſt (whoſe divinity is concealed there)

muſt not throw himſelf down from the top of the temple, becauſe this would have been *tempting God*. But in the poem it is applied to the Demon, and his attempt upon Chriſt ; who is thereby declared to be the *Lord his God.   Calton.*

561. *Tempt not the Lord thy God : he ſaid and ſtood :*] Here is what we may call after Ariſtotle the ἀναγνώρισις, or the diſcovery. Chriſt declares himſelf to be the God and Lord of the Tempter ; and to prove it, ſtands upon the pinnacle. This was evidently the poet's meaning. 1. The miracle ſhows it to be ſo ; which is otherwiſe impertinently introduc'd, and againſt the rule,

Nec Deus interſit, niſi dignus
   vindice nodus
Inciderit. ⸺

It proves nothing but what the Tempter knew, and allow'd before. 2. There is a connection between Chriſt's *ſaying* and *ſtanding*, which demonſtrates that he *ſtood*, in proof of ſomething he had *ſaid*. Now the prohibition, *Tempt not the Lord*

For it is written, He will give command
Concerning thee to his Angels, in their hands
They ſhall up lift thee, leſt at any time
Thou chance to daſh thy foot againſt a ſtone.
 To whom thus Jeſus; Alſo it is written,   560
Tempt not the Lord thy God: he ſaid and ſtood :

                                              But

Lord thy God, as alleged in the Goſpels from the Old Teſtament, was in no want of ſuch an atteſtation : but a miracle was wanting to juſtify the application of it to the Tempter's attack upon Chriſt ; it was for this end therefore that he ſtood.   *Calton.*
I cannot entirely approve this learned Gentleman's expoſition, for I am for underſtanding the words, *Alſo it is written Tempt not the Lord thy God*, in the ſame ſenſe, in which they were ſpoken in the Goſpels; becauſe I would not make the poem to differ from the Goſpel account, farther than neceſſity compels, or more than the poet himſelf has made it. The Tempter ſet our Saviour on a pinnacle of the temple, 'and there required of him a proof of his divinity, either by ſtanding, or by caſting himſelf down as he might ſafely do, if he was the Son of God, according to the quotation from the Pſalmiſt. To this our Saviour anſwers, as he anſwers in the Goſpels, *It is written again Thou ſhalt not tempt the Lord thy God*, tacitly inferring that his

caſting himſelf down would be tempting of God. *He ſaid*, he gave this reaſon for not caſting himſelf down, *and ſtood*. His *ſtanding* properly makes the diſcovery, and is the principal proof of his progeny that the Tempter requir'd : *Now ſhow thy progeny*. His *ſtanding* convinces Satan.   His *ſtanding* is conſidered as the diſplay of his divinity, and the immediate cauſe of Satan's *fall* ; and the grand contraſt is formed between the *ſtanding* of the one and the *fall* of the other.

—— He ſaid, and *ſtood :*
But Satan ſmitten with amazement *fell.*

and afterwards ver. 571.

Fell whence he ſtood to ſee his
          victor fall.

and ver. 576

So ſtruck with dread and anguiſh
    fell the Fiend.

and ver. 581.

So Satan *fell.*

        O 2   563. *As*

But Satan fmitten with amazement fell.

As when earth's fon Antæus (to compare

Small things with greateft) in Iraffa ftrove

With Jove's Alcides, and oft foil'd ftill rofe,   565

Receiving from his mother earth new ftrength,

Frefh from his fall, and fiercer grapple join'd,

Throttled at length in th' air, expir'd and fell;

So after many a foil the Tempter proud,

Renewing frefh affaults, amidft his pride   570

Fell whence he ftood to fee his victor fall.

And as that Theban monfter that propos'd

Her

---

563. *As when earth's fon Antæus*]
This fimile in the perfon of the poet
amazingly fine.   *Warburton.*

564.   —— *in Iraffa ftrove*
With Jove's Alcides,] *Iraffa* is a
place in Libya, mention'd by He-
rodotus, IV. 158. εϛι δε τῳ χωρῳ
τȣτῳ κιȣμα Ιϛασα, and from him
by Stephanus Byzant, who fays,
Ιϛασα, τοπ Λιϛνς, εις ον με-
τηγαγον Βατλον δι Λιϛυες, ὡς Ηϛο-
δοτ —— where Berkelius notes,
Hujus urbis quoque meminit Pin-
darus Pyth. IX. fed *duplicis* (read
duplici s) fcribitur:

Οιοι Λιϛυσσας αμ-
φι γυιαικ ιϛαν
Ιϛασσαν πϛ πυλιν Αϛιϛι-
ȣ, μετα καλλικομον
μιαϛηϛις αγακλια κȣϛαν.

Ad quem locum fic fcribit Scho-
liaftes: Ιϛασσα πολις Λιϛυης, ην
ωκησεν Αϛιϛι, ȣχ ὁ παλαισας
Ηϛακλει, εκειν γαϛ διαλλασσει
τοις χϛοιοις, ον και ανειλεν Ηϛα-
κλης. Pindarus nomen urbis genere
fœm. protulit, quod Schol. alio lo-
co numero multitudinis & genere
neut. effert: Ενιοι γαϛ φασιν, ὁτι
ὁ απο Ηϛακλεȣς καταγονισθεις
Αϛιϛι, Ιϛασσευς ην, απο Ιϛασ-
σων των εν τη Τϛιτωιιδι λιμιη, ὡς
φησι Φεϛεκυδης. From whence we
may obferve, that in Herodotus
and Stephanus, *Irafa* is the name
of a place, in Pindar and his Scho-
liaft, the name of a town: that the
name is *Irofa* in Herodotus, *Hirafa*
in Stephanus, (though perhaps it
fhould be *Iraja,* Ιϛασα, there)
Iraffa in Pindar and his Scholiaft:
that

Her riddle', and him who folv'd it not, devour'd,

That once found out and folv'd, for grief and fpite

Caft herfelf headlong from th' Ifmenian fteep;   575

So ftruck with dread and anguifh fell the Fiend,

And to his crew, that fat confulting, brought

Joylefs triumphals of his hop'd fuccefs,

Ruin, and defperation, and difmay,

Who durft fo proudly tempt the Son of God.   580

So Satan fell ; and ftrait a fiery globe

Of Angels on full fail of wing flew nigh,

Who on their plumy vans receiv'd him foft

From

that the Scholiaft fays, *Antæus* dwelt at *Iraffa*, not he who wreftled with *Hercules*, but one later than him; which, if true, makes againft Milton : that he afterwards adds, that according to the opinion of fome, the *Antæus* whom *Hercules* overcame was Ἰραϲϲευϲ, απο Ἰραϲϲωϲ, which Berkelius takes to be the genitive of τα Ἰραϲϲα, though it may be of ἁι Ἰραϲϲαι.   Jortin. *Antæus* dwelt at the city *Iraffa*, according to Pindar.   But it was not there that he wreftled with *Hercules*, but at *Lixos*, according to Pliny.   Lixos vel fabulofiffime antiquis narrata.   Ibi regia Antæi, certamenque cum Hercule.   Nat. Hift. Lib. 5. cap. 1. *Meadowcourt*.
    572. *And as that Theban monfter* &c] The Sphinx, whofe riddle be-

ing refolved by Oedipus, fhe threw herfelf into the fea. Statius Theb. I. 66.

    Si Sphingos iniquæ
    Callidus ambages te præmon-
ftrante refolvi.

    581. —— *and ftrait a fiery globe Of Angels* &c]   There is a peculiar foftnefs and delicacy in this defcription, and neither circumftances nor words could be better felected to give the reader an idea of the eafy and gentle defcent of our Saviour, and to take from the imagination that horror and uneafinefs which it is naturally fill'd with in contemplating the dangerous and uneafy fituation he was left in.
                                                      Thyer.
So Pfyche was carried down from
                O 3   the

From his uneafy ftation, and upbore
As on a floting couch through the blithe air,   585
Then in a flow'ry valley fet him down
On a green bank, and fet before him fpread
A table of celeftial food, divine,
Ambrofial fruits, fetch'd from the tree of life,
And from the fount of life ambrofial drink,   590
That foon refrefh'd him wearied, and repair'd
What hunger, if ought hunger had impair'd,
Or thirft; and as he fed, angelic quires
Sung heav'nly anthems of his victory
Over temptation, and the Tempter proud.   595

True

the rock by zephyrs, and laid
lightly on a green and flowry bank,
and there entertain'd with invifible
mufic. See Apuleius. Lib. IV.
                Richardfon.
  585. *As on a floting couch through
    the blithe air,*] Which way fo-
ever I turn this term *blithe*, it con-
veys no idea to me fuitable to the
place it occupies : nor do my dic-
tionaries aid me in the leaft. The
place is certainly corrupted, and
ought to run fo,

    —— through the *lithe* air.

Our author ufes the word in his
Paradife Loft in the fenfe requir'd
here,

        —— and wreath'd
His *lithe* probofcis. IV. 347.

I make no doubt of the certainty
of this conjecture.   *Sympfon.*
I queftion whether others will have
fo good an opinion of this emen-
dation, as the Gentleman feems to
entertain of it himfelf. I conceive
through the blithe air to be much
the fame as if he had faid *through
the glad air*, and the propriety of
fuch a metaphor wants no juftifica-
tion or explanation.

  593.   —— *angelic quires
Sung heav'nly anthems of his vic-
tory*] As Milton in his Para-
dife Loft had reprefented the Angels
finging triumph upon the Meffiah's
victory over the rebel Angels ; fo
here again with the fame propriety
they are defcribed celebrating his
                                    fuccefs

True Image of the Father, whether thron'd
In the bofom of blifs, and light of light
Conceiving, or remote from Heav'n, infhrin'd
In flefhly tabernacle, and human form,
Wand'ring the wildernefs, whatever place,   600
Habit, or ftate, or motion, ftill expreffing
The Son of God, with God-like force indued
Againft th' attempter of thy Father's throne,
And thief of Paradife ; him long of old
Thou didft debel, and down from Heaven caft 605
With all his army, now thou haft aveng'd
Supplanted Adam, and by vanquifhing

Temptation,

fuccefs againft temptation, and to
be fure he could not have poffibly
concluded his work with greater
dignity and folemnity, or more
agreeably to the rules of poetic de-
corum.   *Thyer.*

596. *True Image of the Father,*
&c]
    Cedite Romani fcriptores, cedite
    Graii.

All the poems that ever were writ-
ten, muft yield, even Paradife Loft
muft yield to Regain'd in the gran-
deur of its clofe. Chrift ftands
triumphant on the pointed emi-
nence. The Demon falls with
amazement and terror, on this full
proof of his being that very Son

of God, whofe thunder forced him
out of Heaven. The bleffed An-
gels receive new knowledge. They
behold a fublime truth eftablifh'd,
which was a fecret to them at the
beginning of the temptation ; and
the great difcovery gives a proper
opening to their hymn on the vic-
tory of Chrift, and the defeat of
the Tempter.   *Calton.*

600.   —— *whatever place,*
Habit, or ftate, or motion,] Pro-
bably not without allufion to Ho-
race Ep. I. XVII. 23.

    Omnis Ariftippum decuit color,
    et ftatus, et res.

605. *Thou didft debel*] Debellare
fuperbos. Virg. Æn. VI. 853.
O 4   619.—*like*

Temptation, haft regain'd loft Paradife ;

And fruftrated the conqueft fraudulent :

He never more henceforth will dare fet foot   610

In Paradife to tempt ; his fnares are broke :

For though that feat of earthly blifs be fail'd,

A fairer Paradife is founded now

For Adam and his chofen fons, whom thou

A Saviour art come down to re-inftall   615

Where they fhall dwell fecure, when time fhall be,,

Of

619. — *like an autumnal ftar Or lightning*] The poet does here, as in other places, imitate profane authors and Scripture both together. *Like an autumnal ftar,* Αςϊρ' οπωριϊῳ εναλιϊκιον. Iliad. V. 5. *Or like lightning fall from Heaven,* Luke X. 18. *I beheld Satan as lightning fall from Heaven.*

624. *Abaddon*] The name of the Angel of the bottomlefs pit. Rev. IX. 11. Here applied to the bottomlefs pit itfelf. In this concluding hymn of the Angels, the poet has taken fome pains, to fhow the fitnefs and propriety of giving the name of Paradife Regain'd to fo confin'd a fubject, as our Saviour's temptation. Confin'd as the fubject was, I make no queftion that he thought the Paradife Regain'd an epic poem as well as the Paradife Loft For in his invocation he undertakes

— to tell of deeds Above heroic:

and he had no notion that an epic poem muft of neceffity be formed after the example of Homer, and according to the precepts of Ariftotle. In the introduction to the fecond book of his *Reafon of Church-Government* he thus delivers his fentiments. " Time ferves not now, " and perhaps I might feem too " profufe to give any certain ac-" count of what the mind at home, " in the fpacious circuits of her " mufing, hath liberty to propofe " to herfelf, though of higheft " hope, and hardeft attempting ; " whether that epic form whereof " the two poems of Homer, and " thofe other two of Virgil and " I alfo are a diffufe, and the book " of Job a brief model : or whe-" ther the rules of Ariftotle here-" in are ftrictly to be kept, or na-" ture to be followed, which in " them that know art, and ufe " judgment, is no tranfgreffion, but " an enriching of art." We fee that

Of Tempter and temptation without fear.

But thou, infernal Serpent, fhalt not long

Rule in the clouds; like an autumnal ftar

Or lightning thou fhalt fall from Heav'n, trod down

Under his feet: for proof, ere this thou feel'ft   621

Thy wound, yet not thy laft and deadlieft wound,

By this repulfe receiv'd, and hold'ft in Hell

No triumph; in all her gates Abaddon rues

Thy bold attempt; hereafter learn with awe   625

To

that he look'd upon the book of Job, as a brief model of an epic poem: and the fubject of Paradife Regain'd is much the fame as that of the book of Job, a good man triumphing over temptation: and the greateft part of it is in dialogue as well as the book of Job, and abounds with moral arguments and reflections, which were more natural to that feafon of life, and better fuited Milton's age and infirmities than gay florid defcriptions. For by Mr. Elwood's account, he had not thought of the Paradife Regain'd, till after he had finifh'd the Paradife Loft: (See the Life of Milton) the firft hint of it was fuggefted by Elwood, while Milton refided at St. Giles Chalfont in Buckinghamfhire during the plague in London; and afterwards when Elwood vifited him in London, he fhow'd him the poem finifh'd, fo that he was not long in conceiving, or long in writing it:

and this is the reafon why in the Paradife Regain'd there are much fewer imitations of, and allufions to other authors, than in the Paradife Loft. The Paradife Loft he was long in meditating, and had laid in a large ftock of materials, which he had collected from all authors ancient and modern: but in the Paradife Regain'd he compofed more from memory, and with no other help from books, than fuch as naturally occurred to a mind fo thoroughly tinctur'd and feafon'd, as his was, with all kinds of learning. Mr. Thyer makes the fame obfervation, particularly with regard to the Italian poets. From the very few allufions, fays he, to the Italian poets in this poem one may draw, I think, a pretty conclufive argument for the reality of thofe pointed out in the notes upon Paradife Loft, and fhow that they are not, as fome may imagin, mere accidental coincidences

To dread the Son of God : he all unarm'd
Shall chace thee with the terror of his voice
From thy demoniac holds, poſſeſſion foul,
Thee and thy legions ; yelling they ſhall fly,
And beg to hide them in a herd of ſwine,   630

Left

dences of great geniuſes writing upon ſimilar ſubjects. Admitting them to be ſuch only, no tolerable reaſon can be aſſign'd why the ſame ſhould not occur in the ſame manner in the Paradiſe Regain'd : whereas upon the other ſuppoſition of their being real, the difference of the two poems in this reſpect is eaſily accounted for. It is very certain, that Milton form'd his firſt deſign of writing an epic poem very ſoon after his return from Italy, if not before, and highly probable that he then intended it after the Italian model, as he ſays, ſpeaking of this deſign in his *Reaſon of Church-Government*, that " he " apply'd himſelf to that reſolu- " tion which Arioſto follow'd a- " gainſt the perſuaſions of Bembo, " to fix all the art and induſtry he " could unite to the adorning of " his native tongue" — and again that he was then meditating " what " king or knight before the Con- " queſt might be choſen in whom " to lay the pattern of a Chriſtian " hero, as Taſſo gave to a prince " of Italy his choice, whether he " would command him to write of " Godfrey's expedition againſt the " Infidels, or Beliſarius againſt the

" Goths, or Charlemain againſt " the Lombards." This would naturally lead him to a frequent peruſal of the choiceſt wits of that country ; and altho' he dropt his firſt ſcheme, and was ſome conſiderable time before he executed the preſent work, yet ſtill the impreſſions he had firſt receiv'd would be freſh in his imagination, and he would of courſe be drawn to imitate their particular beauties, tho' he avoided following them in his general plan. The caſe was far otherwiſe when the Paradiſe Regain'd was compos'd. As Mr. Elwood informs us, Milton did not ſo much as think of it till he was advanced in years, and it is not very likely, conſidering the troubles and infirmities he had long labor'd under, that his ſtudies had been much employ'd about that time among the ſprightly Italians, or indeed any writers of that turn. Conſiſtent with this ſuppoſition we find it of a quite different ſtamp, and inſtead of alluſions to poets either ancient or modern, it is full of moral and philoſophical reaſonings, to which ſort of thoughts an afflicted old age muſt have turned our author's mind.

Left he command them down into the deep
Bound, and to torment fent before their time.
Hail Son of the moft high, heir of both worlds,
Queller of Satan, on thy glorious work
Now enter, and begin to fave mankind.   635
   Thus they the Son of God our Saviour meek
Sung victor, and from heav'nly feaft refrefh'd
Brought on his way with joy ; he unobferv'd
Home to his mother's houfe private return'd.

T H E   E N D.

F. Hayman inv.

C. Grignion sculp

SAMSON AGONISTES,

A

DRAMATIC POEM.

The AUTHOR

JOHN MILTON.

Ariſtot. Poet. Cap. 6.

Τραγωδια μιμησις πραξεως σπεδαιας, &c.

Tragœdia eſt imitatio actionis feriæ, &c. per miſeri-
cordiam et metum perficiens talium affectuum
luſtrationem.

Of that fort of Dramatic Poem which is called Tragedy.

TRAGEDY, as it was anciently compos'd, hath been ever held the graveft, moraleft, and moft profitable of all other poems : therefore faid by Ariftotle to be of power by raifing pity and fear, or terror, to purge the mind of thofe and fuch like paffions, that is, to temper and reduce them to juft meafure with a kind of delight, ftirr'd up by reading or feeing thofe paffions well imitated. Nor is Nature wanting in her own effects to make good his affertion : for fo in phyfic things of melancholic hue and quality are us'd againft melancholy, four againft four, falt to remove falt humors. Hence philofophers and other graveft writers, as Cicero, Plutarch and others, frequently cite out of tragic poets, both to adorn and illuftrate their difcourfe. The Apoftle Paul himfelf thought it not unworthy to infert * a verfe of Euripides into the text of Holy Scripture, 1 Cor. XV. 33. and Paræus commenting on the Revelation, divides the whole book as a tragedy, into acts diftinguifh'd each by a chorus of heavenly harpings and fong between. Heretofore men in higeft dignity have labor'd not a little to be thought able to compofe a tragedy. Of that honor Dionyfius the elder was no lefs ambitious, than before of his attaining to the tyranny. Auguftus Cæfar alfo had begun his Ajax, but unable to pleafe his own judgment with what he had begun, left it unfinifh'd. Seneca the philofopher is by fome thought the author of thofe tragedies (at leaft the beft of them) that go under that name. Gregory Nazianzen, a Father of the Church, thought it not unbefeeming the fanctity of his

---

* *a verfe of Euripides*] The verfe here quoted is *Evil communications corrupt good manners:* but I am inclin'd to think that Milton is miftaken in calling it a verfe of *Euripides*; for Jerome and Grotius (who publifh'd the fragments of Menander) and the beft commentators, ancient and modern, fay that it is taken from the Thais of *Menander*, and it is extant among the fragments of Menander. p. 79. Le Clerc's Edit.

Φθείρεσιν ήθη χρησθ' ομιλίαι κακαι.

Such flips of memory may be found fometimes in the beft writers. As we obferved before, Diodorus Siculus cites Eupolis inftead of Ariftophanes.

perfon

perfon to write a tragedy, which is intitled *Chrift fuffering*. This is mention'd to vindicate tragedy from the fmall efteem, or rather infamy, which in the account of many it undergoes at this day with other common interludes ; hap'ning through the poets error of intermixing comic ftuff with tragic fadnefs and gravity ; or introducing trivial and vulgar perfons, which by all judicious hath been counted abfurd ; and brought in without difcretion, corruptly to gratify the people. And though ancient tragedy ufe no prologue, yet ufing fometimes, in cafe of felf-defenfe, or explanation, that which Martial calls an epiftle ; in be-half of this tragedy coming forth after the ancient manner, much different from what among us paffes for beft, thus much before-hand may be epiftled ; that chorus is here in-troduc'd after the Greek manner, not ancient only but mo-dern, and ftill in ufe among the Italians. In the modeling therefore of this poem, with good reafon, the Ancients and Italians are rather follow'd, as of much more authority and fame. The meafure of verfe us'd in the chorus is of all forts, call'd by the Greeks Monoftrophic, or rather Apolelymenon, without regard had to Strophe, Antiftrophe, or Epod, which were a kind of ftanza's fram'd only for the mufic, then us'd with the chorus that fung; not effential to the poem, and therefore not material ; or being divided into ftanza's or paufes, they may be call'd Allæoftropha. Divifion into act and fcene referring chiefly to the ftage (to which this work never was intended) is here omitted.

It fuffices if the whole drama be found not produc'd be-yond the fifth act. Of the ftile and uniformity, and that commonly call'd the plot, whether intricate or explicit, which is nothing indeed but fuch œconomy, or difpofition of the fable as may ftand beft with verfimilitude and deco-rum ; they only will beft judge who are not unacquainted with Æfchylus, Sophocles, and Euripides, the three tragic poets unequal'd yet by any, and the beft rule to all who en-devor to write tragedy. The circumfcription of time, where-in the whole drama begins and ends, is according to ancient rule, and beft example, within the fpace of 24 hours.

THE ARGUMENT.

Samſon made captive, blind, and now in the priſon at Gaza, there to labor as in a common work-houſe, on a feſtival day, in the general ceſſation from labor, comes forth into the open air to a place nigh, ſomewhat retir'd, there to ſit a while and bemoan his condition. Where he happens at length to be viſited by certain friends and equals of his tribe, which make the Chorus, who ſeek to comfort him what they can ; then by his old father Manoah, who endevors the like, and withal tells him his purpoſe to procure his liberty by ranſome ; laſtly, that this feaſt was proclamed by the Philiſtines as a day of thankſgiving for their deliverance from the hands of Samſon, which yet more troubles him. Manoah then departs to proſecute his endevor with the Philiſtian lords for Samſon's redemption ; who in the mean while is viſited by other perſons ; and laſtly by a public officer to require his coming to the feaſt before the lords and people, to play or ſhow his ſtrength in their preſence ; he at firſt refuſes, diſmiſſing the public officer with abſolute denial to come ; at length perſuaded inwardly that this was from God, he yields to go along with him, who came now the ſecond time with great threatnings to fetch him : the Chorus yet remaining on the place, Manoah returns full of joyful hope, to procure ere long his ſon's deliverance ; in the midſt of which diſcourſe an Hebrew comes in haſte, confuſedly at firſt, and afterward more diſtinctly relating the cataſtrophe, what Samſon had done to the Philiſtines, and by accident to himſelf ; wherewith the tragedy ends.

THE PERSONS.

Samson.

Manoah, the Father of Samſon.

Dalila, his Wife.

Harapha of Gath.

Public Officer.

Meſſenger.

Chorus of Danites.

The Scene before the Priſon in Gaza.

SAMSON AGONISTES.

SAMSON.

A Little onward lend thy guiding hand
To thefe dark fteps, a little further on;
For yonder bank hath choice of fun or fhade :
There I am wont to fit, when any chance
Relieves me from my tafk of fervile toil,   5
Daily' in the common prifon elfe injoin'd me,
Where I a prifoner chain'd, fcarce freely draw
The air imprifon'd alfo, clofe and damp,
Unwholefome draught : but here I feel amends,

The

Samfon Agonifles]The fubject but a very indifferent one for a dramatic fable. However he has made the beft of it. He feems to have chofen it for the fake of the fatire on bad wives.   *Warburton.*

Samfon Agonifles] That is Samfon an actor, Samfon reprefented in a play. Αγωνιςης, ludio, hiftrio, actor fcenicus.

Samfon] Milton after the example of the Greek tragedians, whom he profeffes to imitate, opens his drama with introducing one of its principal perfonages explaining the ftory upon which it is founded.   *Thyer.*

1. *A little onward lend thy guiding hand*

To thefe dark fteps.] So Tirefias in Euripides, Phœniffæ ver. 841.

Ηγε προπαροιθε θυγατερ, ως τυφλω ποδ. &c.   *Richardfon.*

3. *For yonder bank*] The fcene of this tragedy is much the fame as that of the Ο δι πους επι κολωιω in Sophocles, where blind Oedipus is conducted in like manner, and reprefented fitting upon a little hill near Athens : but yet I think there is fcarcely a fingle thought the fame in the two pieces, and I am fure the Greek tragedy can have no pretence to be efteemed better, but only becaufe it is two thoufand years older.

The breath of Heav'n frefh blowing, pure and fweet,

With day-fpring born; here leave me to refpire. 11

This day a folemn feaft the people hold

To Dagon their fea-idol, and forbid

Laborious works; unwillingly this reft

Their fuperftition yields me; hence with leave 15

Retiring from the popular noife, I feek

This unfrequented place to find fome eafe,

Eafe to the body fome, none to the mind

From reftlefs thoughts, that like a deadly fwarm

Of hornets arm'd, no fooner found alone, 20

But rufh upon me thronging, and prefent

Times paft, what once I was, and what am now.

O wherefore was my birth from Heav'n foretold

Twice by an Angel, who at laft in fight

Of both my parents all in flames afcended 25

From

13. *To Dagon their fea-idol.*] For
Milton both here and in the Para-
dife Loft follows the opinion of
thofe, who defcribe this idol as
part man, part fifh. l. 462.

    Dagon his name, fea monfter,
      upward man
    And downward fifh.

24. *Twice by an Angel,*] Once
to his mother, and again to his fa-
ther Manoah and his mother both,

and the fecond time the Angel
afcended in the flame of the altar.
Judges XIII. 3, 11, 20.

    28. —— *and from fome great act,*]
Mr. Sympfon fays that the true
reading is

    —— *as* from fome great act:

but the poet would hardly fay *As* in
a fiery column &c *as* from fome
great act &c; and therefore we may
retain *and*, and *as* may be under-
ftood

From off the altar, where an offering burn'd,
As in a fiery column charioting
His god-like prefence, and from fome great act
Or benefit reveal'd to Abraham's race?
Why was my breeding order'd and prefcrib'd   30
As of a perfon feparate to God,
Defign'd for great exploits; if I muft die
Betray'd, captiv'd, and both my eyes put out,
Made of my enemies the fcorn and gaze;
To grind in brazen fetters under tafk   35
With this Heav'n-gifted ftrength? O glorious ftrength
Put to the labor of a beaft, debas'd
Lower than bondflave! Promife was that I
Should Ifrael from Philiftian yoke deliver;
Afk for this great deliverer now, and find him   40
Eyelefs in Gaza at the mill with flaves,

Himfelf

ftood tho' not exprefs'd *As in a fiery column charioting &c, and as from fome great act &c.*

33. *Betray'd, captiv'd,*] It fhould be pronounced with the accent upon the laft fyllable, as afterwards ver. 694.

To dogs and fowls a prey, or elfe *captiv'd.*

I think we commonly pronounce it with the accent upon the firft

fyllable *cáptiv'd*: but our old authors give it the fame pronunciation as Milton. Spenfer. Faery Queen. B. 2. Cant. 4. St. 16.

Thus when as Guyon Furor had
   captiv'd:

and B. 3. Cant. 1. St. 2.

But the *captiv'd* Aerafia he fent:

and Fairfax Cant. 19. S. 95.

Free was Erminia, but *captiv'd*
   her heart.

P 3   53. *But*

Himfelf in bonds under Philiftian yoke :
Yet ftay, let me not rafhly call in doubt
Divine prediction ; what if all foretold
Had been fulfill'd but through mine own default,
Whom have I to complain of but myfelf ?   46
Who this high gift of ftrength committed to me,
In what part lodg'd, how eafily bereft me,
Under the feal of filence could not keep,
But weakly to a woman muft reveal it,   50
O'ercome with importunity and tears.
O impotence of mind, in body ftrong !
But what is ftrength without a double fhare
Of wifdom, vaft, unwieldy, burdenfome,
Proudly fecure, yet liable to fall   55
By weakeft fubtleties, not made to rule,
But to fubferve where wifdom bears command !
God, when he gave me ftrength, to fhow withal
How flight the gift was, hung it in my hair.
But peace, I muft not quarrel with the will   60
                                          Of

53. *But what is ftrength without
    a double fhare
Of wifdom,* &c] Ovid. Met. XIII.
363.
     Tu vires fine mente geris —
     — tu tantum corpore prodes,

Nos animo; quantoque ratem qui
    temperat &c.   *Jortin.*

Hor. Od. III. IV. 65.

Vis confili expers mole ruit fua.
                         Richardfon.
                         69.—*or*

SAMSON AGONISTES. 215

Of higheſt diſpenſation, which herein
Haply had ends above my reach to know:
Suffices that to me ſtrength is my bane,
And proves the ſource of all my miſeries;
So many, and ſo huge, that each apart   65
Would aſk a life to wail, but chief of all,
O loſs of fight, of thee I moſt complain!
Blind among enemies, O worſe than chains,
Dungeon, or beggery, or decrepit age!
Light the prime work of God to me' is extinct,   70
And all her various objects of delight
Annull'd, which might in part my grief have eas'd,
Inferior to the vileſt now become
Of man or worm; the vileſt here excel me,
They creep, yet ſee, I dark in light expos'd   75
To daily fraud, contempt, abuſe and wrong,
Within doors, or without, ſtill as a fool,
In pow'r of others, never in my own;
Scarce half I ſeem to live, dead more than half.

O

69. —— *or decrepit age!*] So it is printed in the firſt edition; the later editors have omitted *or*, concluding I ſuppoſe that it made the verſe a ſyllable too long. Mr. Calton propoſes to read

—— beggery *in* decrepit age!

Want join'd to the weakneſſes of helpleſs age, ſays he, would render it a very real miſery.

P 4   87. *And*

O dark, dark, dark, amid the blaze of noon,　　80
Irrecoverably dark, total eclipse
Without all hope of day !
O firſt created beam, and thou great Word,
Let there be light, and light was over all ;
Why am I thus bereav'd thy prime decree ?　　85
The ſun to me is dark
And ſilent as the moon,
When ſhe deſerts the night
Hid in her vacant interlunar cave.
Since light ſo neceſſary is to life,　　90
And almoſt life itſelf, if it be true

That

87. *And ſilent as the moon*, &c]
There cannot be a better note on
this paſſage than what Mr. War-
burton has written on this verſe
of Shakeſpear 2 Henry VI. Act I.
Sc. 8.

　Deep night, dark night, the ſi-
　lent of the night.

The ſilent of the night is a claſſical
expreſſion, and means an interlu-
nar night —— *amica ſilentia lunæ.*
So Pliny, Inter omnes verò con-
venit, utiliſſime in coitu ejus ſterni,
quem diem alii *interlunii,* alii *ſilen-
tis* lunæ appellant. Lib. 16. cap. 39.
In imitation of this language, Mil-
ton ſays,

　The ſun to me is dark,

And *ſilent* as the moon,
When ſhe deſerts the night
Hid in her vacant *interlunar* cave.

89. *Hid in her vacant interlunar
cave.*] *Silens luna* is the moon
at or near the change, and in con-
junction with the ſun. Plin. 1. Lib.
16. c. 39. The interlunar cave is
here called *vacant,* quia luna ibi
vacat opere et miniſterio ſuo, be-
cauſe the moon is idle, and uſeleſs,
and makes no return of light.
　　　　　　　　　Meadowcourt.
Alluding, I ſuppoſe to the ſame
notion, which he has adopted from
Heſiod in his Paradiſe Loſt. VI. 4.
　—— There is a cave
　Within the mount of God, faſt
　by his throne,

　　。　Where

That light is in the foul,

She all in every part; why was the fight

To fuch a tender ball as th' eye confin'd,

So obvious and fo eafy to be quench'd ? 95

And not as feeling through all parts diffus'd,

That fhe might look at will through every pore ?

Then had I not been thus exil'd from light,

As in the land of darknefs, yet in light,

To live a life half dead, a living death, 100

And bury'd ; but O yet more miferable !

Myfelf my fepulchre, a moving grave,

Bury'd, yet not exempt

By

Where light and darknefs in per-
petual round
Lodge and diflodge by turns.
See the note on this place. *Thyer.*

90. *Since light fo neceffary is to
life, &c.*] This intermixing of
his philofophy very much weakens
the force and pathos of Samfon's
complaint, which in the main is
excellent, but I think not altoge-
ther fo fine as the poet's lamenta-
tion of his own blindnefs at the
beginning of the third book of the
Paradife Loft ; fo much better does
every body write from his own
feeling and experience, than when
he imagines only what another
would fay upon the fame occafion.
100. *To live a life half dead, a*

living death,] The fame thought
occurs in the following paffage of
Euripides, Supp. 966.

Και νυν απαις, ατικι⊙·
Γηρασκω δυσηνοτατ⊙·,
Ουτ' εν τοις φθιμενοις,
Ουτ' εν ζωσιν αριθμυμενη,
Χωρις δη τινα τωνδ' ισχυσα μοι-
ραν.

So alfo in Sophocles, Antig. 1283.

———— τας γαρ ηδονας
'Οταν προδωσιν ανδρες, 8 τιθημ'
εγω
Ζην τυτον, αλλ' εμψυχον ηγε-
μαι νεκρον.   Thyer.

102. *Myfelf my fepulchre, a mov-
ing grave,*] This thought is not
very

By privilege of death and burial
From worſt of other evils, pains and wrongs,   105
But made hereby obnoxious more
To all the miſeries of life,
Life in captivity
Among inhuman foes.
But who are theſe? for with joint pace I hear   110
The tread of many feet ſteering this way;
Perhaps my enemies, who come to ſtare
At my affliction, and perhaps t' inſult,
Their daily practice to afflict me more.

CHORUS.

This, this is he ; ſoftly a while,   115
Let us not break in upon him ;
O change beyond report, thought, or belief!
See how he lies at random, careleſly diffus'd,
With languiſh'd head unprop,

As

very unlike that of Gorgias Le-
ontinus, who called vultures *living
ſepulchres,* γυπες εμψυχοι ταφοι,
for which he incurred the in-
dignation of Longinus ; whether
juſtly or no I ſhall not ſay.
        Jortin.

111. —— *ſteering this way ;*] If
this be the right reading, the meta-
phor is extremely hard and abrupt.

A common man would have ſaid
bearing this way.   Warburton.

118. *See how he lies at random,
     careleſly diffus'd,*] This beauti-
ful application of the word *diffus'd*
Milton has borrow'd from the
Latins.   So Ovid ex Ponto. III.
III. 7.
  Publica me requies curarum ſom-
    nus habebat,
                        Fuſaque

As one paſt hope, abandon'd, 120
And by himſelf given over ;
In ſlaviſh habit, ill-fitted weeds
O'er-worn and ſoil'd ;
Or do my eyes miſrepreſent ? Can this be he,
That heroic, that renown'd, 125
Irreſiſtible Sampſon ? whom unarm'd
No ſtrength of man, or fierceſt wild beaſt could
   withſtand ;
Who tore the lion, as the lion tears the kid,
Ran on imbattel'd armies clad in iron,
And weaponleſs himſelf, 130
Made arms ridiculous, uſeleſs the forgery
Of brazen ſhield and ſpear, the hammer'd cuiraſs,
Chaly'bean temper'd ſteel, and frock of mail
Adamantean proof ;
But ſafeſt he who ſtood aloof, 135
                                          When

Fuſaque erant toto languida
membra toro.   *Thyer.*

133. *Chaly'bean temper'd ſteel,*]
That is, the beſt temper'd ſteel by
the *Chalybes,* who were famous
among the Ancients for their iron
works. Virg. Georg. I. 58.

   At Chalybes nudi ferrum ——

The adjective ſhould be pronounc'd

Chalybéan with the third ſyllable
long according to Heinſius's read-
ing of that verſe of Ovid. Faſt. IV.
405.

   Æs erat in pretio : Chalybeïa
      maſſa latebat :

but Milton makes it ſhort by the
ſame poetical liberty, with which
he had before uſed *Ægéan* for
Ægéanſ and *Thyéſtean* for *Thyéſtéan.*
136. *When*

When infupportably his foot advanc'd,
In fcorn of their proud arms and warlike tools,
Spurn'd them to death by troops. The bold Afcalonite
Fled from his lion ramp, old warriors turn'd
Their plated backs under his heel;   140
Or grov'ling foil'd their crefted helmets in the duft.
Then with what trivial weapon came to hand,
The jaw of a dead afs, his fword of bone,
A thoufand fore-fkins fell, the flow'r of Paleftine, 144
In Ramath-lechi famous to this day.   [bore
Then by main force pull'd up, and on his fhoulders
The gates of Azza, poft, and maffy bar,
Up to the hill by Hebron, feat of giants old,

                                                        No

136. *When infupportably his foot advanc'd,*] For this nervous expreffion Milton was probably indebted to the following lines of Spenfer. Faery Queen, B. 1. Cant. 7. St. 11.

That when the knight he fpy'd, he 'gan *advance*
With huge force, and *infupportable* main.   *Thyer.*

138. *The bold Afcalonite*] The inhabitant of *Afcalon*, one of the five principal cities of the Philiftines, mention'd 1. Sam. VI. 17.

145. *In Ramath-lechi famous to this day:*] Judges XV. 17.—

he caft away the jaw-bone out of his hand, and called that place Ramath-lechi, that is, *the lifting up of the jaw-bone*, or *cafting away of the jaw-bone*, as it is render'd in the margin of our bibles.

147. *The gates of Azza.*] If the poet did not think the alliteration too great, he poffibly would have wrote

    The gates of *Gaza.*

So he does within fix lines of the end of this play,

—— whence *Gaza* mourns.

I can't help remarking the great difference

No journey of a fabbath-day, and loaded fo ;
Like whom the Gentiles feign to bear up Heaven.
Which fhall I firft bewail   151
Thy bondage or loft fight,
Prifon within prifon
Infeparably dark ?
Thou art become (O worft imprifonment !)   155
The dungeon of thyfelf ; thy foul
(Which men enjoying fight oft without caufe com-   [plain)
Imprifon'd now indeed,
In real darknefs of the body dwells,
Shut up from outward light   160
T' incorporate with gloomy night ;

For

difference there is betwixt Ben
Johnfon's Chorus's, and our au-
thor's. Old Ben's are of a poor
fimilar regular contexture ; our au-
thor's truly Grecian, and noble,
diverfified with all the meafures
our language and poetry are ca-
paple of, and I am afraid not to be
read in the manner Milton defign'd
them.   *Sympfon.*
147. —— *poft*, *and maffy bar*,]
Mr. Meadowcourt propofes to read
pofts, as being more conformable
to Scripture, Judg. XVI. 3. *And
Samfon lay till midnight, and arofe at
midnight, and took the doors of the
gate of the city, and the* two pofts,

*and went away with them, bar and
all :* and *pofts* is certainly better on
this account, but perhaps Milton
might prefer *poft* as fomewhat of a
fofter found.
148. —— *Hebron, feat of giants
old,*] For Hebron was the city
of Arba, the father of Anak, and
the feat of the Anakims. Jofh. XV.
13, 14. And the Anakims were
giants, which come of the giants.
Numb. XIII. 33.
157. —— *oft without caufe com-
plain*] So Milton himfelf cor-
rected it, but all the editions con-
tinue the old erratum *complain'd.*

For inward light alas

Puts forth no vifual beam.

O mirror of our fickle ftate,

Since man on earth unparallel'd !   165

The rarer thy example ftands,

By how much from the top of wondrous glory,

Strongeft of mortal men,

To loweft pitch of abject fortune thou art fall'n.

For him I reckon not in high eftate   170

Whom long defcent of birth

Or the fphere of fortune raifes ;

But thee whofe ftrength, while virtue was her mate,

Might have fubdued the earth,

Univerfally

162. *For inward light alas*
Puts forth no vifual beam.] The expreffion is fine, and means the *ray of light*, which occafions *vifion.* Mr. Pope borrow'd the expreffion in one of his juvenile poems,

He from thick films fhall purge
the *vifual ray,*
And on the fightlefs eye-ball pour
the day.

Either he miftook his original, and fuppofed Milton meant by *vifual ray* the *fight,* or at leaft thought himfelf at liberty to ufe it in that highly figurative fenfe. See what is faid on the paffage in the laft edition of Mr. Pope's works.
Warburton.

172. *Or the fphere of fortune raifes* ;] Fortune is painted on a globe, which by her influence is in a perpetual rotation on its axis.   *Warburton.*

178. *He fpeaks,*] We have follow'd Milton's own edition ; moft of the others have it *He fpake.*

181. *From Efhtaol and Zora's fruitful vale*] Thefe were two towns of the tribe of Dan. Jofh. XIX. 41. the latter the birth-place of Samfon Judg. XIII. 2. and they were near one another. *And the Spirit of the Lord began to move him at times in the camp of Dan between Zorah and Efhtaol,* Judg. XIII. 25. And they were both fituated *in the valley,* Jofh. XV. 33. and

Univerfally crown'd with higheft praifes.   175

SAMSON.

I hear the found of words, their fenfe the air
Diffolves unjointed ere it reach my ear.

CHORUS.

He fpeaks, let us draw nigh. Matchlefs in might,
The glory late of Ifrael, now the grief;
We come thy friends and neighbours not unknown
From Efhtaol and Zora's fruitful vale   181
To vifit or bewail thee, or if better,
Counfel or confolation we may bring,
Salve to thy fores; apt words have pow'r to fwage
The tumors of a troubled mind,   185

And

and therefore the poet with great
exactnefs fays *Efhtaol and Zora's
fruitful vale.*

182. *To vifit or bewail thee,*] The
poet dictated

To vifit *and* bewail thee:

The purpofe of their vifit was to
bewail him; or *if better*, (that is if
they found it more proper) to *ad-
vife* or *comfort* him. Veniebat au-
tem ad Eumenem utrumque genus
hominum, et qui propter odium
*fructum oculis ex ejus cafu capere vel-
lent*, [See above ver. 112. *to ftare
at my affliction*] et qui propter vete-
rem amicitiam *colloqui confolarique
cuperent.* Corn. Nepos in vita Eu-
menis.   *Calton.*

184. —— *apt words have pow'r
to fwage &c*] Alluding to thefe
lines in Æfchylus. Prom. Vinct.
377.

Ουκ̄ν Προμηθευ τ̄το γινωσκεις,
ὁτι

Οργης ιοσ̄σης εισιν ιατροι λογοι.

Or to this paffage in Menander.

Λογ☉ γαρ εςι λυπης φαρμακον
μονον.   Thyer.

Or perhaps to Horace, Epift. I.
I. 34.

Sunt verba et voces, quibus hunc
  lenire dolorem
Poffis, et magnam morbi depo-
  nere partem.

195. *Yet*

And are as balm to fefter'd wounds.

SAMSON.

Your coming, Friends, revives me, for I learn
Now of my own experience, not by talk,
How counterfeit à coin they are who friends
Bear in their fuperfcription, (of the moft   190
I would be underftood) in profp'rous days
They fwarm, but in adverfe withdraw their head,
Not to be found though fought. Ye fee, O Friends,
How many evils have inclos'd me round;   194
Yet that which was the worft now leaft afflicts me,
Blindnefs, for had I fight, confus'd with fhame,
How could I once look up, or heave the head,
Who like a foolifh pilot have fhipwrack'd

My

195. *Yet that which was the worft now leaft afflicts me,*] There is no inconfiftence in this with what he had faid before ver. 66.

—— but chief of all,
O lofs of fight, of thee I moft complain.

When he was by himfelf, he con-fider'd his blindnefs as the *worft* of evils ; but *now*, upon his friends coming in and feeing him in this wretched condition, it *leaft afflicts me*, fays he, as being fome cover to his fhame and confufion.

210. *Tax not divine difpofal* ; &c] As this whole play, fo particularly

the part of the Chorus is written in the very fpirit of the Ancients, and is formed exactly according to the precepts of Horace. De Arte Poet. 193.

Actoris partes Chorus, officium-que virile
Defendat ; neu quid medios in-tercinat actus,
Quod non propofito conducat et hæreat apte.
Ille bonis faveatque, et concilie-tur amicis ;
Et regat iratos, et amet pacare tumentes :

Ille

My veſſel truſted to me from above,
Glorioúſly rigg'd ; and for a word, a tear,   200
Fool, have divulg'd the ſecret gift of God
To a deceitful woman ? tell me, Friends,
Am I not ſung and proverb'd for a fool
In every ſtreet ? do they not ſay, how well
Are come upon him his deſerts ? yet why ?   205
Immeaſurable ſtrength they might behold
In me, of wiſdom nothing more than mean ;
This with the other ſhould, at leaſt, have pair'd,
Theſe two proportion'd ill drove me tranſverſe.

CHORUS.

Tax not divine diſpoſal ; wiſeſt men   210
Have err'd, and by bad women been deceiv'd ;

And

Ille dapes laudet menſæ brevis ;
ille ſalubrem
Juſtitiam, legeſque, et apertis
otia portis :
Ille tegat commiſſa, Deoſque
precetur et oret,
Ut redeat miſeris, abeat fortuna
ſuperbis.

The Chorus muſt ſupport an ac-
tor's part ;
Defend the virtuous, and adviſe
with art ;
Govern the choleric, the proud
appeaſe,
And the ſhort feaſts of frugal
tables praiſe ;

The laws and juſtice of well-
govern'd ſtates,
And peace triumphant with her
open gates.
Intruſted ſecrets let them ne'er
betray,
But to the righteous Gods with
ardor pray,
That fortune with returning
ſmiles may bleſs
Afflicted worth, and impious
pride depreſs.
Yet let their ſongs with apt co-
herence join,
Promote the plot, and aid the
main deſign.   · *Francis.*

And fhall again, pretend they ne'er fo wife.

Dejeƈt not then fo overmuch thyfelf,

Who haft of forrow thy full load befides ;

Yet truth to fay, I oft have heard men wonder   215

Why thou fhouldft wed Philiftian women rather

Than of thy own tribe fairer, or as fair,

At leaft of thy own nation, and as noble.

SAMSON.

The firft I faw at Timna, and fhe pleas'd

Me, not my parents, that I fought to wed   220

The daughter of an infidel : they knew not

That what I motion'd was of God ; I knew

From intimate impulfe, and therefore urg'd

The marriage on ; that by occafion hence

I might begin Ifrael's deliverance,   225

The work to which I was divinely call'd.

She proving falfe, the next I took to wife

(O that I never had ! fond wifh too late,)

Was

Such is the charaƈter and office of the Chorus, as prefcrib'd by this great critic and poet, and it was never exemplified more fully than in the Chorus of Milton.

216. — *Philiftian women rather*] So it is printed in Milton's own edition, and *woman* is a miftake of the other editions ; for more than one are mention'd afterwards. *The*

firft I faw at Timna &c. ver. 219. *the next I took to wife* &c. ver. 227.

219. *The firft I faw at Timna,*] Judg. XIV. 1. *And Samfon went down to Timnath, and faw a woman in Timnath of the daughters of the Philiftines.* &c.

222. *That what I motion'd was of God ;*] It was printed *mention'd* which is fenfe indeed, but Milton

Was in the vale of Sorec, Dalila,
That ſpecious monſter, my accompliſh'd ſnare. 230
I thought it lawful from my former act,
And the ſame end; ſtill watching to oppreſs
Iſrael's oppreſſors : of what now I ſuffer
She was not the prime cauſe, but I myſelf,
Who vanquiſh'd with a peal of words (O weakneſs !)
Gave up my fort of ſilence to a woman. 236

CHORUS.

In ſeeking juſt occaſion to provoke
The Philiſtine, thy country's enemy,
Thou never waſt remiſs, I bear thee witneſs :
Yet Iſraël ſtill ſerves with all his ſons. 240

SAMSON.

That fault I take not on me, but transfer
On Iſrael's governors, and heads of tribes,
Who ſeeing thoſe great acts, which God had done
Singly by me againſt their conquerors,

Acknow-

Milton himſelf in the table of Er-
rata ſubſtituted *motion'd* which is
better : but the firſt error hath ſtill
prevailed in all the editions.
229. *Was in the vale of Sorec,
Dalila,*] Judg. XVI. 4. *And
it came to paſs afterward, that he
loved a woman in the valley of So-
rek, whoſe name was Dalilah,* &c.
230. —— *my accompliſh'd ſnare.*]

There ſeems to be a quibble in the
uſe of this epithet. *Warburton.*
241. *That fault* &c] Milton cer-
tainly intended to reproach his
countrymen indirectly, and as plain-
ly as he dared, with the Reſtora-
tion of Charles II, which he ac-
counted the reſtoration of ſlavery,
and with the execution of the Re-
gicides. He purſues the ſame ſub-
ject

Q 2

Acknowledg'd not, or not at all confider'd   245
Deliverance offer'd : I on th' other fide
Us'd no ambition to commend my deeds,   [doer ;
The deeds themfelves, though mute, fpoke loud the
But they perfifted deaf, and would not feem   249
To count them things worth notice, till at length
Their lords the Philiftines with gather'd pow'rs
Enter'd Judea feeking me, who then
Safe to the rock of Etham was retir'd,
Not flying, but forecafting in what place
To fet upon them, what advantag'd beft :   255
Mean while the men of Judah, to prevent
The harrafs of their land, befet me round ;
I willingly on fome conditions came
Into their hands, and they as gladly yield me
To the uncircumcis'd a welcome prey,   260
Bound with two cords ; but cords to me were threds
Touch'd with the flame : on their whole hoft I flew
                              Unarm'd,

jeft again 678 to 700. I wonder
how the licenfers of thofe days let
it pafs.   Jortin.
    247. Us'd no ambition] Going a-
bout with ftudioufnefs and affecta-
tion to gain praife, as Mr. Richard-
fon fays, alluding to the origin of
the word in Latin.
    253. Safe to the rock of Etham
    was retir'd, &c] Judg. XV. 8.

And he went down, and dwelt in the
top of the rock Etam. Then the Phi-
liftines went up, and pitched in Ju-
dah &c.
    268. But what more oft in nations
    grown corrupt, &c] Here Mr.
Thyer has anticipated me by ob-
ferving that Milton is very uniform,
as well as juft, in his notions of li-
berty, always attributing the lofs
                                      of

Unarm'd, and with a trivial weapon fell'd
Their choiceſt youth ; they only liv'd who fled.
Had Judah that day join'd, or one whole tribe,   265
They had by this poſſeſs'd the tow'rs of Gath,
And lorded over them whom now they ſerve :
But what more oft in nations grown corrupt,
And by their vices brought to ſervitude,
Than to love bondage more than liberty,   270
Bondage with eaſe than ſtrenuous liberty ;
And to deſpiſe, or envy, or ſuſpect
Whom God hath of his ſpecial favor rais'd
As their deliverer ; if he ought begin,
How frequent to deſert him, and at laſt   275
To heap ingratitude on worthieſt deeds ?

CHORUS.

Thy words to my remembrance bring
How Succoth and the fort of Penuel
Their great deliverer contemn'd,

The

of it to vice and corruption of
morals : but in this paſſage he very
probably intended alſo a ſecret ſatir
upon the Engliſh nation, which ac-
cording to his republican politics
had by reſtoring the King choſen
bondage with eaſe rather than *ſtre-
nuous liberty.* And let me add that
the ſentiment is very like that of
Æmilius Lepidus the conſul in his

oration to the Roman people a-
gainſt Sulla, preſerved among the
fragments of Salluſt —— annuite
legibus impoſitis ; accipite otium
cum ſervitio ; —— but for myſelf
——potior viſa eſt periculoſa liber-
tas, quieto ſervitio.
278. *How Succoth and the fort of
Penuel* &c] The men of Succoth
and of the tower of Penuel re-
fuſed

The matchlefs Gideon in purfuit   280
Of Madian and her vanquifh'd kings :
And how ingrateful Ephraim
Had dealt with Jephtha,, who by argument,
Not worfe than by his fhield and fpear,
Defended Ifrael from the Ammonite,   285
Had not his prowefs quell'd their pride
In that fore battel, when fo many dy'd
Without reprieve adjudg'd to death,
For want of well pronouncing Shibboleth.

S A M S O N.

Of fuch examples add me to the roll,   290
Me eafily indeed mine may neglect,
But God's propos'd deliverance not fo.

C H O R U S.

Juft are the ways of God,
And juftifiable to men ;

Unlefs

---

fufed to give loaves of bread to
Gideon and his three hundred men
purfuing after Zebah and Zalmun-
na kings of Midian. See Judg.
VIII. 4—9.
   282. *And how ingrateful Ephraim*
&c.] Jephtha fubdued the children
of Ammon ; and he is faid to have
defended Ifrael by argument not worfe
than by arms on account of the mef-
fage which he fent unto the king

of the children of Ammon Judg. XI.
15- 27. For his victory over the Am-
monites the Ephraimites envied and
quarrel'd with him ; and threaten'd
to burn his houfe with fire : but
Jephthah and the men of Gilead
fmote Ephraim, and took the paf-
fages of Jordan before the Ephra-
imites, and there flew thofe of them
who could not rightly pronounce
the word *Shibboleth,* and there fell at
that

Unlefs there be who think not God at all :   295
If any be, they walk obfcure ;
For of fuch doctrine never was there fchool,
But the heart of the fool,
And no man therein doctor but himfelf.   299
    Yet more there be who doubt his ways not juft,
As to his own edicts found contradicting,
Then give the reigns to wandring thought,
Regardlefs of his glory's diminution ;
Till by their own perplexities involv'd
They ravel more, ftill lefs refolv'd,   305
But never find felf-fatisfying folution.
    As if they would confine th' Interminable,
And tie him to his own prefcript,
Who made our laws to bind us, not himfelf,
And hath full right t'exempt   310
Whom fo it pleafes him by choice

From

that time two and forty thoufand
of them. See Judg. XII. 1—6.
    298. *But the heart of the fool,*]
Alluding to Pfal. XIV. 1. and the
fentiment is not very unlike that of
a celebrated divine. " *The fool*
" *hath faid in his heart, There is no*
" *God :* and who but a fool would
" have faid fo ? "
    299. *And no man therein doctor*
    but himfelf.] There is fome-

thing rather too quaint and fanci-
ful in this conceit, and it appears
the worfe, as this fpeech of the
Chorus is of fo ferious a nature,
and fill'd with fo many deep and
folemn truths.   *Thyer.*
    303. *Regardlefs of his glory's di-*
    minution ;] This expreffion is
ftrong as anciently underftood. Ci-
cero de Orat. II. 39. *Majeftatem*
pop. Rom. minuere is the fame as cri-
men

From national obftriction, without taint
Of fin, or legal debt;
For with his own laws he can beft difpenfe.

He would not elfe who never wanted means, 315
Nor in refpect of th' enemy juft caufe
To fet his people free,
Have prompted this heroic Nazarite,
Againft his vow of ftricteft purity,
To feek in marriage that fallacious bride,   320
Unclean, unchafte.

Down reafon then, at leaft vain reafonings down,
Though reafon here aver
That moral verdict quits her of unclean :
Unchafte was fubfequent, her ftain not his,   325

But fee here comes thy reverend Sire
With careful ftep, locks white as down,
Old Manoah : advife

Forth-

men læfæ majeftatis. Corn. Nepos
Agef. 4. *religionem minuere* is vio-
lare.   *Richardfon.*
    319. —— *vow of ftricteft purity,*]
Not a vow of celibacy, but of
ftricteft purity from Mofaical and
legal uncleannefs.   *Warburton.*
    324. *That moral verdict quits her
    of unclean :*] That is, By the
law of nature a Philiftian woman
was not unclean, yet the law of
Mofes held her to be fo.   I don't
know why the poet thought fit to
make his hero fcepticize on a point,
as irreconcileable to reafon, which
may be very well accounted for by
the beft rules of human prudence
and policy. The inftitution of Mo-
fes was to keep the Jewifh people
diftinct and feparate from the na-
tions,

Forthwith how thou oughtſt to receive him.

SAMSON.

Ay me, another inward grief awak'd   330
With mention of that name renews th' aſſault.

MANOAH.

Brethren and men of Dan, for ſuch ye ſeem,
Though in this uncouth place; if old reſpect,
As I ſuppoſe, tow'ards your once glory'd friend,
My ſon now captive, hither hath inform'd   335
Your younger feet, while mine caſt back with age
Came lagging after; ſay if he be here.

CHORUS.

As ſignal now in low dejected ſtate,
As earſt in high'eſt, behold him where he lies.

MANOAH.

O miſerable change! is this the man,   340
That invincible Samſon, far renown'd,

The

---

tions. This the lawgiver effected by a vaſt variety of means: one of which was to hold all other nations under a legal *impurity*; the beſt means of preventing intermarriages with them. *Warburton.*

336.— *while mine caſt back with age*] This is very artfully and properly introduc'd, to account for the Chorus coming to Samſon

before Manoah, for it is not to be ſuppoſed that any of his friends ſhould be more concern'd for his welfare, or more deſirous to viſit him than his father.

340. *O miſerable change!* &c] This ſpeech of Manoah's is in my opinion very beautiful in its kind. The thoughts are exactly ſuch as one may ſuppoſe would occur to the

The dread of Iſrael's foes, who with a ſtrength
Equivalent to Angels walk'd their ſtreets,
None offering fight ; who ſingle combatant
Duel'd their armies rank'd in proud array,   345
Himſelf an army, now unequal match
To ſave himſelf againſt a coward arm'd
At one ſpear's length.   O ever failing truſt
In mortal ſtrength ! and oh what not in man
Deceivable and vain ? Nay what thing good   350
Pray'd for, but often proves our woe, our bane ?

I

the mind of the old man, and are expreſſed with an earneſtneſs and impatience very well ſuited to that anguiſh of mind he muſt be in at the fight of his ſon under ſuch miſerable afflicted circumſtances. It is not at all unbecoming the pious grave character of Manoah to repreſent him, as Milton does, even complaining and murmuring at this diſpoſition of Heaven, in the firſt bitterneſs of his ſoul. Such ſudden ſtarts of infirmity are aſcribed to ſome of the greateſt perſonages in Scripture, and it is agreeable to that well known maxim, that religion may regulate, but can never eradicate natural paſſions and affections.
        Thyer.

352. *I pray'd for children, and thought barrenneſs In wedlock a reproach ;*] Some lines from a fragment of Euripides

may be introduced here. They are very beautiful, and not impertinent.

Γυναι, φιλον μεν φεγγ᾿ ηλιυ
        τοδε,
Καλον δε πονle χευμ᾿ ιδειν ευη-
        νεμον,
Γητ᾿ ηρινον θαλλυσα, πλυσιον θ᾿
        υδωρ
Πολλων τ᾿ επαινον εςι μοι λεξαι
        καλων·
Αλλ᾿ υδεν υτω λαμπρον, υδ᾿ ιδειν
        καλον,
Ως τοις απαισι, και ποθω δε-
        δηγμενοις,
Παιδων νεογνων εν δομοις ιδειν
        φαθ᾿.

Mulier, amicum ſolis hoc magni
        jubar,
Dulce et tueri maria cum venti
        ſilent :
                    Dulce

I pray'd for children, and thought barrenneſs
In wedlock a reproach; I gain'd a ſon,
And ſuch a ſon as all men hail'd me happy;
Who would be now a father in my ſtead ? 355
O wherefore did God grant me my requeſt,
And as a bleſſing with ſuch pomp adorn'd ?
Why are his gifts deſirable, to tempt
Our earneſt pray'rs, then giv'n with ſolemn hand
As graces, draw a ſcorpion's tail behind ? 560
For this did th' Angel twice deſcend ? for this

Ordain'd

Dulce eſt et amnis largus, et ver-
nans humus :
Sunt aliis pulchra multa, quæ
poſſum addere.
Sed crede nullum gratius ſpecta-
culum eſt,
*Quam poſt querelas orbitatis te-
tricæ,*
Conſpicere florem liberûm orientem
dcmi.

Eurip. Barnes. p. 443.   *Calton.*

354. *And ſuch a ſon &c*] It is
very hard that the editors of Mil-
ton have never taken the pains to
correct the errors of the firſt edi-
tion, which he had himſelf cor-
rected. This verſe at firſt was print-
ed imperfect, and it has been fol-
low'd in all the editions,

    Such a ſon as all men hail'd me
    happy;

And was wanting in the beginning,

And ſuch a ſon as all men hail'd
me happy;

ſo Milton himſelf corrected it, and
ſo Mr. Jortin and Mr. Sympſon
conjectur'd it ſhould be read. And
at the time of writing this, in all
probability the author remember'd
the happy father in Terence. An-
dria I. 1. 69.

Cum id mihi placebat, tum uno
    ore omnes omnia
Bona diçere, et laudare fortunas
    meas,
Qui natum haberem tali ingenio
    præditum.

359.——— *then giv'n with ſolemn
    hand*
*As graces, draw a ſcorpion's tail
    behind?*] He has rais'd this
                        beautiful

Ordain'd thy nurture holy, as of a plant
Select, and sacred, glorious for a while,
The miracle of men ; then in an hour
Insnar'd, assaulted, overcome, led bound,   365
Thy foes derision, captive, poor and blind,
Into a dungeon thrust, to work with slaves ?
Alas methinks whom God hath chosen once
To worthiest deeds, if he through frailty err,
He should not so o'erwhelm, and as a thrall   370
Subject him to so foul indignities,
Be it but for honor's sake of former deeds.

SAMSON.

Appoint not heav'nly disposition, Father;
Nothing of all these evils hath befall'n me
But justly; I myself have brought them on,   375
Sole author I, sole cause : if ought seem vile,
As vile hath been my folly, who' have profan'd
The mystery of God giv'n me under pledge
Of vow, and have betray'd it to a woman,
A Canaanite, my faithless enemy.   380
This well I knew, nor was at all surpris'd,

But

beautiful imagery on the following   *him a scorpion ?* He was not always
text, Luke XI. 12. *If a son shall*   so happy.   *Warburton.*
ask of his father an egg, will be offer   373. *Appoint*] That is, arraign,
                                            summon

But warn'd by oft experience : did not ſhe
Of Timna firſt betray me, and reveal
The ſecret wreſted from me in her highth
Of nuptial love profeſs'd, carrying it ſtrait   385
To them who had corrupted her, my ſpies,
And rivals ? In this other was there found
More faith, who alſo in her prime of love,
Spouſal embraces, vitiated with gold,
Though offer'd only, by the ſent conceiv'd   390
Her ſpurious firſt-born, treaſon againſt me ?
Thrice ſhe aſſay'd with flattering pray'rs and ſighs,
And amorous reproaches, to win from me
My capital ſecret, in what part my ſtrength
Lay ſtor'd, in what part ſumm'd, that ſhe might know;
Thrice I deluded her, and turn'd to ſport   396
Her importunity, each time perceiving
How openly, and with what impudence
She purpos'd to betray me, and (which was worſe
Than undiſſembled hate) with what contempt   400
She ſought to make me traitor to myſelf ;
Yet the fourth time, when muſt'ring all her wiles,
                                                                    With

fummon to anſwer.   *Warburton.*   401. *She ſought*] So it is in Mil-
    391.—*treaſon againſt me?*] By our   ton's own ediſion; in moſt of the
laws called pettytreaſon.*Richardſon.*   others *She thought*.

                                                                    411.—C

With blandifh'd parlies, feminine affaults;
Tongue-batteries, fhe furceas'd not day nor night
To ftorm me over-watch'd, and weary'd out,   405
At times when men feek moft repofe and reft,
I yielded, and unlock'd her all my heart,
Who with a grain of manhood well refolv'd
Might eafily have fhook off all her fnares :
But foul effeminacy held me yok'd   410
Her bond-flave ; O indignity, O blot
To honor and religion ! fervile mind
Rewarded well with fervile punifhment !
The bafe degree to which I now am fall'n,
Thefe rags, this grinding is not yet fo bafe   415
As was my former fervitude, ignoble,
Unmanly, ignominious, infamous,
True flavery, and that blindnefs worfe than this,
That faw not how degenerately I ferv'd.

MANOAH.

I cannot praife thy marriage choices, Son,   420

Rather

411.——*O indignity ! O blot* &c]
Nothing could give the reader a
better idea of a great and heroic
fpirit in the circumftances of Sam-
fon, than this fudden guft of in-
dignation and paffionate felf-re-
proach upon the mentioning of his
weaknefs. Befides there is fome-
thing vaftly grand and noble in his
reflection upon his prefent condi-
tion on this occafion,

Thefe

Rather approv'd them not; but thou didſt plead
Divine impulſion prompting how thou might'ſt
Find ſome occaſion to infeſt our foes.
I ſtate not that; this I am ſure, our foes
Found ſoon occaſion thereby to make thee   425
Their captive, and their triumph; thou the ſooner
Temptation found'ſt, or over-potent charms
To violate the ſacred truſt of ſilence
Depoſited within thee; which to have kept
Tacit, was in thy pow'r: true; and thou bear'ſt   430
Enough, and more, the burden of that fault;
Bitterly haſt thou pay'd, and ſtill art paying
That rigid ſcore.   A worſe thing yet remains,
This day the Philiſtines a popular feaſt
Here celebrate in Gaza; and proclame   435
Great pomp, and ſacrifice, and praiſes loud
To Dagon, as their God, who hath deliver'd
Thee, Samſon, bound and blind into their hands,
Them out of thine, who ſlew'ſt them many a ſlain.

So

Theſe rags, this grinding is not
yet ſo baſe &c.   *Thyer.*

434. *This day the Philiſtines a po-
pular feaſt* &c] Judg. XVI. 23.
Then the lords of the Philiſtines ga-
thered them together, for to offer a
great ſacrifice unto Dagon their God,
and to rejoice; for they ſaid, Our
God hath delivered Samſon our enemy
into our hand. &c.   This incident
the poet hath finely improv'd, and
with

So Dagon ſhall be magnify'd, and God,   440
Beſides whom is no God, compar'd with idols,
Diſglorify'd, blaſphem'd, and had in ſcorn
By the idolatrous rout amidſt their wine ;
Which to have come to paſs by means of thee,
Samſon, of all thy ſufferings think the heavieſt, 445
Of all reproach the moſt with ſhame that ever
Could have befall'n' thee and thy father's houſe.

SAMSON.

Father, I do acknowledge and confeſs
That I this honor, I this pomp have brought
To Dagon, and advanc'd his praiſes high   450
Among the Heathen round ; to God have brought
Diſhonor, obloquy, and op'd the mouths
Of idoliſts, and atheiſts ; have brought ſcandal
To Iſrael, diffidence of God, and doubt
In feeble hearts, propenſe enough before   455
To waver, or fall off, and join with idols ;
Which is my chief affliction, ſhame and ſorrow,
The anguiſh of my ſoul, that ſuffers not

Mine

with great judgment he hath put
this reproach of Samſon into the
mouth of the father, rather than
any other of the dramatis perſonæ.

472.   and theſe words
I as a prophecy receive ;] This
method of one perſon's taking an
omen from the words of another
was

Mine eye to harbour fleep, or thoughts to reft.
This only hope relieves me, that the ftrife   460
With me hath end ; all the contéft is now
'Twixt God and Dagon ; Dagon hath prefum'd,
Me overthrown, to enter lifts with God,
His deity comparing and preferring
Before the God of Abraham.   He, be fure,   465
Will not connive, or linger, thus provok'd,
But will arife, and his great name affert :
Dagon muft ftoop, and fhall ere long receive
Such a difcomfit, as fhall quite defpoil him
Of all thefe boafted trophies won on me,   470
And with confufion blank his worfhippers.

MANOAH.

With caufe this hope relieves thee, and thefe words
I as a prophecy receive ; for God,
Nothing more certain, will not long defer
To vindicate the glory of his name   475
Againft all competition, nor will long
Indure it doubtful whether God be Lord,

Or

was frequently practic'd among the Ancients : and in thefe words the downfall of Dagon's worfhippers is artfully prefignified, as the death of Samfon is in other places ; but Manoah, as it was natural, accepts the good omen without thinking of the evil that is to follow.

Or Dagon.   But for thee what fhall be done?
Thou muft not in the mean while here forgot
Lie in this miferable loathfome plight   480
Neglected.   I already have made way
To fome Philiftian lords, with whom to treat
About thy ranfome : well they may by this
Have fatisfy'd their utmoft of revenge   484
By pains and flaveries, worfe than death inflicted
On thee, who now no more canft do them harm.

SAMSON.

Spare that propofal, Father, fpare the trouble
Of that folicitation ; let me here,
As I deferve, pay on my punifhment;
And expiate, if poffible, my crime,   490
Shameful garrulity.   To have reveal'd
Secrets of men, the fecrets of a friend,
How hainous had the fact been, how deferving
Contempt, and fcorn of all, to be excluded

All

500. *That Gentiles in their parables condemn* &c.] Alluding to the ftory of Tantalus, who for revealing the fecrets of the Gods was condemn'd to pains in Hell. Cicero Tufc. Difp. IV. 16. —— poetæ impendere apud inferos faxum Tantalo faciunt ob fcelera, animique impotentiam, et fuperbiloquentiam.   Euripides affigns the fame punifhment, and for the fame reafon.   Oreftes 8.

—— ὁτι θεοις ανθρωπ⌖ ων
Κοινης τραπεζης αξιωμ' εχων
ισον,

Axo-

All friendſhip, and avoided as a blab,   495
The mark of fool ſet on his front?
But I God's counſel have not kept, his holy ſecret
Preſumptuouſly have publiſh'd, impiouſly,
Weakly at leaſt, and ſhamefully : a ſin
That Gentiles in their parables condemn   500
To their abyſs and horrid pains confin'd.

MANOAH.

Be penitent and for thy fault contrite,
But act not in thy own affliction, Son ;
Repent the ſin, but if the puniſhment
Thou canſt avoid, ſelf-preſervation bids ;   505
Or th' execution leave to high diſpoſal,
And let another hand, not thine, exact
Thy penal forfeit from thyſelf; perhaps
God will relent, and quit thee all his debt ;
Who ever more approves and more accepts   510
(Beſt pleas'd with humble' and filial ſubmiſſion)

Him

Ἀκόλαϛον εϛχε γλωσσαν, αισχιϛην νοσον.

Mr. Warburton's remark is that " the ancient myſtagogues taught, " that the Gods puniſhed both the " revealers and the violators of " their myſteries. Milton had here

" in his eye that fine paſſage of " Virgil, Æn. VI. 617.

— ſedet, æternumque ſedebit Infelix Theſeus, Phlegyaſque mi- ſerrimus omnes Admonet, et magna teſtatur vo- ce per umbras &c.

R 2   531.—_none_

Him who imploring mercy fues for life,
Than who felf-rigorous choofes death as due ;
Which argues over-juft, and felf-difpleas'd
For felf-offenfe, more than for God offended.   515
Reject not then what offer'd means ; who knows
But God hath fet before us, to return thee
Home to thy country and his facred houfe,
Where thou may'ft bring thy offerings, to avert
His further ire, with pray'rs and vows renew'd ?   520

SAMSON.

His pardon I implore ; but as for life,
To what end fhould I feek it ? when in ftrength
All mortals I excell'd, and great in hopes
With youthful courage and magnanimous thoughts
Of birth from Heaven foretold, and high exploits,
Full of divine inftinct, after fome proof   526
Of acts indeed heroic, far beyond
The fons of Anak, famous now and blaz'd,

Fearlefs

531.——*none daring my affront.*] None daring to contend with me, and meet me face to face, according to the etymology of the word. See the note on Paradife Loft, IX. 330.

535.—— *hallow'd pledge*] This is the genuin reading of the firft edition ; in moft of the others it is abfurdly corrupted into *hollow pledge.*

538. —— *all my precious fleece,*] Read *of* my precious fleece. Thus in Paradife Loft, I. 596. the fun in a mift is fhorn *of* his beams : and IX.

Fearlefs of danger, like a petty God
I walk'd about, admir'd of all and dreaded   530
On hoftile ground, none daring my affront.
Then fwoll'n with pride into the fnare I fell
Of fair fallacious looks, venereal trains,
Soften'd with pleafure and voluptuous life;
At length to lay my head and hallow'd pledge 535
Of all my ftrength in the lafcivious lap
Of a deceitful concubine, who fhore me
Like a tame weather, all my precious fleece,
Then turn'd me out ridiculous, defpoil'd,
Shav'n, and difarm'd among mine enemies.   540

CHORUS.

Defire of wine and all delicious drinks,
Which many a famous warrior overturns,
Thou couldft reprefs, nor did the dancing ruby
Sparkling, out-pour'd, the flavor, or the fmell,
Or tafte that chears the hearts of Gods and men, 545

Allure

IX. 1059. Samfon from the harlot-
lap wak'd fhorn *of* his ftrength.
Meadowcourt.
543. —— *nor did the dancing ruby*
&c] The poet here probably al-
ludes to Prov. XXIII. 31. *Look not
thou upon the wine when it is red,
when it giveth his color in the cup,*

when it moveth itfelf aright. Mr.
Thyer has made the fame obfer-
vation.
545. *Or tafte that chears the heart
of Gods and men,*] Taken from
Judg. IX. 13.—— *wine which chear-
eth God and man.* Milton fays *Gods,*
which is a juft paraphrafe, mean-
ing

R 3

Allure thee from the cool cryſtallin ſtream.

SAMSON.

Wherever fountain or freſh current flow'd
Againſt the eaſtern ray, tranſlucent, pure
With touch ethereal of Heav'n's fiery rod,
I drank, from the clear milky juce allaying   550
Thirſt, and refreſh'd ; nor envy'd them the grape
Whoſe heads that turbulent liquor fills with fumes.

CHORUS.

O madneſs, to think uſe of ſtrongeſt wines
And ſtrongeſt drinks our chief ſupport of health,
When God with theſe forbidd'n made choice to rear
His mighty champion, ſtrong above compare,   556
Whoſe drink was only from the liquid brook.

SAMSON.

ing the *Hero-Gods* of the Heathen.
Jotham is here ſpeaking to an ido-
latrous city, that *ran a whoring af-*
ter Baalim, and made Baal-berith
their God : A God ſprung from
among men, as may be partly col-
lected from his name, as well as
from diverſe other circumſtances
of the ſtory.   Heſiod in a ſimilar
expreſſion ſays that *the vengeance of*
the fates purſued the crimes of Gods
and men. Theog. v. 220.

Αιτ' ανδζων τε θεωνε &c.
Warburton.

Gods *and* men is the reading of
Milton's own edition, and more
agreeable to the text of Scripture
than in the common editions Gods
or men.

547. *Wherever fountain or freſh*
current flow'd
Againſt the eaſtern ray, &c] This
circumſtance was very probably
ſuggeſted to our author by the
following lines of Taſſo's poem
del Mondo creato. Giornata 3.
St. 8.

O

SAMSON.

But what avail'd this temp'rance, not complete
Againſt another objeƈt more enticing?
What boots it at one gate to make defenſe, 560
And at another to let in the foe,
Effeminately vanquiſh'd? by which means,
Now blind, diſhearten'd, ſham'd, diſhonor'd, quell'd,
To what can I be uſeful, wherein ſerve
My nation, and the work from Heav'n impos'd,
But to ſit idle on the houſhold hearth, 566
A burd'nous drone; to viſitants a gaze,
Or pity'd objeƈt, theſe redundant locks
Robuſtious to no purpoſe cluſtring down,
Vain monument of ſtrength; till length of years

And

O liquidi criſtalli, onde s' eſtin-
gua
L'ardente ſete a miſeri mortali :
Ma piu ſalubre é, ſe tra viue
pietre
Rompendo l' argentate, e fredde
corna,
Incontra il nuouo ſol, che il puro
argento
Co' raggi indora —— *Thyer.*

557. *Whoſe drink* &c] Samſon
was a Nazarite, Judge XIII. 7.
therefore to drink no wine, nor

ſhave his head. See Numb. VI.
Amos II. 12. *Richardſon.*

566. *But to ſit idle on the houſhold
hearth,* &c] It is ſuppos'd,
with probability enough, that Mil-
ton choſe Samſon for his ſubjeƈt,
becauſe he was fellow-ſuffcrer with
him in the loſs of his eyes ; how-
ever one may venture to ſay, that
the ſimilitude of their circumſtances
in this reſpeƈt has enrich'd the
poem with ſeveral very pathetic
deſcriptions of the miſery of blind-
neſs. *Thyer.*

R 4 571.—*craze*

And ſedentary numneſs craze my limbs   571
To a contemptible old age obſcure ?
Here rather let me drudge and earn my bread,
Till vermin or the draff of ſervile food
Conſume me, and oft-invocated death   575
Haſten the welcome end of all my pains.

MANOAH.

Wilt thou then ſerve the Philiſtines with that gift
Which was expreſly giv'n thee to annoy them ?
Better at home lie bed-rid, not only idle,
Inglorious, unemploy'd, with age outworn.   580
But God who caus'd a fountain at thy prayer
From the dry ground to ſpring, thy thirſt t' allay
After the brunt of battel, can as eaſy

Cauſe

571.—— *craze my limbs*] He uſes the word *craze* much in the ſame manner as in the Paradiſe Loſt XII. 210. where ſee the note ; and I would always recommend it to the reader, when an uncommon word eſpecially occurs in two or more different places, to compare the places together for the better underſtanding of our author. I cannot always refer to the particular places in theſe notes, but the indexes may be of uſe for this purpoſe.

581. *But God who caus'd a fountain at thy prayer*

From the dry ground to ſpring, &c] Judg. XV. 18, 19. *And he was ſore athirſt, and called on the Lord, and ſaid, Thou haſt given this great deliverance into the hand of thy ſervant, and now ſhall I die for thirſt, and fall into the hand of the uncircumciſed? But God clave an hollow place that was in the jaw, and there came water thereout ; and when he had drunk, his ſpirit came again, and he revived.* We ſee that Milton differs from our tranſlation. Our tranſlation ſays that God clave an hollow place that was in the jaw : but Milton ſays

Caufe light again within thy eyes to fpring,

Wherewith to ferve him better than thou haft; 585

And I perfuade me fo; why elfe this ftrength

Miraculous yet remaining in thofe locks?

His might continues in thee not for nought,

Nor fhall his wondrous gifts be fruftrate thus.

S A M S O N.

All otherwife to me my thoughts portend, 590

That thefe dark orbs no more fhall treat with light,

Nor th' other light of life continue long,

But yield to double darknefs nigh at hand:

So much I feel my genial fpirits droop,

My hopes all flat, nature within me feems 595

In all her functions·weary of herfelf,

My

fays that *God caus'd a fountain from the dry ground to fpring,* and herein he follows the Chaldee paraphraft and the beft commentators, who underftand it that God made a cleft in fome part of the ground or rock, in the place called Lehi, *Lehi* fignifying both a jaw and a place fo called.

588. *His might continues* &c] A fine preparative, which raifes our expectation of fome great event to be produced by his ftrength.
Warburton.

594. *So much I feel my genial fpirits droop,* &c] Here Milton in the perfon of Samfon defcribes exactly his own cafe, what he felt, and what he thought in fome of his melancholy hours. He could not have wrote fo well but from his own feeling and experience, and the very flow of the verfes is melancholy, and excellently adapted to the fubject. As Mr. Thyer expreffes it, there is a remarkable folemnity and air of melancholy in the very found of thefe verfes, and the reader will find it very difficult to pronounce them without that grave and ferious tone of voice which is proper for the occafion.
600—*and*

My race of glory run, and race of fhame,
And I fhall fhortly be with them that reft.

MANOAH.

Believe not thefe fuggeftions which proceed
From anguifh of the mind and humors black, 600
That mingle with thy fancy.   I however
Muft not omit a father's timely care
To profecute the means of thy deliverance
By ranfome, or how elfe: mean while be calm,
And healing words from thefe thy friends admit.

SAMSON.

O that torment fhould not be confin'd   606
To the body's wounds and fores,
With maladies innumerable
In heart, head, breaft and reins;
But muft fecret paffage find   610

To

---

600.   — and humors black,
That mingle with thy fancy.] This
very juft notion of the mind or
fancy's being affected and as it
were tainted with the vitiated hu-
mors of the body Milton had be-
fore adopted in his Paradife Loft,
where he introduces Satan in the
fhape of a toad at the ear of Eve.
IV. 804.
    Or if, infpiring venom, he might
        taint

Th' animal fpirits &c.
So again in the Mafk,

        — 'tis but the lees
And fettlings of a melancholy
    blood.   Thyer.

606. O that torment fhould not be
confin'd &c.] Milton, no doubt,
was apprehenfive that this long de-
fcription of Samfon's grief and
                            mifery

To th' inmoſt mind,
There exercife all his fierce accidents,
And on her pureſt ſpirits prey,
As on entrails, joints, and limbs,
With anſwerable pains, but more intenſe,   615
Though void of corporal ſenſe.
     My griefs not only pain me
As a lingring diſeaſe,
But finding no redreſs, ferment and rage,
Nor leſs than wounds immedicable   620
Rankle, and feſter, and gangrene,
To black mortification.
Thoughts my tormentors arm'd with deadly ſtings
Mangle my apprehenſive tendereſt parts,
Exaſperate, exulcerate, and raiſe   625
Dire inflammation, which no cooling herb

                                          Or

mifery might grow tedious to the reader, and therefore here with great judgment varies both his manner of expreſſing it and the verſification. Theſe fudden ſtarts of impatience are very natural to perſons in ſuch circumſtances, and this rough and unequal meaſure of the verſes is very well ſuited to it. *Thyer.*
     623. *Thoughts my tormentors arm'd with deadly ſtings*

Mangle &c] This defcriptive imagery is fine and well purfued. The idea is taken from the effects of poifonous falts in the ſtomach and bowels, which ſtimulate, tear, inflame and exulcerate the tender fibres, and end in a mortification, which he calls *death's benumming opium,* as in that ſtage the pain is over.   *Warburton.*

                              637. *Or*

Or medicinal liquor can affwage,
Nor breath of vernal air from fnowy Alp.
Sleep hath forfook and giv'n me o'er
To death's benumming opium as my only cure : 630
Thence faintings, fwoonings of defpair,
And fenfe of Heav'n's defertion.

  I was his nurfling once, and choice delight,
His deftin'd from the womb,
Promis'd by heav'nly meffage twice defcending. 635
Under his fpecial eye
Abftemious I grew up, and thriv'd amain ;
He led me on to mightieft deeds
Above the nerve of mortal arm
Againft th' uncircumcis'd, our enemies :   640
But now hath caft me off as never known,

                                                    And

627. *Or medicinal liquor can af-fwage,*] Here *medicinal* is pro-nounc'd with the accent upon the laft fyllable but one, as in Latin : which is more mufical than as we commonly pronounce it *medicinal* with the accent upon the laft fylla-ble but two, or *med'cinal* as Milton has ufed it in the Mafk. The fame mufical pronunciation occurs in Shakefpear. Othello Act 5. Sc. 10.
    Drop tears as faft as the Arabian
    trees

Their *medicinal* gum.

628. ——*from fnowy Alp.*] He ufes *Alp* for mountain in general, as in the Paradife Loft II. 620.
    O'er many a frozen, many a
    fiery *Alp*.

Alp in the ftrict etymology of the word fignifies a mountain white with fnow. We have indeed ap-propriated the name to the high mountains which feparate Italy from France and Germany ; but
                                               any

SAMSON AGONISTES. 253

And to thofe cruel enemies,
Whom I by his appointment had provok'd,
Left me all helplefs with th' irreparable lofs
Of fight, referv'd alive to be repeated   645
The fubject of their cruelty or fcorn.
Nor am I in the lift of them that hope ;
Hopelefs are all my evils, all remedilefs ;
This one prayer yet remains, might I be heard,
No long petition, fpeedy death,   650
The clofe of all my miferies, and the balm.

CHORUS.

Many are the fayings of the wife
In ancient and in modern books inroll'd,
Extolling patience as the trueft fortitude ;
And to the bearing well of all calamities,   655

All

any high mountain may be fo cal-
led, and fo Sidonius Apollinaris
calls mount Athos, fpeaking of
Xerxes cutting through it, Carmen
II. 510.

——cui ruptus Athos, cui remige
Medo
Turgida fylvofam currebant ve-
la per *Alpem.*

And the old Gloffary interprets Alps
by οϕη ιψηλα high mountains.
633. I was his nurfling once &c]

This part of Samfon's fpeech is
little more than a repetition of
what he had faid before, ver. 23.

O wherefore was my birth from
Heav'n foretold
Twice by an Angel &c.

But yet it cannot juftly be imputed
as a fault to our author. Grief
though eloquent is not tied to
forms, and is befides apt in its own
nature frequently to recur to and
repeats its fource and object. *Thyer.*
656. *All*

All chances incident to man's frail life,

Confolatories writ

With ftudy'd argument, and much perfuafion fought

Lenient of grief and anxious thought:

But with th' afflicted in his pangs their found   660

Little prevails, or rather feems a tune

Harfh, and of diffonant mood from his complaint;

Unlefs he feel within

Some fource of confolation from above,

Secret refrefhings, that repair his ftrength,   665

And fainting fpirits uphold.

   God of our fathers, what is man!

That thou tow'ards him with hand fo various,

Or might I fay contrarious,

Temper'ft

656. *All chances incident to man's frail life*, &c] There is a full ftop at the end of this line in all the editions, but there fhould be only a comma, as the fenfe evinces, the conftruction being *And confola-tories writ with* &c *to the bearing well* &c. Milton himfelf corrected it in the firft edition; but when an error is once made, it is fure to be perpetuated through all the editions.

658.—*and much perfuafion fought*] I fuppofe an error of the prefs for *fraught*.   Warburton.

I conceive the conftruction to be,

confolatories are *writ with ftudy'd argument, and much perfuafion* is *fought* &c.

659. *Lenient of grief*] Exprefs'd from what we quoted before from Horace Epift. l. l. 34.

   Sunt verba et voces quibus hunc
     lenire dolorem
Poffis.

660. *But with th' afflicted* &c] Here was another error perpetuated through all the editions,

   But *to* th' afflicted &c.

Milton himfelf corrected it, and certainly

Temper'ft thy providence through his fhort courfe,

Not ev'nly, as thou rul'ft   671

Th' angelic orders and inferior creatures mute,

Irrational and brute.

Nor do I name of men the common rout,

That wand'ring loofe about   675

Grow up and perifh, as the fummer flie,

Heads without name no more remember'd,

But fuch as thou haft folemnly elected,

With gifts and graces eminently adorn'd

To fome great work, thy glory,   680

And people's fafety, which in part they' effect :

Yet toward thefe thus dignify'd, thou oft

Amidft their highth of noon

Changeft

certainly *their found prevails* with *th' afflicted* is better than *prevails* to *th' afflicted.*

661. — *or rather feems a tune Harfh, and of diffonant mood* &c] Alluding to Ecclus. XXII. 6. *A tale out of feafon is as mufic in mourning.*   Thyer.

667. *God of our fathers, what is man!* &c] This and the following paragraph to ver. 705. feems to be an imitation of the Chorus in Seneca's Hippolytus, where the immature and undeferved fate of that young hero is lamented, Act IV. 971.

—— fed cur idem,
Qui tanta regis, fub quo vafti
Pondera mundi librata fuos
Ducunt orbes, hominum nimium
Securus abes; non follicitus
Prodeffe bonis, nocuiffe malis ?
&c. to the end.   Thyer.

677. *Heads without name no more remember'd,*] Milton here probably had in view the Greek term for this lower clafs of mortals. They ftile them αναριθμοι or αναριθμητοι, men not number'd, or not worth the numbring.   Thyer.

693.—*their*

Changeſt thy count'nance, and thy hand with no regard
Of higheſt favors paſt   68 5
From thee on them, or them to thee of ſervice.

Nor only doſt degrade them, or remit
To life obſcur'd, which were a fair diſmiſſion,   [high,
But throw'ſt them lower than thou didſt exalt them

                                              Unſeemly

693. ―――― *their carcaſes*
To dogs and fowls a prey,] Plainly
alluding to Homer's Iliad I. 4.

      ―――― αυτες δ' ελωρια τευχε
      κυνεσσιν
Οιωνοισι πασι.

695. *Or to th' unjuſt tribunals,*
under charge of times, &c]
Here no doubt Milton reflected
upon the trials and ſufferings of his
party after the Reſtoration ; and
probably he might have in mind
particularly the caſe of Sir Harry
Vane, whom he has ſo highly ce-
lebrated in one of his ſonnets.   *If*
theſe they ſcape, perhaps in poverty
&c ; this was his own caſe ; he
eſcaped with life. but lived in po-
verty, and though he was always
very ſober and temperate, yet he
was much afflicted with the gout
and other *painful diſeaſes in crude*
old age, cruda jenectus, when he was
not yet a very old man :

      Though not diſordinate, yet
          cauſeleſs ſuff'ring
      The puniſhment of diſſolute days.

Some time after I had written
this, I had the pleaſure to find that

I had fallen into the ſame vein of
thinking with Mr. Warburton : but
he has open'd and purſued it much
farther with a penetration and live-
lineſs of fancy peculiar to himſelf.

      God of our fathers ――――
                to ver. 704.

is a bold expoſtulation with Provi-
dence for the ill ſucceſs of the *good*
old cauſe.

      But ſuch as thou haſt ſolemnly
          elected,
      With *gifts and graces* eminently
          adorn'd
      To ſome great work, thy glory,

In theſe three lines are deſcribed
the characters of the Heads of the
Independent Enthuſiaſts,

      ――――which *in part* they effect :

That is by the overthrow of the
monarchy, without being able to
raiſe their projected republic.

      Yet toward theſe thus dignify'd,
          thou oft
      Amidſt their highth of noon
      Changeſt thy count'nance ――――

                                    After

Unfeemly falls in human eye,   690
Too grievous for the trefpafs or omiffion ;
Oft leav'ft them to the hoftile fword
Of Heathen and profane, their carcafes
To dogs and fowls a prey, or elfe captiv'd ;   694
Or to th' unjuft tribunals, under change of times,

                                                        And

After Richard had laid down, all power came into the hands of the enthufiaftic Independent Republicans, when a fudden revolution, by the return of Charles II, broke all their meafures.

—— with no regard
Of higheft favors paft
From thee on them, or *them to thee of fervice*.

That is without any regard of thofe favors fhown by thee to them in their wonderful fucceffes againft tyranny and fuperftition [Church and State] or of thofe fervices they paid to thee in declaring for religion and liberty [Independency and a Republic].

Nor only doft degrade &c
Too grievous for the *trefpafs* or *omiffion* ;

By the *trefpafs* of thefe precious faints Milton means the quarrels among themfelves : and by the *omiffion* the not making a clear ftage in the conftitution, and newmodeling the *law* as well as national religion as Ludlow advifed.
—— *captiv'd* ;

Several were condemned to perpetual imprifonment, as Lambert and Martin.

Or to th' *unjuft tribunals* under change of times &c.

The trials and condemnation of Vane and the Regicides. The concluding verfes defcribe his own cafe,

If thefe they fcape, perhaps in *poverty* ——
Painful difcafes and deform'd ——
Though not difordinate, yet caufelefs fuff'ring
The punifhment of diffolute days :

His loffes in the Excife, and his gout not caufed by intemperance. But Milton was the moft heated enthufiaft of his time ; fpeaking of Charles the firft's murder in his Defenfe of the People of England he fays——Quanquam ego hæc divino potius inftinctu gefta effe crediderim, quoties memoria repeto &c.

And condemnation of th' ingrateful multitude.
If thefe they fcape, perhaps in poverty
With ficknefs and difeafe thou bow'ft them down,
Painful difeafes and deform'd,
In crude old age ;   700
Though not difordinate, yet cauflefs fuff'ring
The punifhment of diffolute days : in fine,
Juft or unjuft alike feem miferable,
For oft alike both come to evil end.   704
    So deal not with this once thy glorious champion,
The image of thy ftrength, and mighty minifter.
What do I beg ? how haft thou dealt already ?
Behold him in this ftate calamitous, and turn
His labors, for thou canft, to peaceful end.

                                                But

700. *In crude old age* ;] *Crude* old age in Virgil and in other writers is *ftrong* and *robuft*,

—— cruda Deo viridifque feneftus.

But Milton ufes *crude* here for *premature* and *coming before its time*, as *cruda funera* in Statius : old age brought on by poverty and by ficknefs, as Hefiod fays Eργ. 93.

Αιψα γαρ εν κακοτητι βροτοι καταγηρασκεσι.   Jortin.

714. *Like a ftately fhip* &c] The thought of comparing a woman to a fhip is not entirely new. Plautus has it in his Pænulus. I. II. 1.

Negotii fibi qui volet vim parare,
Navem et mulierem, hæc duo comparato.
Nam nullæ magis res duæ plus negotii
Habent, forte fi occeperis ornare, &c.

Of Tarfus, there is frequent mention

But who is this, what thing of fea or land ? 710
Female of fex it feems,
That fo bedeck'd, ornate, and gay,
Comes this way failing
Like a ftately fhip
Of Tarfus, bound for th' iles 715
Of Javan or Gadire
With all her bravery on, and tackle trim,
Sails fill'd, and ftreamers waving,
Courted by all the winds that hold them play,
An amber fent of odorous perfume 720
Her harbinger, a damfel train behind;
Some rich Philiftian matron fhe may feem,
And now at nearer view, no other certain

Than

tion in Scripture of the *fhips of Tarfhifh*, which Milton as well as fome commentators might conceive to be the fame as *Tarfus* in Cilicia: *bound for th' iles of Javan*, that is Greece, for *Javan* or *Ion* the fourth fon of Japheth is faid to have peopled Greece and Ionia: or *Gadire*, Γαδειρα, Gades, Cadiz. Mr. Warburton in his notes upon Skakefpear, Merry Wives of Windfor Act III. Sc. 8. fpeaking of *the fhip-tire*, fays " it was an open " head-drefs, with a kind of fcarf " depending from behind. Its

" name of *fhip-tire* was, I pre-
" fume, from its giving the wearer
" fome refemblance of a *fhip* (as
" Shakefpear fays) *in all her trim :*
" with all her pennants out, and
" flags and ftreamers flying. Thus
" Milton in Samfon Agoniftes
" paints Dalila. This was an
" image familiar with the poets
" of that time. Thus Beaumont
" and Fletcher in their play of
" Wit without mony ———— *She*
" *fpreads fattens as the king's fhips*
" *do canvas* &c."

Than Dalila thy wife. 724

SAMSON.

My Wife, my Traitrefs, let her not come near me.

CHORUS.

Yet on fhe moves, now ftands and eyes thee fix'd,
About t' have fpoke, but now, with head declin'd
Like a fair flow'r furcharg'd with dew, fhe weeps,
And words addrefs'd feem into tears diffolv'd,
Wetting the borders of her filken veil : 730
But now again fhe makes addrefs to fpeak.

DALILA.

With doubtful feet and wavering refolution
I came, ftill dreading thy difpleafure, Samfon,
Which to have merited, without excufe,
I cannot but acknowledge; yet if tears 735
May

726. *Yet on fhe moves, &c*] Like Ifmene in the Antigone of Sophocles ver. 532.

Και μην προ πυλων ηδ' Ισμηνη
Φιλαδελφα κατω · δακρυ' ειβο-
μοιη
Νηφελη δ' οφρυων υπερ, αιμα-
τοεν
Ρεθ῀ αισχυνει,
Τεγγυσ' ενωπα παρειαν.

Mr. Jortin and Mr. Thyer both concurr'd in the fame obfervation,

and therefore it is more likely to be true.

729. *And words addrefs'd &c*] This verfe is printed imperfect in moft of the editions,

And words addrefs'd feem tears diffolv'd,

that being wanted which is in the firft edition,

And words addrefs'd feem *into* tears diffolv'd.

Mr. Jortin conjectur'd it fhould be fo

May expiate (though the fact more evil drew
In the perverfe event than I forefaw)
My penance hath not flacken'd, though my pardon
No way affur'd. But conjugal affection
Prevailing over fear, and timorous doubt, 740
Hath led me on, defirous to behold
Once more thy face, and know of thy eftate,
If ought in my ability may ferve
To lighten what thou fuffer'ft, and appeafe
Thy mind with what amends is in my power, 745
Though late, yet in fome part to recompenfe
My rafh but more unfortunate mifdeed.

S A M S O N.

Out, out Hyæna ; thefe are thy wonted arts,
And arts of every woman falfe like thee,

To

fo read, without feeing the firft
edition.

732. *With doubtful feet* &c] The
fcene between Samfon and Dalila
is drawn up with great judgment.
and particular beauty. One cannot
conceive a more artful, foft, and
perfuafive eloquence than that
which is put into the mouth of Da-
lila, nor is the part of Samfon lefs
to be admir'd for that ftern and re-
folute firmnefs which runs through
it. What alfo gives both parts a
great additional beauty is their

forming fo fine a contraft to each
other. *Thyer.*

748. *Out, out Hyæna;*] The
hyæna is a creature fomewhat like
a wolf, and is faid to imitate a hu-
man voice fo artfully as to draw
people to it and then devour them.
So Solinus, the tranfcriber of Pliny,
cap. 27 Multa de ea mira : pri-
mum quod fequitur ftabula pafto-
rum, et auditu affiduo addifcit vo-
camen, quod exprimere poffit imi-
tatione vocis humanæ, ut in homi-

S 3   nem

To break all faith, all vows, deceive, betray,   750
Then as repentant to fubmit, befeech,
And reconcilement move with feign'd remorfe,
Confefs, and promife wonders in her change,
Not truly penitent, but chief to try
Her hufband, how far urg'd his patience bears,
His virtue or weaknefs which way to affail :   756
Then with more cautious and inftructed fkill
Again tranfgreffes, and again fubmits ;
That wifeft and beft men full oft beguil'd,
With goodnefs principled not to reject   760
The penitent, but ever to forgive,
Are drawn to wear out miferable days,
Intangled with a pois'nous bofom fnake,
If not by quick deftruction foon cut off
As I by thee, to ages an example.   765

DALILA.

Yet hear me, Samfon ; not that I endevor
To leffen or extenuate my offenfe,
But that on th' other fide if it be weigh'd

By'

nem aftu accitum nocte fæviat.   A
celebrated tragic writer makes ufe
of the fame comparifon. Orphan.
Act 2.

'Tis thus the falfe hyæna makes
  her moan,
To draw the pitying traveler to
  her den ;

Your

By' itfelf, with aggravations not furcharg'd,
Or elfe with juft allowance counterpois'd,   770
I may, if poffible, thy pardon find
The eafier towards me, or thy hatred lefs.
Firft granting, as I do, it was a weaknefs
In me, but incident to all our fex,
Curiofity, inquifitive, importune   775
Of fecrets, then with like infirmity
To publifh them, both common female faults :
Was it not weaknefs alfo to make known
For importunity, that is for nought,
Wherein confifted all thy ftrength and fafety ? 780
To what I did thou fhowd'ft me firft the way.
But I to enemies reveal'd, and fhould not :
Nor fhould'ft thou have trufted that to woman's frailty:
Ere I to thee, thou to thyfelf waft cruel.
Let weaknefs then with weaknefs come to parle 785
So near related, or the fame of kind,
Thine forgive mine ; that men may cenfure thine
The gentler, if feverely thou exact not

                                              More

Your fex are fo, fuch falfe dif-   Otway to the men ; which with the
femblers all, &c.   greater juftice, let the critics and
                                   the ladies determin.
Milton applies it to a woman, but
                          S 4   840. Knowing

More ftrength from me than in thyfelf was found.

And what if love, which thou interpret'ft hate,   790

The jealoufy of love, pow'rful of fway

In human hearts, nor lefs in mine tow'rds thee,

Caus'd what I did ? I faw thee mutable

Of fancy, fear'd leſt one day thou would'ft leave me

As her at Timna, fought by all means therefore   795

How to indear, and hold thee to me firmeft :

No better way I faw than by impórtuning

To learn thy fecrets, get into my power

Thy key of ftrength and fafety : thou wilt fay,

Why then reveal'd ? I was affur'd by thofe   800

Who tempted me, that nothing was defign'd

Againft thee but fafe cuftody, and hold :

That made for me ; I knew that liberty

Would draw thee forth to perilous enterprifes,

While I at home fat full of cares and fears,   805

Wailing thy abfence in my widow'd bed ;

Here I fhould ftill enjoy thee day and night

Mine and love's prifoner, not the Philiftines,

Whole to myfelf, unhazarded abroad,

Fearlefs at home of partners in my love.   810

Thefe reafons in love's law have paft for good,

Though

Though fond and reafonlefs to fome perhaps;
And love hath oft, well meaning, wrought much woe,
Yet always pity' or pardon hath obtain'd.
Be not unlike all others, not auftere   815
As thou art ftrong, inflexible as fteel.
If thou in ftrength all mortals doft exceed,
In uncompaffionate anger do not fo.

S A M S O N.

How cunningly the forcerefs difplays
Her own tranfgreflions, to upbraid me mine?   820
That malice not repentance brought thee hither,
By this appears : I gave, thou fay'ft, th' example,
I led the way ; bitter reproach, but true ;
I to myfelf was falfe ere thou to me ;
Such pardon therefore as I give my folly,   825
Take to thy wicked deed ; which when thou fee'ft
Impartial, felf-fevere, inexorable,
Thou wilt renounce thy feeking, and much rather
Confefs it feign'd : weaknefs is thy excufe,
And I believe it, weaknefs to refift   830
Philiftian gold : if weaknefs may excufe,
What murderer, what traitor, parricide,
Inceftuous, facrilegious, but may plead it ?

All

All wickednefs is weaknefs : that plea therefore
With God or Man will gain thee no remiſſion.   835
But love conſtrain'd thee ; call it furious rage
To fatisfy thy luſt : love ſceks to' have love ;
My love how could'ſt thou hope, who took'ſt the way
To raiſe in me inexpiable hate,
Knowing, as needs I muſt, by thee betray'd ?   840
In vain thou ſtriv'ſt to cover ſhame with ſhame,
Or by evaſions thy crime uncover'ſt more.

DALILA.

Since thou determin'ſt weaknefs for no plea
In man or woman, though to thy own condemning,
Hear what aſſaults I had, what ſnares beſides,   845
What ſieges girt me round, ere I conſented ;
Which might have aw'd the beſt reſolv'd of men,
The conſtanteſt, to' have yielded without blame.
It was not gold, as to my charge thou lay'ſt,
That wrought with me : thou know'ſt the magiſtrates

And

840. *Knowing, as needs I muſt, by thee betray'd ?*] The fame manner of ſpeaking as in Paradife Loſt. IX. 792.

And knew not eating death : where fee Mr. Richardſon's note.

842. *Or by evaſions*] This is the reading of the old editions, and particularly of Milton's own : the later ones have
For by evaſions ——
which is not fo plain and intelligible.

850.—*thou*

And princes of my country came in perfon,   851
Solicited, commanded, threaten'd, urg'd,
Adjur'd by all the bonds of civil duty
And of religion, prefs'd how juft it was,
How honorable, how glorious to intrap   855
A common enemy, who had deftroy'd
Such numbers of our nation : and the prieft
Was not behind, but ever at my ear,
Preaching how meritorious with the Gods
It would be to infnare an irreligious   860
Difhonorer of Dagon : what had I
T' oppofe againft fuch pow'rful arguments?
Only my love of thee held long debate,
And combated in filence all thefe reafons
With hard conteft : at length that grounded maxim
So rife and celebrated in the mouths   866
Of wifeft men, that to the public good
Private refpects muft yield, with grave authority

Took

850. —— thou know'ft the ma-
    giftrates
And princes of my country came in
    perfon,] Judg. XVI. 5. And the
lords of the Philiftines came up unto
her, and faid unto her &c. So exact
is Milton in all the particulars of
the ftory, and improves every in-
cident.
    864. —— all thefe reafons] We
follow the reading of Milton's own
edition, and not of the others ——
all their reafons.

934. Thy

Took full poffeffion of me and prevail'd ;
Virtue, as I thought, truth, duty fo injoining.   870
S A M S O N.

I thought where all thy circling wiles would end ;
In feign'd religion, fmooth hypocrify.
But had thy love ftill odioufly pretended,
Been, as it ought, fincere, it would have taught thee
Far other reafonings, brought forth other deeds. 875
I before all the daughters of my tribe
And of my nation chofe thee from among
My enemies, lov'd thee, as too well thou knew'ft,
Too well, unbofom'd all my fecrets to thee,
Not out of levity, but over-power'd   880
By thy requeft, who could deny thee nothing ;
Yet now am judg'd an enemy.   Why then
Didft thou at firft receive me for thy hufband,
Then, as fince then, thy country's foe profefs'd ?
Being once a wife, for me thou waft to leave   885
Parents and country ; nor was I their fubject,
Nor under their protection but my own,
Thou mine, not theirs : if ought againft my life
Thy country fought of thee, it fought unjuftly,
Againft the law of nature, law of nations,   890
No

No more thy country, but an impious crew
Of men confpiring to uphold their ftate
By worfe than hoftile deeds, violating the ends
For which our country is a name fo dear;   894
Not therefore to be' obey'd. But zeal mov'd thee;
To pleafe thy Gods thou didft it; Gods unable
T' acquit themfelves and profecute their foes
But by ungodly deeds, the contradiction
Of their own deity, Gods cannot be;
Lefs therefore to be pleas'd, obey'd, or fear'd.   900
Thefe falfe pretexts and varnifh'd colors failing,
Bare in thy guilt how foul muft thou appear ?

D A L I L A.

In argument with men a woman ever
Goes by the worfe, whatever be her caufe.   904

S A M S O N.

For want of words no doubt, or lack of breath;
Witnefs when I was worried with thy peals.

D A L I L A.

I was a fool, too rafh, and quite miftaken
In what I thought would have fucceeded beft.
Let me obtain forgivenefs of thee, Samfon,
Afford me place to fhow what recompenfe   910

Tow'ards

Tow'rds thee I intend for what I have mifdone,
Mifguided; only what remains paft cure
Bear not too fenfibly, nor ftill infift
T' afflict thyfelf in vain : though fight be loft,
Life yet hath many folaces, enjoy'd   915
Where other fenfes want not their delights
At home in leifure and domeftic eafe,
Exempt from many a care and chance to which
Eye-fight expofes daily men abroad.
I to the lords will intercede, not doubting   920
Their favorable ear, that I may fetch thee
From forth this loathfome prifon-houfe, to abide
With me, where my redoubled love and care
With nurfing diligence, to me glad office,
May ever tend about thee to old age   925
With all things grateful chear'd, and fo fupply'd,
That what by me thou' haft loft thou leaft fhalt mifs.

S A M S O N.

No, no, of my condition take no care;

It

934. *Thy fair inchanted cup, and warbling charms*] Alluding no doubt to the ftory of Circe and the Sirens, but did not our author's fondnefs for Greek learning make him here forget that it is a little out of character to reprefent Samfon acquainted with the mythology of that country? It feems the more odd as the allufion to the adder immediately following is taken from Scripture.   *Thyer.*

He

It fits not; thou and I long fince are twain :
Nor think me fo unwary or accurs'd,   930
To bring my feet again into the fnare
Where once I have been caught ; I know thy trains
Though dearly to my coft, thy gins, and toils ;
Thy fair inchanted cup, and warbling charms
No more on me have pow'r, their force is null'd,
So much of adder's wifdom I have learn'd   936
To fence my ear againft thy forceries.
If in my flower of youth and ftrength, when all men
Lov'd, honor'd, fear'd me, thou alone could'ft hate me
Thy hufband, flight me, fell me, and forego me; 940
How wouldft thou ufe me now, blind, and thereby
Deceivable, in moft things as a child
Helplefs, thence eafily contemn'd, and fcorn'd,
And laft neglected ? How wouldft thou infult,
When I muft live uxorious to thy will   945
In perfect thraldom, how again betray me,
Bearing my words and doings to the lords

To

He might as well be fuppofed to know the ftory of Circe and the Sirens as of Tantalus &c before ver. 500. and there is no more impropriety in the one than in the other.

936. *So much of adder's wifdom I have learn'd*] The allufion is to Pfal. LVIII. 4, 5. *They are like the deaf adder, that ftoppeth her ear ; which will not hearken to the voice of charmers, charming never fo wifely.*
973. *On*

To glofs upon, and cenfuring, frown or fmile?

This jail I count the houfe of liberty   949

To thine, whofe doors my feet fhall never enter.

DALILA.

Let me approach at leaft, and touch thy hand.

SAMSON.

Not for thy life, left fierce remembrance wake

My fudden rage to tear thee joint by joint.

At diftance I forgive thee, go with that;

Bewail thy falfhood, and the pious works   955

It hath brought forth to make thee memorable

Among illuftrious women, faithful wives:

Cherifh thy haften'd widowhood with the gold

Of matrimonial treafon: fo farewel.

DALILA.

I fee thou art implacable, more deaf   960

To

---

973. *On both his wings, one black, the other white,*
Bears greateft names in his wild aery flight.] I think Fame has paffed for a *Goddefs* ever fince Heſiod deify'd her: 'Εϱγ. 763.

Φημη δ' 8 τις παμπαν απολλυ-
ται, ἡν τινα πολλοι
Λαοι Φημιζδσι. Θεῶ· ιυ τις εςί
και αυτη.

Fama vero nulla prorfus perit, quam quidem multi
Populi divulgant, quippe dea quidem eft et ipfa.

Milton makes her a *God*, I know not why, unlefs fecundum eos, qui dicunt utriufque fexus participatio-nem habere numina. So in his Lycidas he fays (unlefs it be a falfe print)

So

To pray'rs, than winds and feas, yet winds to feas
Are reconcil'd at length, and fea to fhore :
Thy anger, unappeafable, ftill rages,
Eternal tempeft never to be calm'd.
Why do I humble thus myfelf, and fuing   965
For peace, reap nothing but repulfe and hate ?
Bid go with evil omen, and the brand
Of infamy upon my name denounc'd ?
To mix with thy concernments I defift
Henceforth, nor too much difapprove my own. 970
Fame if not double-fac'd is double-mouth'd,
And with contrary blaft proclames moft deeds ;
On both his wings, one black, the other white,
Bears greateft names in his wild aery flight.
My name perhaps among the circumcis'd   975
In Dan, in Judah, and the bordering tribes,

To

So may fome gentle Mufe
With lucky words favor my de-
ftin'd urn,
And as *he* paffes turn,
And bid fair peace be to my fa-
ble fhroud.

Where *Mufe* is the mafculine for
poet is very bold. Perhaps it fhould
be :

Bears greateft names in his *wide*
aery flight.

What Milton fays of Fame's bear-
ing great names on his wings,
feems to be partly from Horace :
Od. II. II. 7.

Illum aget penna metuente folvi
Fama fuperftes.   *Jortin*,

To all pofterity may ftand defam'd,
With malediction mention'd, and the blot
Of falfhood moft unconjugal traduc'd.
But in my country where I moft defire,   980
In Ecron, Gaza, Afdod, and in Gath,
I fhall be nam'd among the famoufeft
Of women, fung at folemn feftivals,
Living and dead recorded, who to fave
Her country from a fierce deftroyer, chofe   985
Above the faith of wedlock-bands, my tomb
With odors vifited and annual flowers;
Not lefs renown'd than in mount Ephraim
Jael, who with inhofpitable guile
Smote Sifera fleeping through the temples nail'd.
Nor fhall I count it hainous to enjoy   991
The public marks of honor and reward
Conferr'd upon me, for the piety

Which

986.   —— *my tomb*
With odors vifited and annual
  flowers;] What is faid in
Scripture of the daughter of Jeph-
thah, *that the daughters of Ifrael*
went yearly to lament her, feems to
imply that this folemn and perio-
dical vifitation of the tombs of emi-
nent perfons was an eaftern cuftom.
                            Thyer.

So it is faid afterwards of Samfon,

  The virgins alfo fhall on feaftful
    days
Vifit his tomb with flowers.

988. *Not lefs renown'd than in*
    mount Ephraim
Jael,] Jael is celebrated in the
noble fong of Deborah and Barak,
                            Judg.

Which to my country I was judg'd to' have fhown.

At this who ever envies or repines,   995

I leave him to his lot, and like my own.

CHORUS.

She's gone, a manifeft ferpent by her fting

Difcover'd in the end, till now conceal'd.

SAMSON.

So let her go, God fent her to debafe me,

And aggravate my folly, who committed   1000

To fuch a viper his moft facred truft

Of fecrefy, my fafety, and my life.

CHORUS.

Yet beauty, though injurious, hath ftrange power,

After offenfe returning, to regain

Love once poffefs'd, nor can be eafily   1005

Repuls'd, without much inward paffion felt

And fecret fting of amorous remorfe.

SAMSON.

Judg. V. and Deborah dwelt *be-tween Ramah and Beth-el in mount Ephraim.* Judg. IV. 5.

995. *At this who ever envies or repines,*
I leave him to his lot, and like my own.] Teucer to the Chorus in Sophocles's Ajax ver. 1060.

'Οτῳ δε μη ταδ' εϛιν εν γνωμη φιλα,
Κειν@· τ' εκεινα ϛεργετω, καγω ταδε.

Cui autem hæc non funt cordi,
Illeque fua amet, et ego mea.
                                        Calton.

1003. *Yet beauty, though injurious,*
T 2   *hath*

SAMSON.

Love-quarrels oft in pleaſing concord end,
Not wedlock-treachery indang'ring life.

CHORUS.

It is not virtue, wiſdom, valor, wit,   1010
Strength, comelineſs of ſhape, or ampleſt merit
That woman's love can win or long inherit ;
But what it is, hard is to ſay,
Harder to hit,
(Which way ſoever men refer it)   1015
Much like thy riddle, Samſon, in one day
Or ſev'n, though one ſhould muſing ſit.
If any of theſe or all, the Timnian bride
Had not ſo ſoon preferr'd
Thy paranymph, worthleſs to thee compar'd,   1020
                                              Succeſſor

hath ſtrange power, &c] This truth Milton has finely exemplified in Adam forgiving Eve, and he had full experience of it in his own caſe, as the reader may ſee in the note upon Paradiſe Loſt, X. 940. for I would not repeat it here.

1008. _Love-quarrels oft in pleaſing concord end,_] Terence Andria III. III. 23.

Amantium iræ, amoris integratio eſt.

1010. _It is not virtue,_ &c] However juſt the obſervation may be, that Milton in his Paradiſe Loſt ſeems to court the favor of the female ſex, it is very certain, that he did not carry the ſame complaiſance into this performance. What the Chorus here ſays outgoes the very bittereſt ſatir of Euripides who was called the Woman-hater. It may be ſaid indeed in excuſe, that the occaſion was very provoking, and that theſe reproaches are rather to be look'd upon as a ſudden ſtart of reſentment, than cool and

Succeſſor in thy bed,
Nor both ſo looſely diſally'd
Their nuptials, nor this laſt ſo treacherouſly
Had ſhorn the fatal harveſt of thy head.
Is it for that ſuch outward ornament   1025
Was laviſh'd on their ſex, that inward gifts
Were left for haſte unfiniſh'd, judgment ſcant,
Capacity not rais'd to apprehend
Or value what is beſt
In choice, but ofteſt to affect the wrong?   1030
Or was too much of ſelf-love mix'd,
Of conſtancy no root infix'd,
That either they love nothing, or not long?
  Whate'er it be, to wiſeſt men and beſt
Seeming at firſt all heav'nly under virgin veil, 1035
                                        Soft,

and ſober reaſoning.   *Thyer.*
Theſe reflections are the more ſe-
vere, as they are not ſpoken by
Samſon, who might be ſuppoſed to
utter them out of pique and reſent-
ment, but are deliver'd by the Cho-
rus as ſerious and important truths.
But by all accounts Milton himſelf
had ſuffer'd ſome uneaſineſs through
the temper and behaviour of two of
his wives; and no wonder there-
fore that upon ſo tempting an oc-
caſion as this he indulges his ſpleen
a little, depreciates the qualifica-
tions of the women, and aſſerts the
ſuperiority of the men, and to give
theſe ſentiments the greater weight
puts them into the mouth of the
Chorus.

1020. *Thy paranymph,*] Bride-
man. *But Samſon's wife was given
to his companion, whom he had uſed
as his friend.* Judg. XIV. 20.
                              Richardſon.
  1034.—— *to wiſeſt men and beſt*]
Read *to the wiſeſt man.* See the
following expreſſions——in *his* way
— draws *him* awry. *Meadowcourt.*

T 3   We

Soft, modeſt, meek, demure,
Once join'd, the contrary ſhe proves, a thorn
Inteſtin, far within defenſive arms
A cleaving miſchief, in his way to virtue
Adverſe and turbulent, or by her charms   1040
Draws him awry inſlav'd
With dotage, and his ſenſe deprav'd
To folly and ſhameful deeds which ruin ends.
What pilot ſo expert but needs muſt wreck
Imbark'd with ſuch a ſteers-mate at the helm ?   1045
   Favor'd of Heav'n who finds
One virtuous rarely found,
That in domeſtic good combines :
Happy that houſe his way to peace is ſmooth ;
But virtue which breaks through all oppoſition,   1050
And all temptation can remove,

                                        Moſt

We have ſuch a change of the number in the Paradiſe Loſt IX. 1183.

— in *women* overtruſting
Lets *her* will rule ; reſtraint *ſhe*
   will not brook,
And left to *herſelf*, &c :

and we juſtified it there by a ſimilar inſtance from Terence.

1048.—*far within defenſive arms A cleaving miſchief,*] The words

a cleaving miſchief allude to the poiſon'd ſhirt ſent to Hercules by his wife Deianira. *Meadowcourt.*

1046. *Favor'd of Heav'n who finds* &c] If Milton like Solomon and the Son of Sirach ſatirizes the women in general, like them too he commends the virtuous and good, and eſteems a good wife a bleſſing from the Lord. Prov. XVIII. 22. *Whoſo findeth*

Moft fhines and moft is acceptable above.

Therefore God's univerfal law

Gave to the man defpotic power

Over his female in due awe,   1055

Nor from that right to part an hour,

Smile fhe or lour :

So fhall he leaft confufion draw

On his whole life, not fway'd

By female ufurpation, or difmay'd.   1060

But had we beft retire, I fee a ftorm ?

SAMSON.

Fair days have oft contracted wind and rain.

CHORUS.

But this another kind of tempeft brings.

SAMSON.

Be lefs abftrufe, my riddling days are paft.

CHORUS.

findeth a wife, findeth a good thing, and obtaineth favor of the Lord. XIX. 14. A prudent wife is from the Lord, Ecclus. XXVI. 1, 2. Bleffed is the man that hath a virtuous wife, for the number of his days fhall be double. A virtuous woman rejoiceth her hufband, and he fhall fulfil the years of his life in peace. &c. This is much better than condemning all without diftinction, as Juvenal and Boileau have done, the former

in his fixth, and the latter in his tenth fatir.

1061. But had we beft retire &c] Read

But we had beft retire ———

or

But had n't we beft retire ———

Sympfon.

T 4   1075 His

Chorus.

Look now for no inchanting voice, nor fear 1065
The bait of honied words; a rougher tongue
Draws hitherward, I know him by his ſtride,
The giant Harapha of Gath, his look
Haughty as is his pile high-built and proud.
Comes he in peace? what wind hath blown him hither
I leſs conjecture than when firſt I ſaw   1071
The ſumptuous Dalila floting this way:
His habit carries peace, his brow defiance.

Samson.

Or peace or not, alike to me he comes.

Chorus.

His fraught we ſoon ſhall know, he now arrives.

Harapha.

I come not, Samſon to condole thy chance, 1706
As theſe perhaps, yet wiſh it had not been,

Though

1075. *His fraught*] For *fraught*
read *fraight*.   Meadowcourt.
  1079. *Men call me Harapha, &c*]
This character is fictitious, but is
properly introduced by the poet,
and not without ſome foundation
in Scripture. *Arapha* or rather
Rapha (ſays Calmet) was father of
the giants of *Rephaim*.   The word

Rapha may likewiſe ſignify ſimply
a giant.   *Of ſtock renown'd as Og*,
for Og the king of Baſhan was of
the race of the Rephaim, whoſe
bed was nine cubits long, and four
broad. Deut. III. 11. *Or Anak*, the
father of the Anakims, *and the
Emims old*, Deut. II. 10, 11. *a peo-
ple great, and many, and tall as the
Anakims*;

Though for no friendly' intent. I am of Gath,
Men call me Harapha, of ſtock renown'd
As Og or Anak and the Emims old 1080
That Kiriathaim held, thou know'ſt me now
If thou at all art known. Much I have heard
Of thy prodigious might and feats perform'd
Incredible to me, in this diſpleas'd,
That I was never preſent on the place 1085
Of thoſe encounters, where we might have try'd
Each other's force in camp or liſted field :
And now am come to ſee of whom ſuch noiſe
Hath walk'd about, and each limb to ſurvey,
If thy appearance anſwer loud report. 1090

SAMSON.

The way to know were not to ſee but taſte.

HARAPHA.

Doſt thou already ſingle me ? I thought

Gyves

Anakims; *which alſo were account-*
ed giants or Rephaim, *as the Ana-*
kims, but the Moabites call them
Emims. That Kiriathaim held,
for Gen. XIV. 5. *Chedorlaomer,*
and the kings that were with him,
ſmote the Rephaims in Aſhteroth
Karnaim, and the Zuzims in Ham,
and the Emims in Shaveh Kiria-

thaim, or the plain of Kiriathaim.

1081. —— *thou know'ſt me now*
If thou at all art known.] He is
made to ſpeak in the ſpirit and al-
moſt in the language of Satan, Pa-
radiſe Loſt IV. 830.

Not to know me argues your-
ſelves unknown,

1093. *Gyves*]

Gyves and the mill had tam'd thee. O that fortune
Had brought me to the field, where thou art fam'd
To' have wrought luch wonders with an afs's jaw ;
I fhould have forc'u thee foon with other arms,   1096
Or left thy carcafs where the afs lay thrown :
So had the glory' of prowefs been recover'd
To Paleftine, won by a Philiftine   1099
From the unforefkinn'd race, of whom thou bear'ft
The higheft name for valiant acts ; that honor
Certain to' have won by mortal duel from thee,
I lofe, prevented by thy eyes put out.

S A M S O N.

Boaft not of what thou wouldft have done, but do
What then thou wouldft, thou feeft it in thy hand.

H A R A P H A.

To combat with a blind man I difdain,   1106
                                             And

1093. *Gyves*] Chains, fetters.
Cymbeline. Act 5. Sc. 3.

—— Muft I repent ?
I cannot do it better than in *gyves.*
Romeo and Juliet. Act 2. Sc. 2.
Juliet to Romeo.

'Tis almoft morning. I would
   have thee gone,
And yet no farther than a wan-
   ton's bird,

That lets it hop a little from her
   hand,
Like a poor prifoner in his twift-
   ed *gyves,*
And with a filk thred plucks it
   back again,
So loving jealous of his liberty,

Fairfax, Cant. 5. St. 42.

Thefe hands were made to fhake
   fharp fpears and fwords.

                                             Not

SAMSON AGONISTES. 283

And thou haſt need much waſhing to be touch'd.
S A M S O N.
Such uſage as your honorable lords
Afford me' aſſaſſinated and betray'd,
Who durſt not with their whole united powers 1110
In fight withſtand me ſingle and unarm'd,
Nor in the houſe with chamber ambuſhes
Cloſe-banded durſt attack me, no not ſleeping,
Till they had hir'd a woman with their gold
Breaking her marriage faith to circumvent me. 1115
Therefore without feign'd ſhifts let be aſſign'd
Some narrow place inclos'd, where ſight may give
        thee,
Or rather flight, no great advantage on me ;
Then put on all thy gorgeous arms, thy helmet
And brigandine of braſs, thy broad habergeon, 1120
                                              Vant-

Not to be ty'd in *gyves* and twiſted cords.

1120. *And brigandine of braſs,* &c] *Brigandine,* a coat of mail, Jer. XLVI. 4,——*furbiſh the ſpears, and put on the* brigandines. LI. 3. *Againſt him that bendeth, let the archer bend his bow, and againſt him that lifteth himſelf up in his* brigandine. *Habergeon,* a coat of mail for the neck and ſhoulders, Job

XLI. 26. *The ſword of him that layeth at him cannot hold, the ſpear, the dart, nor the* habergeon. Spenſer Faery Queen. B. 2. Cant. 6. St. 29.

    Their mighty ſtrokes, their *ha-*
        bergeons diſmail'd,
    And naked made each other's
        manly ſpalles.

Spalles that is ſhoulders. Fairfax Cant. 1. St. 72.

                        Some

Vant-braſs and greves, and gauntlet, add thy ſpear,

A weaver's beam, and ſeven-times-folded ſhield,

I only with an oaken ſtaff will meet thee,

And raiſe ſuch outcries on thy clatter'd iron,   1124

Which long ſhall not withhold me from thy head,

That in a little time while breath remains thee,

Thou oft ſhalt wiſh thyſelf at Gath to boaſt

Again in ſafety what thou wouldſt have done

To Samſon, but ſhall never ſee Gath more.

HARAPHA.

Thou durſt not thus diſparage glorious arms,

Which greateſt heroes have in battel worn,   1131

Their ornament and ſafety, had not ſpells

And black inchantment, ſome magician's art,

Arm'd

Some ſhirts of mail, ſome coats of plate put on,
— and ſome a *habergeon.*

Vant-braſs or *Vantbrace*, avant-bras, armour for the arms. Troilus and Creſſida. Act 1. Sc. 6. Neſtor ſpeaks.

> I'll hide my ſilver beard in a gold beaver,
> And in my *vantbrace* put this wither'd brawn.

Fairfax. Cant. 20. St. 139.

> His left arm wounded had the knight of France,

His ſhield was pierc'd, his *vantbrace* cleft and ſplit.

Greves, armour for the legs. 1 Sam. XVII. 6. *And he had* greves *of braſs upon his legs.* *Gauntlet,* an iron glove. 2 Henry IV. Act 1. Sc. 3. old Northumberland ſpeaks.

> ——Hence therefore, thou nice crutch;
> A ſcaly *gauntlet* now with joints of ſteel
> Muſt glove this hand.

1121. —— *add thy ſpear,* &c]
This is Milton's own reading: the other

Arm'd thee or charm'd thee ftrong, which thou from
   Heaven   .
Feign'dft at thy birth was giv'n thee in thy hair,   1135
Where ftrength can leaft abide, though all thy hairs
Were briftles rang'd like thofe that ridge the back
Of chaf'd wild boars, or ruffled porcupines.

S A M S O N.

I know no fpells, ufe no forbidden arts ;
My truft is in the living God, who gave me   1140
At my nativity this ftrength diffus'd
No lefs through all my finews, joints and bones,
Than thine, while I preferv'd thefe locks unfhorn,
The pledge of my unviolated vow.
For proof hereof, if Dagon be thy God,   1145
                                         Go

other editions have *and thy fpear*, which is not fo proper, for it cannot well be faid in conftruction, *put on thy fpear*. *A weaver's beam*, as Goliath's was, 1 Sam. XVII. 7. *And the ftaff of his fpear was like a weaver's beam*, and his brother's, 2 Sam. XXI. 19. *the ftaff of whofe fpear was like a weaver's beam. And fev'n-times folded fhield*, as was Ajax's, *clypei* dominus *feptemplicis* Ajax, Ovid. Met. XIII. 2.

1132. —— *had not fpells* &c] This is natural enough in the mouth of Harapha, and no ways inconfiftent with the manners of the age in which this fcene is laid, fince we are informed in Scripture that they were at that time much addicted to magical fuperftition. But yet it is very probable, that Milton adopted this notion from the Italian Epics, who are very full of inchanted arms, and fometimes reprefent their heroes invulnerable by this art. So Ariofto's Orlando is defcribed.   *Thyer.*

1138 —— *or ruffled porcupines.*] Who can doubt that Milton here had Shakefpear in mind ? Hamlet Act 1. Sc. 8.
                    .

                                         And

Go to his temple, invocate his aid
With folemneft devotion, fpread before him
How highly it concerns his glory now
To fruftrate and diffolve thefe magic fpells,
Which I to be the power of Ifrael's God   1150
Avow, and challenge Dagon to the teft,
Offering to combat thee his champion bold,
With th' utmoft of his Godhead feconded :
Then thou fhalt fee, or rather to thy forrow   1154
Soon feel, whofe God is ftrongeft, thine or mine.

H A R A P H A.

Prefume not on thy God, whate'er he be,
Thee he regards not, owns not, hath cut off
Quite from his people, and deliver'd up
Into thy enemies hand, permitted them   1159
To put out both thine eyes, and fetter'd fend thee
Into the common prifon, there to grind
Among the flaves and affes, thy comrádes,
As good for nothing elfe, no better fervice
With thofe thy boift'rous locks, no worthy match

For

And each particular hair to ftand on end,
Like quills upon the fretful porcupine.

1162. —— *thy comrádes,*] With the accent upon the laft fyllable as in 1 Henry IV. Act 4. Sc. 2.

And

For valor to affail, nor by the fword   1165
Of noble warrior, fo to ftain his honor,
But by the barber's razor beft fubdued.

S A M S O N.

All thefe indignities, for fuch they are
From thine, thefe evils I deferve and more,
Acknowledge them from God inflicted on me 1170
Juftly, yet defpair not of his final pardon
Whofe ear is ever open, and his eye
Gracious to re-admit the fuppliant ;
In confidence whereof I once again
Defy thee to the trial of mortal fight,   1175
By combat to decide whofe God is God,
Thine or whom I with Ifrael's fons adore.

H A R A P H A.

Fair honor that thou doft thy God, in trufting
He will accept thee to defend his caufe,
A Murderer, a Revolter, and a Robber.   1180

S A M S O N.   [thefe ?

Tongue-doughty Giant, how doft thou prove me
H A-

And his *comrádes*, that daft the
world afide
And bid it pafs.
1181. *Tongue-doughty*] *Doughty*

that is valiant. See Skinner. 9ρα-
συρομ☉. Æfchylus. Septem con-
tra Thebas. 617.   *Richardfon.*

1222. *Who*

Harapha.

Is not thy nation fubject to our lords?
Their magiftrates confefs'd it, when they took thee
As a league-breaker, and deliver'd bound
Into our hands : for hadft thou not committed 1185
Notorious murder on thofe thirty men
At Afcalon, who never did thee harm,
Then like a robber ftripp'dft them of their robes?
The Philiftines, when thou hadft broke the league,
Went up with armed powers thee only feeking, 1190
To others did no violence nor fpoil.

Samson.

Among the daughters of the Philiftines
I chofe a wife, which argued me no foe;
And in your city held my nuptial feaft :
But your ill-meaning politician lords,   1195
Under pretence of bridal friends and guefts,
Appointed to await me thirty fpies,
Who threatning cruel death conftrain'd the bride
To wring from me and tell to them my fecret,
That folv'd the riddle which I had propos'd.   1200
When I perceiv'd all fet on enmity,

As

1222. *Who now defies thee thrice*] arms to give the challenge and to
This was the cuftom and the law of found the trumpet *thrice.* In al-
lufion

As on my enemies, wherever chanc'd,
I us'd hoftility, and took their fpoil
To pay my underminers in their coin.
My nation was fubjected to your lords.　　1205
It was the force of conqueft; force with force
Is well ejected when the conquer'd can.
But I a private perfon, whom my country
As a league-breaker gave up bound, prefum'd
Single rebellion, and did hoftile acts.　　1210
I was no private but a perfon rais'd
With ftrength fufficient and command from Heaven
To free my country; if their fervile minds
Me their deliverer fent would not receive,
But to their mafters gave me up for nought,　1215
Th' unworthier they; whence to this day they ferve.
I was to do my part from Heav'n affign'd,
And had perform'd it, if my known offenfe
Had not difabled me, not all your force :
Thefe fhifts refuted, anfwer thy appellant　　1220
Though by his blindnefs maim'd for high attempts,
Who now defies thee thrice to fingle fight,

As

lufion to the fame practice Edgar　*by the third found of the trumpet,*
appears to fight with the Baftard　Lear. Act 5. Sc. 7.

As a petty enterprife of fmall enforce.

HARAPHA.

With thee a man condemn'd, a flave inroll'd,
Due by the law to capital punifhment?   1225
To fight with thee no man of arms will deign.

SAMSON.

Cam'ft thou for this, vain boafter, to furvey me,
To defcant on my ftrength, and give thy verdict?
Come nearer, part not hence fo flight inform'd;
But take good heed my hand furvey not thee. 1230

HARAPHA.

O Baal-zebub! can my ears unus'd
Hear thefe difhonors, and not render death?

SAMSON.

No man withholds thee, nothing from thy hand
Fear I incurable; bring up thy van,
My heels are fetter'd, but my fift is free.   1235

HARAPHA.

This infolence other kind of anfwer fits.

SAMSON.

1231. O *Baal-zebub!*] He is
properly made to invoke *Baal-zebub*, as afterwards to fwear by
Aftaroth, that is the deities of the
Philiftines and neighb'ring nations,
of whom we have faid fomething

in the notes on the Paradife Loft,
and the learned reader may fee
more in Selden.

1248. *Though fame divulge him
&c.*] So it plainly fhould be as
Milton

SAMSON.

Go baffled coward, left I run upon thee,
Though in thefe chains, bulk without fpirit vaft,
And with one buffet lay thy ftructure low,
Or fwing thee in the air, then dafh thee down   1240
To th' hazard of thy brains and fhatter'd fides.

HARAPHA.

By Aftaroth ere long thou fhalt lament
Thefe braveries in irons loaden on thee.

CHORUS.

His giantfhip is gone fomewhat creft-faln,
Stalking with lefs unconfcionable ftrides,   1245
And lower looks, but in a fultry chafe.

SAMSON.

I dread him not, nor all his giant-brood,
Though fame divulge him father of five fons,
All of gigantic fize, Goliah chief.

CHORUS.

He will directly to the lords, I fear,   1250

And

Milton himfelf corrected it, and not *divulg'd* as it is in all the editions. *Father of five fons* &c. The ftory of Goliath of Gath is very well known; and the other four are mention'd 2 Sam. XXI.15--22. *Thefe four were born to the giant* or to Harapha *in Gath, and fell by the hand of David, and by the hand of his fervants.*

And with malicious counſel ſtir them up
Some way or other yet further to afflict thee.

SAMSON.

He muſt allege ſome cauſe, and offer'd fight
Will not dare mention, leſt a queſtion riſe
Whether he durſt accept th' offer or not,   1255
And that he durſt not plain enough appear'd.
Much more affliction than already felt
They cannot well impoſe, nor I ſuſtain;
If they intend advantage of my labors,   1259
The work of many hands, which earns my keeping
With no ſmall profit daily to my owners.
But come what will, my deadlieſt foe will prove
My ſpeedieſt friend, by death to rid me hence,
The worſt that he can give, to me the beſt.
Yet ſo it may fall out, becauſe their end   1265
Is hate, not help to me, it may with mine
Draw their own ruin who attempt the deed.

CHORUS.

Oh how comely it is, and how reviving
To the ſpirits of juſt men long oppreſs'd!
When God into the hands of their deliverer   1270
Puts invincible might

To

To quell the mighty of the earth, th' oppreſſor,
The brute and boiſt'rous force of violent men
Hardy and induſtrious to ſupport
Tyrannic pow'r, but raging to purſue   1275
The righteous, and all ſuch as honor truth;
He all their ammunition
And feats of war defeats
With plain heroic magnitude of mind
And celeſtial vigor arm'd,   1280
Their armories and magazines contemns,
Renders them uſeleſs, while
With winged expedition
Swift as the lightning glance he executes
His errand on the wicked, who ſurpris'd   1285
Loſe their defenſe diſtracted and amaz'd.
    But patience is more oft the exerciſe
Of ſaints, the trial of their fortitude,
Making them each his own deliverer,
And victor over all   1290
That tyranny or fortune can inflict.
Either of theſe is in thy lot,
Samſon, with might indued
Above the ſons of men; but ſight bereav'd

May chance to number thee with thofe   1295
Whom patience finally muft crown.
   This idcl's day hath been to thee no day of reft,
Laboring thy mind
More than the working day thy hands.
And yet perhaps more trouble is behind,   1300
For I defcry this way
Some other tending, in his hand
A fcepter or quaint ftaff he bears,
Comes on amain, fpeed in his look.
By his habit I difcern him now   1305
A public officer, and now at hand.
His meffage will be fhort and voluble.

OFFICER.

Hebrews, the pris'ner Samfon here I feek.

CHORUS.

His manacles remark him, there he fits.

OFFICER.

Samfon, to thee our lords thus bid me fay;

This

1309. —— *remark him*,] Di-
ftinguifh him, point him out.
               Richardfon.
1313.—*furpaffing human rate*,]
In the firft edition it was printed
race, but in the table of Errata we
are defired to read *rate*. No won-
der the firft reading is followed in
all the editions, when it is fenfe ;
for it would have been followed in
all probability, though it had made
nonfenfe.

1325.—*mum-*

This day to Dagon is a folemn feaft,   1311
With facrifices, triumph, pomp, and games;
Thy ftrength they know furpafling human rate,
And now fome public proof thereof require
To honor this great feaft, and great aſſembly; 1315
Rife therefore with all ſpeed and come along,
Where I will fee thee hearten'd and freſh clad
To' appear as fits before th' illuftrious lords.

SAMSON.

Thou know'ft I am an Hebrew, therefore tell them,
Our law forbids at their religious rites   1320
My prefence; for that caufe I cannot come.

OFFICER.

This anfwer, be affur'd, will not content them.

SAMSON.

Have they not fword-players, and every fort
Of gymnic artifts, wreftlers, riders, runners,
Juglers and dancers, antics, mummers, mimics, 1325
But they muft pick me out with fhackles tir'd,

And

1325. ——mummers, mimics,] It was printed mummers, mimirs; mummers are maſkers according to Junius, Skinner, and the other etymologiſts; but what are mimirs? The table of Errata to the firſt edition hath fet us right, inftructing us to read mimics, but not one of the editions have followed it.

1347. Perhaps

And over-labor'd at their public mill,
To make them fport with blind activity?
Do they not feek occafion of new quarrels
On my refufal to diftrefs me more,   1330
Or make a game of my calamities?
Return the way thou cam'ft, I will not come.

OFFICER.

Regard thyfelf, this will offend them highly.

SAMSON.

Myfelf? my confcience and internal peace.
Can they think me fo broken, fo debas'd   1335
With corporal fervitude, that my mind ever
Will condefcend to fuch abfurd commands?
Although their drudge, to be their fool or jefter,
And in my midft of forrow and heart-grief   1339
To fhow them feats, and play before their God,
The worft of all indignities, yet on me
Join'd with extreme contempt? I will not come.

OFFICER.

My meffage was impos'd on me with fpeed,

Brooks

1347. *Perhaps thou fhalt have caufe to forrow indeed.*] Here the cataftrophe is anticipated, as before ver. 1266.

—— it may with mine
Draw their own ruin who attempt the deed.

And

Brooks no delay: is this thy refolution? 1344

SAMSON.

So take it with what fpeed thy meffage needs.

OFFICER.

I am forry what this ftoutnefs will produce.

SAMSON.

Perhaps thou fhalt have caufe to forrow' indeed.

CHORUS.

Confider, Samfon; matters now are ftrain'd
Up to the highth, whether to hold or break;
He's gone, and who knows how he may report 1350
Thy words by adding fuel to the flame?
Expect another meffage more imperious,
More lordly thund'ring than thou well wilt bear.

SAMSON.

Shall I abufe this confecrated gift
Of ftrength, again returning with my hair 1355
After my great tranfgreffion, fo requite
Favor renew'd, and add a greater fin
By proftituting holy things to idols;

A

And fuch anticipations are ufual with the beft dramatic writers, who knowing their own plan open it by degrees, and drop fuch hints as cannot be perfectly comprehended, till they are fully explain'd by the event. The fpeaker himfelf can only be fuppofed to have fome general

A Nazarite in place abominable
Vaunting my ftrength in honor to their Dagon ?
Befides how vile, contemptible, ridiculous,   1361
What act more execrably unclean, profane ?

CHORUS.

Yet with this ftrength thou ferv'ft the Philiftines,
Idolatrous, uncircumcis'd, unclean.

SAMSON.

Not in their idol-worfhip, but by labor   1365
Honeft and lawful to deferve my food
Of thofe who have me in their civil power.

CHORUS.

Where the heart joins not, outward acts defile not.

SAMSON.

Where outward force conftrains, the fentence holds.
But who conftrains me to the temple' of Dagon, 1370
Not dragging ? the Philiftian lords command.
Commands are no conftraints.   If I obey them,

I

general meaning, and not a diftinct conception of all the particulars, fomewhat like the high prieft in the Gofpel, who prophefied without his knowing it.

1377. *Yet that he may difpenfe &c*] Milton here probably had in view the ftory of Naaman the Sy-

rian's begging a difpenfation of this fort from Elifha, which he feemingly grants him. See 2 Kings V. 18, 19.   *Thyer.*

1384. *I with this meffenger will go along,*] With what meffenger ? It was not exprefsly faid before that the meffenger was coming;

I do it freely, vent'ring to diſpleaſe
God for the fear of Man, and Man prefer,
Set God behind : which in his jealouſy   1375
Shall never, unrepented, find forgiveneſs.
Yet that he may diſpenſe with me or thee
Preſent in temples at idolatrous rites
For ſome important cauſe, thou need'ſt not doubt.

CHORUS.

How thou wilt here come off ſurmounts my reach.

SAMSON.

Be of good courage, I begin to feel   1381
Some rouſing motions in me which diſpoſe
To ſomething extraordinary my thoughts.
I with this meſſenger will go along,
Nothing to do, be ſure, that may diſhonor   1385
Our Law, or ſtain my vow of Nazarite.
If there be ought of preſage in the mind,
This day will be remarkable in my life

By

---

ing ; it was implied indeed in what the Chorus had ſaid,

   How thou wilt here come off ſurmounts my reach :

and this might very well be underſtood by a man, who could ſee the meſſenger coming as well as the Chorus, but ſeems hardly a ſufficient intimation to a blind man, unleſs we ſuppoſe him to know that the meſſenger was coming by the ſame impulſe that he felt rouſing him to ſomething extraordinary.

1404. Maſter;;

By fome great act, or of my days the laft.   1389

Chorus.

In time thou haft refolv'd, the man returns.

Officer.

Samfon, this fecond meffage from our lords
To thee I am bid fay. Art thou our flave,
Our captive, at the public mill our drudge,
And dar'ft thou at our fending and command
Difpute thy coming ? come without delay;   1395
Or we fhall find fuch engins to affail
And hamper thee, as thou fhalt come of force,
Though thou wert firmlier faften'd than a rock.

Samson.

I could be well content to try their art,   1399
Which to no few of them would prove pernicious.
Yet knowing their advantages too many,
Becaufe they fhall not trail me through their ftreets
Like a wild beaft, I am content to go.
Mafters commands come with a pow'r refiftlefs
To fuch as owe them abfolute fubjection ;   1405
And for a life who will not change his purpofe ?

(So

1404. *Mafter's commands* &c]
This was a feint, but it had be-
tray'd itfelf had it not been cover'd
by ver. 1408.

Yet

(So mutable are all the ways of men)
Yet this be fure, in nothing to comply
Scandalous or forbidden in our Law.

OFFICER.

I praife thy refolution : doff thefe links :   1410
By this compliance thou wilt win the lords
To favor, and perhaps to fet thee free.

SAMSON.

Brethren farewel ; your company along
I will not wifh, left it perhaps offend them
To fee me girt with friends ; and how the fight 1415
Of me as of a common enemy,
So dreaded once, may now exafperate them
I know not : lords are lordlieft in their wine ;
And the well-feafted prieft then fooneft fir'd
With zeal, if ought religion feem concern'd ;   1420
No lefs the people on their holy-days
Impetuous, infolent, unquenchable :
Happen what may, of me expect to hear
Nothing difhonorable, impure, unworthy
Our God, our Law, my Nation, or myfelf,   1425

The

Yet this be fure &c. *Warburton.*   That is of going, not what he faid
1410. *I praife thy refolution :*]   laft.   *Richardfon.*
                                              1463. *That*

The laſt of me or no I cannot warrant.

Go, and the Holy One
Of Iſrael be thy guide
To what may ſerve his glory beſt, and ſpread his name
Great among the Heathen round ;   1430
Send thee the Angel of thy birth, to ſtand
Faſt by thy ſide, who from thy father's field
Rode up in flames after his meſſage told
Of thy conception, and be now a ſhield
Of fire ; that Spirit that firſt ruſh'd on thee   1435
In the camp of Dan
Be efficacious in thee now at need.

For never was from Heav'n imparted
Meaſure of ſtrength ſo great to mortal ſeed,
As in thy wondrous actions hath been ſeen.   1440
But wherefore comes old Manoah in ſuch haſte
With youthful ſteps ? much livelier than ere while
He ſeems : ſuppoſing here to find his ſon,
Or of him bringing to us ſome glad news ?

Peace with you, Brethren; my inducement hither
                                                      Was

1463. *That part moſt reverenc'd   I doubt not, in this place indulges
Dagon and his prieſts:*] Milton,   that inveterate ſpleen, which he
                                     always

Was not at prefent here to find my fon,   1446
By order of the lords new parted hence
To come and play before them at their feaft.
I heard all as I came, the city rings,
And numbers thither flock, I had no will,   1450
Left I fhould fee him forc'd to things unfeemly.
But that which mov'd my coming now, was chiefly
To give ye part with me what hope I have
With good fuccefs to work his liberty.   1454

Chorus.

That hope would much rejoice us to partake
With thee; fay, reverend Sire, we thirft to hear.

Manoah.

I have attempted one by one the lords
Either at home, or through the high ftreet paffing,
With fupplication prone and father's tears,
T' accept of ranfome for my fon their pris'ner. 1460
Some much averfe I found and wondrous harfh,
Contemptuous, proud, fet on revenge and fpite;
That part moft reverenc'd Dagon and his priefts:
Others more moderate feeming, but their aim
Private reward, for which both God and State 1465
                                                        They

always had againft public and efta- application forSamfon's deliverance
blifh'd reli___ ___ ___ight alfo pr- gr___ce at his own cafe after the
h___ ___ ___ of Manoah's Reftoration.   *Thyer.*

They eafily would fet to fale : a third
More generous far and civil, who confefs'd
They had enough reveng'd, having reduc'd
Their foe to mifery beneath their fears,
The reft was magnanimity to remit,   1470
If fome convenient ranfome were propos'd.
What noife or fhout was that ? it tore the fky.

CHORUS.

Doubtlefs the people fhouting to behold
Their once great dread, captive, and blind before them,
Or at fome proof of ftrength before them fhown,

MANOAH.

His ranfome, if my whole inheritance   1476
May compafs it, fhall willingly be paid
And number'd down : much rather I fhall choofe
To live the pooreft in my tribe, than richeft,
And he in that calamitous prifon left.   1480
No, I am fix'd not to part hence without him.
For his redemption all my patrimony,

If

1490. *It fhall be my delight* &c]
The character of a fond parent is
extremely well fupported in the
perfon of Manoah quite through
the whole performance ; but there
is in my opinion fomething parti-
cularly natural and moving in this
fpeech. The circumftance of the
old man's feeding and foothing
his fancy with the thoughts of
tending his fon and contemplating
him ennobled with fo many fa-
mous

If need be, I am ready to forgo
And quit: not wanting him I fhall want nothing.

CHORUS.

Fathers are wont to lay up for their fons,   1485
Thou for thy fon art bent to lay out all:
Sons wont to nurfe their parents in old age,
Thou in old age car'ft how to nurfe thy fon
Made older than thy age through eye-fight loft.

MANOAH.

It fhall be my delight to tend his eyes,   1490
And view him fitting in the houfe, ennobled
With all thofe high exploits by him achiev'd,
And on his fhoulders waving down thofe locks,
That of a nation arm'd the ftrength contain'd:
And I perfuade me God had not permitted   1495
His ftrength again to grow up with his hair
Garrifon'd round about him like a camp
Of faithful foldiery, were not his purpofe
To ufe him further yet in fome great fervice,

Not

mous exploits is vaftly expreffive of the doating fondnefs of an old father. Nor is the poet lefs to be admir'd for his making Manoah under the influence of this pleaf-ing imagination go ftill further, and flatter himfelf even with the hopes of God's reftoring his eyes a-gain. Hope as naturally arifes in the mind in fuch a fituation, as doubts and fears do when it is overclouded with gloominefs and melancholy.

Not to fit idle with fo great a gift   1500
Ufelefs, and thence ridiculous about him.
And fince his ftrength with eye-fight was not loft,
God will reftore him eye-fight to his ftrength.

CHORUS.

Thy hopes are not ill founded nor feem vain
.Of his delivery, and thy joy thereon   1505
Conceiv'd, agreeable to a father's love,
In both which we, as next, participate.

MANOAH.

I know your friendly minds and --- O what noife!
Mercy of heav'n, what hideous noife was that!
Horribly loud, unlike the former fhout.   1510

CHORUS.

Noife call you it or univerfal groan,
As if the whole inhabitation perifh'd!

Blood,

1504. *Thy hopes are not ill founded nor feem vain Of his delivery,*] This is very proper and becoming the gravity of the Chorus, as much as to intimate that his other hopes were fond and extravagant. And the art of the poet cannot be fufficiently admired in raifing the hopes and expectations of his perfons to the higheft pitch juft before the dreadful cataftrophe. How great and how fudden is the change from good to bad! The one renders the other more ftriking and affecting.

1508. *— and — O what noife!* &c.] It muft be very pleafing to the reader to obferve with what art and judgment Milton prepares him for the relation of the cataftrophe of this tragedy. This abrupt ftart of Manoah upon hearing

Blood, death, and deathful deeds are in that noise,
Ruin, destruction at the utmost point.

MANOAH.

Of ruin indeed methought I heard the noise:
Oh it continues, they have slain my son.　1516

CHORUS.

Thy son is rather slaying them, that outcry
From slaughter of one foe could not ascend.

MANOAH.

Some dismal accident it needs must be;
What shall we do, stay here or run and see? 1520

CHORUS.

Best keep together here, lest running thither
We unawares run into danger's mouth.
This evil on the Philistines is fall'n;
From whom could else a general cry be heard?

The

---

ing the hideous noise, and the description of it by the Chorus in their answer, in terms so full of dread and terror, naturally fill the mind with a presaging horror proper for the occasion. This is still kept up by their suspense and reasoning about it, and at last raised to a proper pitch by the frighted and distracted manner of the Messenger's coming in, and his hesitation and backwardness in telling what had happen'd. What gives it the greater strength and beauty is the sudden transition from that soothing and flattering prospect with which Manoah was entertaining his thoughts to a scene so totally opposit. *Thyer*.

1512.—*inhabitation*] Οικχμιη. Richardson.

1514. —— *at the utmost point.*] Al ultimo segno. *Richardson*.

The fufferers then will fcarce moleft us here,   1525
From other hands we need not much to fear.
What if his eye-fight (for to Ifrael's God
Nothing is hard) by miracle reftor'd,
He now be dealing dole among his foes,
And over heaps of flaughter'd walk his way?   1530

MANOAH.

That were a joy prefumptuous to be thought.

CHORUS.

Yet God hath wrought things as incredible
For his people of old; what hinders now?

MANOAH.

He can I know, but doubt to think he will;
Yet hope would fain fubfcribe, and tempts belief.
A little ftay will bring fome notice hither.   1536

CHORUS.

1529. — *be dealing dole*] Diftributing his gifts and portions among his enemies, from a Saxon word fays Skinner, but Mr. Upton in his remarks upon Ben. Johnfon's three plays p. 31. derives the word *dole* from the Greek απο τʋ διαλειν, diftribuere. By the way we may obferve, that the Chorus here entertains the fame pleafing hope of Samfon's *eye-fight* being *by miracle reftor'd*, which he had before tacitly reproved in Manoah, and Manoah who had before encourag'd the fame hope in himfelf, now defponds and reckons it *prefumptuous* in another. Such changes of our thoughts are natural and common, efpecially in any change of our fituation and circumftances. Fear and hope ufually fucceed each other like ague and fever. And it was not a flight obfervation of mankind, that could have enabled Milton to have underftood and defcrib'd the human paffions fo exactly.

CHORUS.

Of good or bad fo great, of bad the fooner;

For evil news rides poft, while good news baits.

And to our wifh I fee one hither fpeeding,

An Hebrew, as I guefs, and of our tribe. 1540

MESSENGER.

O whither fhall I run, or which way fly

The fight of this fo horrid fpectacle,

Which erft my eyes beheld and yet behold?

For dire imagination ftill purfues me.

But providence or inftinct of nature feems, 1545

Or reafon though difturb'd, and fcarce confulted,

To' have guided me aright, I know not how,

To thee firft reverend Manoah, and to thefe

My countrymen, whom here I knew remaining,

As

1536. *A little ftay will bring fome notice hither.*] The text of the firft edition wants the nine lines preceding this, and the line that follows it: but they are fupplied in the Errata. This line in that edition is in the part of the Chorus, as I think it ought to be: and fo is the next but one, in that and all the editions; though it feems to belong rather to Manoah. The line between them, which is wanting (as I juft now obferved) in the text of the firft edition, in the Errata and in all the editions fince is given to the Chorus, but the poet certainly intended both them and Manoah a fhare in it.

    CHOR. A little ftay will bring fome notice hither

Of good or bad fo great. MAN. Of bad the fooner;

For evil news rides poft, while good news baits.

    CHOR. And to our wifh I fee one hither fpeeding,

An Hebrew, as I guefs, and of our tribe. *Calton.*

1552. — *and*

As at fome diftance from the place of horror, 1550
So in the fad event too much concern'd.

MANOAH.

The accident was loud, and here before thee
With rueful cry, yet what it was we hear not;
No preface needs, thou feeft we long to know.

MESSENGER.

It would burft forth, but I recover breath
And fenfe diftract, to know well what I utter. 1556

MANOAH.

Tell us the fum, the circumftance defer.

MESSENGER.

Gaza yet ftands, but all her fons are fall'n,
All in a moment overwhelm'd and fall'n.

MANOAH.

Sad, but thou know'ft to Ifraelites not faddeft
The defolation of a hoftile city.   1561

MESSENGER.

Feed on that firft, there may in grief be furfeit.

MANOAH.

1552. —— and here before thee] Here again the old error was carefully preferved through all the editions. In the firft edition it was printed and heard before thee; but we have corrected it, as Milton himfelf corrected it in the table of Errata, to which correction as well as the reft no regard was paid in any edition, though it improves the fenfe greatly.

1554. No preface needs,] No preface

MANOAH.

Relate by whom.

MESSENGER.

By Samſon.

MANOAH.

That ſtill leſſens
The ſorrow, and converts it nigh to joy.

MESSENGER.

Ah Manoah, I refrain, too ſuddenly   1565
To utter what will come at laſt too ſoon;
Left evil tidings with too rude irruption
Hitting thy aged ear ſhould pierce too deep.

MANOAH.

Suſpenſe in news is torture, ſpeak them out.

MESSENGER.

Take then the worſt in brief, Samſon is dead.

MANOAH.

The worſt indeed, O all my hope's defeated 1571
To free him hence! but death who ſets all free

Hath

---

face is wanting. *Needs* is a verb neuter here as in Paradiſe Loſt X. 80. where ſee the note.

1556. *And ſenſe diſtract.*] The word is uſed likewiſe as an adjec- tive in Shakeſpear. Julius Cæſar Act 4. Sc. 4.

— With this ſhe fell *diſtract,*
And (her attendents abſent) ſwal-
low'd fire.

Hath paid his ranfome now and full difcharge.

What windy joy this day had I conceiv'd

Hopeful of his delivery, which now proves   1575

Abortive as the firft-born bloom of fpring

Nipt with the lagging rear of winter's froft!

Yet ere I give the reins to grief, fay firft,

How dy'd he; death to life is crown or fhame.

All by him fell thou fay'ft, by whom fell he, 1580

What glorious hand gave Samfon his death's wound ?

MESSENGER.

Unwounded of his enemies he fell.

MANOAH.

Wearied with flaughter then or how ? explain.

MESSENGER.

By his own hands.

MANOAH.

Twelfth-Night Act 5. Sc. 5.

They fay, poor gentleman! he's much *diſtract*.

1576. *Abortive as the firſt-born bloom of fpring* &c.] As Mr. Thyer fays, this fimilitude is to be admired for its remarkable juft-nefs and propriety: One cannot poffibly imagin a more exact and perfect image of the dawning hope which Manoah had conceived from the favorable anfwer he had met

with from fome of the Philiftian lords, and of its being fo fuddenly extinguifh'd by this return of ill fortune, than that of the early bloom, which the warmth of a few fine days frequently pufhes forward in the fpring, and then it is cut off by an unexpected return of winterly weather. As Mr. Warburton obferves, this beau-tiful paffage feems to be taken from Shakefpear. Henry VIII. Act 3. Sc. 6.

This

MANOAH.

Self-violence? what cause

Brought him so soon at variance with himself   1585
Among his foes?

MESSENGER.

Inevitable cause

At once both to deftroy and be deftroy'd;

The edifice, where all were met to fee him,

Upon their heads and on his own he pull'd.

MANOAH.

O laftly over-ftrong againft thyfelf!   1590

A dreadful way thou took'ft to thy revenge.

More than enough we know; but while things yet

Are in confufion, give us if thou canft,

Eye-witnefs of what firft or laft was done,

Relation

This is the ftate of man; to day he puts forth
The tender leaves of hopes, to morrow bloffoms,
And bears his blufhing honors thick upon him;
The third day comes a froft, a killing froft;
And when he thinks, good eafy man, full furely
His greatnefs is a ripening, nips his root;
And then he falls, as I do. ——

Upon which Mr. Warburton remarks, that as fpring frofts are not injurious to the *roots* of fruit-trees, he fhould imagin the poet wrote *fhoot*, that is, the tender *fhoot* on which are the young *leaves* and *bloffoms*. The comparifon, as well as expreffion of *nips*, is jufter too in this reading. Shakefpear has the fame thought in Love's Labor Loft.

Byron is like an envious fneaping froft

That

Relation more particular and diſtinct.   4595

MESSENGER.

Occaſions drew me early to this city,

And as the gates I enter'd with ſun-riſe,

The morning trumpets feſtival proclam'd

Through each high ſtreet: little I had diſpatch'd,

When all abroad was rumor'd that this day   1600

Samſon ſhould be brought forth, to ſhow the people

Proof of his mighty ſtrength in feats and games;

I ſorrow'd at his captive ſtate, but minded

Not to be abſent at that ſpectacle.

The

That bites the firſt-born infants of the ſpring.

See Warburton's Shakeſpear. Vol. 5. p. 413.

1596. *Occaſions drew me early* &c] As I obſerved before, that Milton had with great art excited the reader's attention to this grand event, ſo here he is no leſs careful to gratify it by the relation. It is circumſtantial, as the importance of it requir'd, but not ſo as to be tedious or too long to delay our expectation. It would be found difficult, I believe, to retrench one article without making it defective, or to add one which ſhould not appear redundant. The picture of Samſon in particular *with head inclin'd and eyes fix'd*, as if he was addreſſing himſelf to that God who had given him ſuch a meaſure of ſtrength, and was ſumming up all his force and reſolution, has a very fine effect upon the imagination. Milton is no leſs happy in the ſublimity of his deſcription of this grand exploit, than judicious in the choice of the circumſtances preceding it. The poetry riſes as the ſubject becomes more intereſting, and one may without rant or extravagance ſay, that the poet ſeems to exert no leſs force of genius in deſcribing than Samſon does ſtrength of body in executing. *Thyer.*

1604. —— *abſent at that ſpectacle*] The language would be more correct, if it was *abſent from* that ſpectacle.

1605. *The building was a ſpacious theatre*

Half-

The building was a fpacious theatre   1605
Half-round on two main pillars vaulted high,
With feats where all the lords and each degree
Of fort, might fit in order to behold;
The other fide was open, where the throng
On banks and fcaffolds under fky might ftand; 1610
I among thefe aloof obfcurely ftood.
The feaft and noon grew high, and facrifice
Had fill'd their hearts with mirth, high chear, and wine,
When to their fports they turn'd.   Immediately
Was Samfon as a public fervant brought,   1615

                                                   In

*Half-round on two main pillars
vaulted high,* &c] Milton has
finely accounted for this dreadful
cataftrophe, and has with great
judgment obviated the common
objection. It is commonly afked,
how fo great a building, contain-
ing fo many thoufands of people,
could reft upon two pillars fo near
placed together : and to this it is
anfwered, that inftances are not
wanting of far more large and ca-
pacious buildings than this, that
have been fupported only by one
pillar. Particularly, Pliny in the
15th chapter of the 36th book of
his natural hiftory, mentions two
theatres built by one C. Curio,
who lived in Julius Cæfar's time ;
each of which was fupported only
by one pillar, or pin, or hinge,
tho' very many thoufands of people
did fit in it together.   See Poole's
Annotations.   Mr. Thyer further
adds, that Dr. Shaw in his travels
obferving upon the eaftern method
of building fays, that the place
where they exhibit their diverfions
at this day is an advanc'd cloyfter,
made in the fafhion of a large
penthoufe, fupported only by one
or two contiguous pillars in the
front, or elfe at the center, and
that upon a fuppofition therefore
that in the houfe of Dagon, there
was a cloyfter'd ftructure of this
kind, the pulling down the front
or center pillars only which fup-
ported it, would be attended with
the like cataftrophe that happen'd
to the Philiftines.   See Shaw's tra-
vels. p. 283.
                    1619 — cata-

In their ſtate livery clad; before him pipes
And timbrels, on each ſide went armed guards,
Both horſe and foot, before him and behind
Archers, and ſlingers, cataphraƈts and ſpears.
At ſight of him the people with a ſhout   1620
Rifted the air, clamoring their God with praiſe,
Who' had made their dreadful enemy their thrall.
He patient but undaunted where they led him,
Came to the place, and what was ſet before him,
Which without help of eye might be aſſay'd, 1625
To heave, pull, draw, or break, he ſtill perform'd
All with incredible, ſtupendious force,
None daring to appear antagoniſt.
At length for intermiſſion ſake they led him
Between the pillars; he his guide requeſted   1630
(For ſo from ſuch as nearer ſtood we heard)
As over-tir'd to let him lean a while
With both his arms on thoſe two maſſy pillars,
That to the arched roof gave main ſupport.
He unſuſpicious led him; which when Samſon 1635
                                                      Felt

1619. ——— cataphraƈts] Men or
horſes completely arm'd, from κα-
ταφϱασσω armis munio.
    1649. With horrible convulſion]

In ſeveral editions it is printed con-
fuſion, but Mr. Thyer, Mr. Symp-
ſon, and every body ſaw that it
ſhould be convulſion, and ſo it is in
                                         Milton's

Felt in his arms, with head a while inclin'd,
And eyes fast fix'd he stood, as one who pray'd,
Or some great matter in his mind revolv'd:
At last with head erect thus cry'd aloud,
Hitherto, Lords, what your commands impos'd 1640
I have perform'd, as reason was, obeying,
Not without wonder or delight beheld:
Now of my own accord such other trial
I mean to show you of my strength, yet greater;
As with amaze shall strike all who behold.   1645
This utter'd, straining all his nerves he bow'd,
As with the force of winds and waters pent,
When mountains tremble, those two massy pillars
With horrible convulsion to and fro,   1649
He tugg'd, he shook, till down they came and drew
The whole roof after them, with burst of thunder
Upon the heads of all who sat beneath,
Lords, ladies, captains, counsellors, or priests,
Their choice nobility and flow'r, not only
Of this but each Philistian city round   1655
                                        Met

318　SAMSON AGONISTES.

Met from all parts to folemnize this feaft.
Samfon with thefe immix'd, inevitably
Pull'd down the fame deftruction on himfelf;
The vulgar only fcap'd who ftood without.

CHORUS.

O dearly-bought revenge, yet glorious!　1660
Living or dying thou haft fulfill'd
The work for which thou waft foretold
To Ifrael, and now ly'ft victorious
Among thy flain felf-kill'd
Not willingly, but tangled in the fold　1665
Of dire neceffity, whofe law in death conjoin'd
Thee with thy flaughter'd foes in number more
Than all thy life had flain before.

SEMICHORUS.

While their hearts were jocond and fublime,
Drunk with idolatry, drunk with wine,　1670
And fat regorg'd of bulls and goats,
Chaunting their idol, and preferring
Before our living Dread who dwells

In

1667. —— in number more Than all thy life had flain before.] Judges XVI. 30. So the dead which he flew at his death, were more than they which he flew in his life. 1674. In Silo] Where the tabernacle and ark were at that time. 1682. So fond are mortal men, &c] Agreeable

In Silo his bright fanctuary:
Among them he a fpi'rit of phrenzy fent,   1675
Who hurt their minds,
And urg'd them on with mad defire
To call in hafte for their deftroyer;
They only fet on fport and play
Unweetingly importun'd   1680
Their own deftruction to come fpeedy upon them.
So fond are mortal men
Fall'n into wrath divine,
As their own ruin on themfelves t'invite,
Infenfate left, or to fenfe reprobate,   1685
And with blindnefs internal ftruck.

Semichorus.

  But he though blind of fight,
Defpis'd and thought extinguifh'd quite,
With inward eyes illuminated,
His fiery virtue rous'd   1690
From under afhes into fudden flame,
And as an evening dragon came,

Affailant

Agreeable to the common maxim,
Quos Deus vult perdere dementat
prius.   *Thyer.*
  1692. *And as an evening dragon*

came &c.] Mr. Calton fays that Milton certainly dictated
  And *not* as an evening dragon
  came.

Samfon

Aſſailant on the perched rooſts,

And neſts in order rang'd

Of tame villatic fowl; but as an eagle   1695

His cloudleſs thunder bolted on their heads.

So virtue giv'n for loſt,

Depreſs'd, and overthrown, as ſeem'd,

Like that ſelf-begotten bird

In the Arabian woods imboſt,   1700

That no ſecond knows nor third,

And lay ere while a holocauſt,

                                  From

Samſon *did not* ſet upon them like an evening dragon; *but* darted ruin on their heads like the thunder-bearing eagle. Mr. Sympſon to the ſame purpoſe propoſes to read

     And *not* as evening dragon came ——*but* as an eagle &c.

Mr. Thyer underſtands it otherwiſe, and explains it without any alteration of the text, to which rather I incline. One might produce (ſays he) authorities enow from the naturaliſts to ſhow that ſerpents devour fowls. That of Aldrovandus is ſufficient, and ſerves fully to juſtify this ſimile. Speaking of the food of ſerpents he ſays, Etenim aves, et potiſſimum avium pullos in nidis adhuc degentes libenter furantur. Aldrov. de Serp. & Drac. Lib. 1. c. 3. It

is common enough among the ancient poets to meet with ſeveral ſimiles brought in to illuſtrate one action, when one cannot be found that will hold in every circumſtance. Milton does the ſame here, introducing this of the dragon merely in alluſion to the order in which the Philiſtians were placed in the amphitheatre, and the ſubſequent one of the eagle to expreſs the rapidity of that vengeance which Samſon took of his enemies.

     1695. —— *villatic fowl*;] *Villaticas alites*, Plin. Lib. 23. Sect. 17.   *Richardſon.*

     1695. —— *but as an eagle* &c] In the Ajax of Sophocles it is ſaid that his enemies, if they ſaw him appear, would be terrify'd like birds at the appearance of the vultur or eagle, ver 167.

                                    Aλλ'

From out her afhy womb now teem'd,
Revives, reflorifhes, then vigorous moft
When moft unactive deem'd,   1705
And though her body die, her fame furvives
A fecular bird ages of lives.

MANOAH.

Come, come, no time for lamentation now,
Nor much more caufe ; Samfon hath quit himfelf
Like Samfon, and heroically hath finifh'd   1710
A life heroic, on his enemies

                         Fully

Ἀλλ' ὅτι γαρ δὴ &c.

The Greek verfes, I think, are faulty, and as I remember, are corrected not amifs by Dawes in his Mifcell. Critic.   *Jortin.*

1700. —— *imboft.*] Conceal'd, cover'd. Spenfer Faery Queen. B. 1. Cant. 3. St. 24.

   A knight her met in mighty arms *imboft.*
               Richardfon.

1702. —— *a holocauft*] An entire burnt-offering. Elfe generally only part of the beaft was burnt.
               Richardfon.
1706. —— *her fame furvives A fecular bird ages of lives.*] The conftruction and meaning of the who'e period I conceive to be this, Virtue giv'n for loft, like the phœnix confum'd and now teem'd from

Vol. I.

out her afhy womb, revives, reflorifhes, and though her body die which was the cafe of Samfon, yet her fame furvives a phœnix many ages : for the comma after *furvives* in all the editions fhould be omitted, as Mr. Calton has obferved as well as myfelf. The phœnix, fays he, liv'd *a thoufand years* according to fome [See Bochart's Hierozoicon.Parsfecunda.p. 817.] and hence it is called here *a fecular bird.* Ergo quoniam fex diebus cuncta Dei opera perfecta funt ; per *fecula fex,* id eft annorum *fex millia,* manere hoc ftatu mundum neceffe eft. Lactantius Div Inft. Lib. 7. c. 14. The fame of virtue (the Semichorus faith) *furvives,* outlives this *fecular bird* many ages. The comma, which is in all the editions after *furvives,* breaks the conftruction.

Y   1713.——*s*

Fully reveng'd, hath left them years of mourning,
And lamentation to the sons of Caphtor
Through all Philiftian bounds; to Ifrael
Honor hath left, and freedom, but let them   1715
Find courage to lay hold on this occasion;
To' himself and father's houfe eternal fame;
And which is beft and happieft yet, all this
With God not parted from him, as was fear'd,
But favoring and affifting to the end.   1720
Nothing is here for tears, nothing to wail
Or knock the breaft, no weaknefs, no contempt,
Difpraife, or blame, nothing but well and fair,
And what may quiet us in a death fo noble.
Let us go find the body where it lies   1725
Sok'd in his enemies blood, and from the ftream
With lavers pure and cleanfing herbs wafh off
The clotted gore.   I with what fpeed the while
(Gaza is not in plight to fay us nay)

Will

1713. — to the fons of Caphtor]
Caphtor it fhould be, and not Chap-
tor as in feveral editions: and the
fons of Caphtor are Philiftines, ori-
ginally of the iland Caphtor or
Crete. The people were called
Caphtorim, Cherethim, Ceretim,
and afterwards Cretians. A colony
of them fettled in Paleftine, and
there went by the name of Philif-
tim.   Meadowcourt.
    1730. Will fend for all my kin-
    dred, all my friends, &c] This
is founded upon what the Scrip-
ture faith, Judg. XVI. 31. which
the poet has finely improv'd. Then
his

Will fend for all my kindred, all my friends, 1730
To fetch him hence, and folemnly attend
With filent obfequy and funeral train
Home to his father's houfe: there will I build him
A monument, and plant it round with fhade
Of laurel ever green, and branching palm, 1735
With all his trophies hung, and acts inroll'd
In copious legend, or fweet lyric fong.
Thither fhall all the valiant youth refort,
And from his memory inflame their breafts
To matchlefs valor, and adventures high: 1740
The virgins alfo fhall on feaftful days
Vifit his tomb with flow'rs, only bewailing
His lot unfortunate in nuptial choice,
From whence captivity and lofs of eyes.

CHORUS.

All is beft, though we oft doubt, 1745
What th' unfearchable difpofe

Of

---

his brethren, and all the houfe of
his father, came down and took him,
and brought him up, and buried
him between Zorah and Efhtaol in
the burying-place of Manoah his fa-
ther.

  1745. *All is beft, though we oft*
    doubt, &c] There is a great

refemblance betwixt this fpeech of
Milton's Chorus, and that of the
Chorus in Æfchylus's Supplices,
beginning at ver. 90.

    Διϴ· ἱμιρϴ· ᴂκ ειθηρατϴ· ἐ-
    τυχθη
  &c to ver. 109. *Thyer.*

Of higheſt wiſdom brings about,

And ever beſt found in the cloſe.

Oft he ſeems to hide his face,

But unexpectedly returns,   1750

And to his faithful champion hath in place

Bore witneſs glorioufly; whence Gaza mourns

And all that band them to refiſt

His uncontrollable intent;

His ſervants he with new acquiſt   1755

Of true experience from this great event

· With peace and confolation hath difmiſt,

And calm of mind all paffion ſpent.

1755. *His ſervants he with new acquiſt*] It is *his ſervant* in moſt of the editions, but the firſt edition has it rightly *his ſervants*, meaning the Chorus and other perſons preſent. *Acquiſt*, the ſame as acquiſition, a word that may be found in Skinner, but I do not remember to have met with it elſewhere.

1757. *With peace and confolation hath difmiſt, And calm of mind all paffion ſpent.*] This moral leſſon in the concluſion is very fine, and excellently ſuited to the beginning. For Milton had choſen for the motto to this piece a paſſage out of Ariſtotle, which may ſhow what was his defign in writing this tragedy, and the ſenſe

of which he hath expreſſed in the preface, that " tragedy is of power " by raiſing pity and fear, or ter- " ror, to purge the mind of thoſe " and ſuch like paffions, &c." and he exemplifies it here in Manoah and the Chorus, after their various agitations of paffion, acquieſcing in the divine difpenfations, and thereby inculcating a moſt inſtructive leſſon to the reader. As this work was not intended for the ſtage, it is not divided into acts, but if any critic ſhould be difpoſed ſo to divide it, he may eaſily do it by beginning the ſecond act at the entrance of Manoah, the third at the entrance of Dalila, the fourth at the entrance of Harapha, and the fifth at the entrance of the public Officer; but the ſtage is is never empty or without perfons, according to the model of the beſt written tragedies among the Ancients. I have faid in the life of Milton, that "Biſhop Atterbury "had an intention of getting "Mr. Pope to divide the Samſon "Agoniſtes into acts and ſcenes, "and of having it acted by the "King's Scholars at Weſtminſter." And ſee what he ſays to that purpoſe in one of his letters to Mr. Pope. "I hope you won't utterly forget "what paſs'd in the coach about "Samſon Agoniſtes. I ſhan't preſs "you as to time, but ſome time "or other, I wiſh you would re- "view, and poliſh that piece. If "upon a new peruſal of it (which "I deſire you to make) you think "as I do, that it is written in the "very ſpirit of the Ancients ; it "deſerves your care, and is capa- "ble of being improved, with "little trouble, into a perfect mo- "del and ſtandard of tragic poetry "—— always allowing for its be- "ing a ſtory taken out of the "Bible, which is an objection that "at this time of day, I know is "not to be got over."

THE END.

Y 3

From

From MILTON's Manuſcript.

The Perſons.

Michael
Heavenly Love
Chorus of Angels
Lucifer
Adam }
Eve } with the Serpent
Conſcience
Death
Labor ⎫
Sickneſs ⎪
Diſcontent ⎬ Mutes
Ignorance ⎪
with others ⎭
Faith
Hope
Charity

The Perſons.

Moſes
Divine Juſtice. Mercy, Wiſdom,
  Heavenly Love
Heſperus the Evening Star
Chorus of Angels
Lucifer
Adam
Eve
Conſcience
Labor
Sickneſs ⎫
Diſcontent ⎪
Ignorance ⎬ Mutes
Fear ⎪
Death ⎭
Faith
Hope
Charity

Other Tragedies.

ADAM in BANISHMENT.

The FLOOD.

ABRAM in EGYPT.

PARADISE LOST.

The Perſons.

Moſes προλογίζει, recounting how he aſſum'd his true body; that it corrupts not, becauſe of his [abode] with God in the mount; declares the like of Enoch and Eliah; beſides the purity of the place, that certain pure winds, dews, and clouds preſerve it from corruption; whence exhorts to the ſight of God; tells they cannot ſee Adam in the ſtate of innocence by reaſon of their ſin.

Juſtice ⎫ debating what ſhou'd
Mercy ⎬ become of Man, if
Wiſdom ⎭ he fall.
Chorus of Angels ſing a hymn of the creation.

Act II.
Heavenly Love.
Evening Star.
Chorus ſing the marriage ſong, and deſcribe Paradiſe.

Act

Act III.

Lucifer contriving Adam's ruin. Chorus fears for Adam, and relates Lucifer's rebellion and fall.

Act IV.

Adam }
Eve } fallen.

Conscience cites them to God's examination.

- Chorus bewails, and tells the good Adam hath loft.

Act V.

Adam and Eve driven out of Paradife :

Prefented by an Angel with Labor, Grief, Hatred ⎫
Envy, War, Famin, Pe- ⎪
ftilence, Sicknefs, Dif- ⎬ Mutes,
content, Ignorance, Fear, ⎪
Death enter'd into the ⎭
world,

to whom he gives their names : likewife Winter, Heat, Tempeft, &c.

Faith ⎫ comfort him and in-
Hope ⎬ ftruct him.
Charity ⎭

Chorus briefly concludes.

The Deluge. Sodom. Dinah. Vide Eufeb. Praeparat. Evang. L. 9. C. 22.

The Perfons.

Dinah.   Hamor.
Debora } Rebecca's Sichem.
        } nurfe   Counfelors 2.
Jacob.   Nuncius.
Simeon.   Chorus.
Levi.

Thamar Cuophorufa, where Judah is found to have been the author of that crime, which he con---- in Thamar. Thamar ex-- in what fhe attempted.

The Golden Calf, or the Maffacre in Horeb.
The Quails, Num. 11.
The Murmurers, Num. 14.
Corah, Dathan, &c. Num. 16, 17.
Moabitides, Num. 25.
Achan, Jofue 7 and 8.
Jofuah in Gibeon, Jof. 10.
Gideon Idoloclaftes, Jud. 6, 7.
Gideon purfuing, Jud. 8.
Abimelech the Ufurper, Jud. 9.
Samfon purfophorus, or Hybriftes, or Samfon marrying or in Ramath Lechi, Jud. 15.
Dagonalia Jud. 16.
Comazontes, or the Benjaminites, or the Rioters, Jud. 19, 20, 21.
Theriftria, a paftoral out of Ruth.
Eliadae, Hophni and Phinehas, Sam. 1, 2, 3, 4, beginning with the firft overthrow of Ifrael by the Philiftins, interlac'd with Samuel's vifion concerning Eli's family.
Jonathan refcued, Sam. 1. 14.
Doeg flandering, Sam. 1. 22.
The Sheepfhearers in Carmel, a paftoral, 1 Sam. 25.
Saul in Gilboa, 1 Sam. 28. 31.
David revolted, 1 Sam. from the 27 c. to the 31.
David adulterous, 2 Sam. c. 11, 12.
Tamar, 2 Sam. 13.
Achitophel, 2 Sam. 15, 16, 17, 18.
Adoniah, 1 Reg. 2.
Solomon Gynaecocratumenus, or Idolomargus, aut Thyfiazufae. Reg. 1. 11.
Rehoboam, 1 Reg. 12. where is difputed of a politic religion.
Abizs Therfaeus. 1 Reg. 14. The queen after much difpute, as the laft

laſt refuge ſent to the prophet Ahias of Shilo ; receives the meſſage. The Epitaſis in that ſhe hearing the child ſhall die as ſhe comes home, refuſes to return, thinking thereby to elude the oracle. The former part is ſpent in bringing the ſick prince forth as it were deſirous to ſhift his chamber and couch as dying men uſe, his father telling him what ſacrifice he had ſent for his health to Bethel and Dan ; his fearleſſneſs of death, and putting his father in mind to ſet [ſend] to Ahiah. The Chorus of the elders of Iſrael, bemoaning his virtues bereft them, and at another time wondring why Jeroboam being bad himſelf ſhould ſo grieve for his ſon that was good, &c.

Imbres, or the Showers, 1 Reg. 18, 19.

Naboth συκοφαντύμενΘ, 1 Reg. 21.

Ahab, 1 Reg. 22. beginning at the ſynod of falſe prophets; ending with relation of Ahab's death ; his body brought ; Zedechiah ſlain by Ahab's friends for his ſeducing. (See Lavater, 2 Chron. 18.)

Elias in the mount, 2 Reg. 1. 'Ορειβάτης, or better, Elias Polemiſtes.

Eliſæus Hudrochoos, 2 Reg. 3. Hudrophantes, Aquator.

Eliſæus Adorodocétas.

Eliſæus Menutes, five in Dothaimis, 2 Reg. 6.

Samaria Liberata, 2 Reg. 7.

Achabæi Cunoborωmeni, 2 Reg. 9. The ſcene Jeſrael: beginning from the watchman's diſcovery of Jehu till he go out : in the mean while, meſſage of things paſſing brought to Jeſebel, &c. Laſtly the 70 heads of Ahab's ſons brought

in, and meſſage brought of Ahaziah's brethren ſlain on the way, c. 10.

Jehu Belicola, 2 Reg. 10.

Athaliah, 2 Reg. 11.

Amaziah Doryalotus, 2 Reg. 14. 2 Chron. 25.

Hezechias πολιορκύμενος, 2 Reg. 18, 19. Heſechia beſieg'd. The wicked hypocriſy of Shebna, ſpoken of in the 11, or thereabout of Iſaiah, and the commendation of Eliakim will afford αφορμας λογου, together with a faction, that ſought help from Egypt.

Joſiah Αιαζomenos, 2 Reg. 23.

Zedechiah νεοτερίζων, 2 Reg. but the ſtory is larger in Jeremiah.

Solymων Haloſis ; which may begin from a meſſage brought to the city, of the judgment upon Zedechiah and his children in Ribla, and ſo ſeconded with the burning and deſtruction of city and temple by Nebuzaradan ; lamented by Jeremiah.

Aſa or Æthiopes, 2 Chron. 14. with the depoſing his Mother, and burning her idol.

The three Children, Dan. 3.

Britiſh. Trag.

1. The cloiſter king Conſtans ſet up by Vortiger.
2. Vortiger poiſon'd by Roena.
3. Vortiger immur'd.

The three following were added afterwards in the margin.

Venutius huſband to Cartiſmandua.

Vortiger marrying Roena. See Speed. reprov'd by Vordin archbiſhop of London. Speed.

The

The maffcre of the Britons by Hengift in their cups at Salibury plain. Malmifbury.

4. Sigher of the Eaft-Saxons revolted from the faith, and reclaim'd by Jarumang.

5. Ethelbert of the Eaft-Angles flain by Offa the Mercian. See Holinfh. L. 6. c. 5. Speed in the Life of Offa and Ethelbert.

· 6. Sebert flain by Penda after he had left his kingdom. See Holinfhed, 116. p.

7. Wulfer flaying his two fons, for being Chriftians.

8. Ofbert of Northumberland flain for ravifhing the wife of Bernbocard, and the Danes brought in. See Stow. Holinfh. L. 6. c. 12. and efpecially Speed, L. 8. c. 2.

9. Edmund laft king of the Eaft-Angles martyr'd by Hinguar the Dane. See Speed, L. 8. c. 2.

10. Sigebert, tyrant of the Weft-Saxons flain by a Swineherd.

11. Edmund brother of Athelftan flain by a thief at his own table. Malmefb.

12. Edwin, fon to Edward the younger, for luft depriv'd of his kingdom, or rather by faction of Monks, whom he hated; together with the impoftor Dunftan.

13. Edward fon of Edgar murder'd by his ftep-mother. To which may be inferted the tragedy ftirr'd up betwixt the Monks and Priefts about marriage.

14. Etheldred, fon of Edgar, a flothful king, the ruin of his land by the Danes.

15. Ceaulin, king of Weft-Saxons, for tyranny depos'd, and banifh'd, and dying.

16. The flaughter of the Monks of Bangor by Edelfride ftirr'd up,

as is faid, by Ethelbert, and he by Auftin the Monk, becaufe the Britons would not receive the rites of the Roman Church. See Bede, Geffrey Monmouth, and Holinfhed, p. 104. which muft begin with the Convocation of Britifh Clergy by Auftin to determin fuperfluous points, which by them was refufed.

17. Edwin by vifion promis'd the kingdom of Northumberland on promife of his converfion, and therein eftablifh'd by Rodoald king of Eaft-Angles.

18. Ofwin king of Deira flain by Ofwie his friend king of Bernitia, through inftigation of flatterers. See Holinfhed, p. 115.

19. Sigibert of the Eaft-Angles keeping company with a perfon excommunicated, flain by the fame man in his houfe, according as the bifhop Cedda had foretold.

20. Egfride king of the Northumbers flain in battle againft the Picts, having before wafted Ireland, and made war for no reafon on men that ever lov'd the Englifh; forewarn'd alfo by Cuthbert not to fight with the Picts.

21. Kinewulf, king of Weft-faxons, flain by Kineard in the houfe of one of his concubines.

22. Gunthildis, the Danifh lady, with her hufband Palingus, and her fon, flain by appointment of the traitor Edrick in king Ethelred's days. Holinfhed, 7. L. c. 5. together with the maffacre of the Danes at Oxford. Speed.

23. Brightrick of Weft-faxons poifon'd by his wife Ethelburge Offa's daughter, who dies miferably alfo in beggery after adultery in a nunnery. Speed in Bithrick.

24. Alfred

24. Alfred in difguife of a mi-
niftrel difcovers the Danes negli-
gence, fets on with a mighty
flaughter; about the fame time the
Devonfhire men :out Hubba and
flay him.
A Heroical poem may be found-
ed fomewhere in Alfred's reign,
efpecially at his iffuing out of Ede-
lingfey on the Danes, whofe ac-
tions are well like thofe of Ulyf-
fes.

25. Altheftan expofing his bro-
ther Edwin to the fea, and repent-
ing.

26. Edgar flaying Ethelwold for
falfe play in wooing, wherein may
be fet out his pride, luft, which he
thought to clofe by favoring Monks
and building Monafteries: alfo the
difpofition of woman in Elfrida to-
ward her hufband.

27. Swane befieging London,
and Ethelred repuls'd by the Lon-
doners.

28 Harold flain in battel by
William the Norman. The firft
fcene may begin with the ghoft of
Alfred, the fecond fon of Ethelred,
flain in cruel manner by Godwin
Harold's father, his mother and
brother diffuading him.

29. Edmond Ironfide defeating
the Danes at Brentford, with his
combat with Canute.

30. Edmund Ironfide murder'd
by Edrick the traitor, and reveng'd
by Canute.

31. Gunilda, daughter to king
Canute and Emma, Wife to Henry
the third Emperor, accus'd of in-
chaftity, is defended by her Englifh
page in combat againft a giant-like
adverfary; who by him at two
blows is flain, &c. Speed in the
Life of Canute.

32. Hardiknute dying in his
cups, an example to riot.

33. EdwardConfeffor's divorcing
and imprifoning his noble wife E-
ditha, Godwin's daughter; where-
in is fhowed his over affection to
ftrangers the caufe of Godwin's in-
furrection, wherein Godwin's for-
bearance of battel prais'd, and the
Englifh moderation on both fides
magnified. His flacknefs to redrefs
the corrupt clergy, and fuperfti-
tious pretence of chaftity.

ABRAM from Morea, or ISAAC
redeem'd.

The Occonomy may be thus.
The fifth or fixth day after Abra-
ham's departure, Eleazer Abram's
fteward, firft alone, and then with
the Chorus, difcourfe of Abra-
ham's ftrange voyage, their miftrefs
forrow and perplexity accompanied
with frightful dreams; and tell the
manner of his rifing by night, tak-
ing his fervants and his fon with
him. Next may come forth Sarah
herfelf; after the Chorus, or If-
mael, or Agar; next fome fhep-
herd or company of merchants
paffing through the mount in the
time that Abram was in the mid-
work, relate to Sarah what they
faw. Hence lamentation, fears,
wonders: the matter in the mean
while divulg'd. Aner or Efchcol,
or Mamre Abram's confederates
come to the houfe of Abram to
be more certain, or to bring news;
in the mean while difcourfing as
the world would of fuch an ac-
tion divers ways, bewailing the fate
of fo noble a man faln from his re-
putation, either through divine ju-
ftice, or fuperftition, or coveting
to

to do fome notable act through zeal. At length a fervant fent from Abram relates the truth ; and laſt he himſelf comes with a great train of Melchizedeck, whoſe ſhepherds being fecret eye-witneſſes of all paſſages had related to their maſter, and he conducted his friend Abraham home with joy.

BAPTISTES.

The Scene, the Court.

Beginning from the morning of Herod's birth-day.

Herod by fome Counſellor perfuaded * on his birth-day to releaſe John Baptiſt, purpoſes it, cauſes him to be fent for to the court from priſon. The Queen hears of it, takes occaſion to paſs where he is, on purpoſe, that under pretence of reconciling to him, or ſeeking to draw a kind retraction from him of his cenſure on the marriage ; to which end ſhe ſends a courtier before to found whether he might be perfuaded to mitigate his ſentence, which not finding, ſhe herſelf craftily aſſays, and on his conſtancy founds an accuſation to Herod of a contumacious affront on ſuch a day before many peers, prepares the king to fome paſſion, and at laſt by her daughter's dancing effects it. There may prologize the Spirit of Philip, Herod's brother. It may alſo be thought, that Herod had well bedew'd himſelf with wine, which made him grant the eaſier to his

wives daughter. Some of his diſciples alſo, as to congratulate his liberty, may be brought in, with whom after certain command of his death many compaſſioning words of his diſciples, bewailing his youth cut off in his glorious courſe, he telling them his work is done, and wiſhing them to follow Chriſt his maſter.

SODOM.

The title, Cupid's funeral pile. Sodom burning.

The Scene before Lot's gate.

The Chorus conſiſts of Lot's ſhepherds comn to the city about fome affairs await in the evening their maſter's return from his evening walk toward the citygates. He brings with him two young men or youths of noble form. After likely diſcourſes prepares for their entertainment. By then fupper is ended, the gallantry of the town paſs by in proceſſion with muſic and fong to the temple of Venus Urania or Peor, and underſtanding of two noble ſtrangers arriv'd, they ſend two of their choiceſt youth with the prieſt to invite them to their city ſolemnities, it being an honor that their city had decreed to all fair perſonages, as being ſacred to their Goddeſs. The Angels being aſkt by the prieſt whence they are, ſay they are of Salem ; the prieſt inveighs againſt the ſtrict reign of Melchizedec. Lot, that knows their

* Or elſe the Queen may plot under pretence of begging for his liberty, to feek to draw him into a ſnare by his freedom of ſpeech.

drift,

drift, anfwers thwartly at laft, of which notice given to the whole affembly, they haften thither, tax him of prefumption, fingularity, breach of city-cuftoms; in fine, after violence, the Chorus of fhepherds prepare refiftance in their mafter's defenfe, calling the reft of the ferviture; but being forc'd to give back, the Angels open the door, refcue Lot, difcover themfelves, warn him to gather his friends and fons in law out of the city. He goes and returns, as having met with fome incredulous. Some other friend or fon in law out of the way, when Lot came to his houfe, overtakes him to know his bufinefs. Here is difputed of incredulity of divine judgments, and fuch like matter: at laft is defcribed the parting from the city; the Chorus depart with their mafter; the Angels do the deed with all dreadful execution; the King and Nobles of the city may come forth, and ferve to fet out the terror; a Chorus of Angels concluding, and the Angels relating the event of Lot's journey and of his wife. The firft Chorus beginning, may relate the courfe of the city each evening every one with miftrefs or Ganymed, gitterning along the ftreets, or folacing on the banks of Jordan, or down the ftream. At the prieft's inviting the Angels to the folemnity, the Angels pitying their beauty may difpute of love, and how it differs from luft, feeking to win them. In the laft fcene, to the King and Nobles, when the fierce thunders begin aloft, the Angel appears all girt with flames, which he faith are the flames of true love, and tells the King, who falls down with terror, his juft fuffering, as alfo Athane's, i. e. Gener, Lot's fon in law, for defpifing the continual admonitions of Lot: then calling to the thunders, lightnings, and fires, he bids them hear the call and command of God to come and deftroy a godlefs nation: he brings them down with fome fhort warning to other nations to take heed.

Chrift born.
Herod maffacring, or Rachel weeping, Matt. II.
Chrift bound.
Chrift crucifi'd.
Chrift rifen.
Lazarus. Joan. XI.

ADAM UNPARADIS'D.

The Angel Gabriel either defcending or entring, fhowing fince this globe was created, his frequency as much on Earth, as in Heaven: defcribes Paradife. Next the Chorus fhewing the reafon of his coming to keep his watch in Paradife after Lucifer's rebellion, by command from God, and withal expreffing his defire to fee and know more concerning this excellent new creature, Man. The Angel Gabriel, as by his name fignifying a prince of power, tracing Paradife with a more free office, paffes by the ftation of the Chorus, and defired by them relates what he knew of Man, as the creation of Eve, with their love and marriage. After this Lucifer appears after his overthrow, bemoans himfelf,

himfelf, feeks revenge on Man. The Chorus prepare refiftance at his firft approach. At laft, after difcourfe of enmity on either fide, he departs; whereat the Chorus fings of the battel, and victory in Heaven againft him and his accomplices; as before, after the firft Act, was fung a hymn of the creation. Here again may appear Lucifer relating and infulting in what he had done to the deftruction of Man. Man next, and Eve having by this time been feduc'd by the ferpent appears confufedly cover'd with leaves. Confcience in a fhape accufes him, Juftice cites him to the place, whither Jehovah call'd for him. In the mean while the Chorus entertains the ftage, and is informed by fome Angel the manner of his fall. Here the Chorus bewails Adam's fall. Adam then and Eve return, accufe one another, but efpecially Adam lays the blame to his wife, is ftubborn in his offenfe. Juftice appears; reafons with him, convinces him. The Chorus admonifheth Adam, and bids him beware Lucifer's example of impenitence. The Angel is fent to banifh them out of Paradife; but before caufes to pafs before his eyes in fhapes a Mafk of all the evils of this life and world. He is humbled, relents, defpairs; at laft appears Mercy, comforts him, promifes the Mefliah; then calls in Faith, Hope, and Charity; inftructs him; he repents, gives God the glory, fubmits to his penalty. The Chorus briefly concludes. Compare this with the former draught.

Scotch Stories, or rather Britifh of the North parts.

ATHIRCO flain by Natholochus, whofe daughter he had ravifht, and this Natholochus ufurping thereon the kingdom, feeks to flay the kindred of Athirco, who fcape him and confpire againft him. He fends to a witch to know the event. The witch tells the meffenger, that he is the man fhall flay Natholochus: he detefts it, but in his journey home changes his mind, and performs it Scotch Chron. Englifh, p. 68, 69.

DUFFE and DONWALD, a ftrange ftory of witchcraft, and murder difcover'd and reveng'd. Scotch Story, 149, &c.

HAIE, the Plowman, who with his two fons that were at plough running to the battel that was between the Scots and Danes in the next field, ftaid the flight of his countrymen, renew'd the battel, and caus'd the victory, &c. Scotch Story, p. 155.

KENNETH, who having privily poifon'd Malcolm Duffe, that his own fon might fucceed, is flain by Fenella. Scotch Hift. p. 157, 158, &c.

MACBETH, beginning at the arrival of Malcolm at Mackduffe. The matter of Duncan may be exprefs'd by the appearing of his ghoft.

MOABITIDES or PHINEAS.

The Epitafis whereof may lie in the contention, firft between the father of Zimri and Eleazer, whether he [ought] to have flain his fon son without law: Next, the embaſſadors of the Moabites expoſtulating about Coſbi a ſtranger and a nóble woman ſlain by Phineas. It may be argued about reformation and puniſhment illegal, and, as it were by tumult: after all arguments driv'n home, then the word of the Lord may be brought acquitting and approving Phineas.

CHRISTUS PATIENS.

The ſcene in the garden beginning from the coming thither till Judas betrays, and the officers lead him away. The reſt by meſſage and Chorus. His agony may receive noble expreſſions.

The end of the Firſt Volume.

Lightning Source UK Ltd.
Milton Keynes UK
UKHW021130270622
405018UK00001B/243